Writers in Conversation
With
CHRISTOPHER BIGSBY

VOLUME THREE

ARTHUR MILLER CENTRE FOR AMERICAN STUDIES

&

UNTHANK BOOKS

First published in 2011 for The Arthur Miller Centre
By Unthank Books
www.unthankbooks.com

Printed and bound in Great Britain by Lightning Source, Milton Keynes

A CIP record for this book is available from the British Library

ISBN 978-0-9564223-4-7

Cover design by Dan Nyman

Contents

Introduction

- Christopher Bigsby -

The interviews collected here were all conducted as part of the Arthur Miller Centre for American Studies International Literary Festival held every autumn at the University of East Anglia (UEA). The festival began in 1991 and in the succeeding years has brought major writers from around the world to the campus, although the audience is drawn from a wide area. In one season a couple even commuted from Germany.

UEA has a reputation not only for studying contemporary writers but also for producing them, or at least for nurturing them. Its creative writing programme is known around the world. Though the Arthur Miller Centre focuses on American Studies, as its title implies it has a wide remit. Any Centre with Arthur Miller's name on the masthead is likely to be catholic in its interests. The Festival itself reaches out not only to novelists, poets and playwrights but to memoirists, biographers, historians, politicians and scientists. The common factor is writing. The Festival was not established with a view to publication and the format was not originally based on interviews, these forming only part of the evening. Over time, however, the interview has become more central.

As discussions of the crisis facing writers have become commonplace – regrets about the disappearance of bookshops, problems in publishing houses, the power of the web – so, apparently paradoxically, we have seen a growth of literary festivals, book clubs and signings. Reading may be a private enterprise but people obviously like to come together to discuss literature, to listen to writers read from their work and to ask them questions. Publishers, of course, see this as a marketing opportunity and writers are frequently leant on to go on the road promoting in a way that would have been unthinkable a generation ago. The surprise, perhaps, is not simply that on the whole they have embraced the necessity, if not always the pleasure, of doing so but that they so often respond with generosity and honesty, exploring the roots of their craft and acknowledging aspects of their lives usually closed to the reader.

Writers are not actors, except in so far as they stage the world they create in their own heads. Some do speak aloud the words they write as they write. Performance, though, was never part of the contract. A few writers are not the best readers of their own work, yet most take pleasure in reading in public, in making apparent rhythms buried in their texts suddenly evident as the words sound out. They also take pleasure in meeting their readers and responding to questions which sometimes offer novel perspectives on their work. Solitude may be the necessary condition to write but it is a rare writer who does not welcome leaving the study to engage with those who know them only through the books they read in equal solitude.

Once or twice in what follows audience questions have been incorporated in my conversations rather than break the text. The conversations have also been edited because as anyone who has ever transcribed a recording knows a literal transcription can be difficult to follow. We are liable to abandon sentences half way through, make redundant asides and punctuate our language with 'sort ofs' and 'kind ofs.' When I worked for the BBC I watched what were then called studio managers 'de-um' tapes, sometimes gaining minutes by doing so. For the most part, though, what you read is what was said and those who write with such apparently fluency speak with the same respect for language observable in their texts. Some of the interviews are brief, because the evening was taken up with rather longer readings than usual. All, however, I trust add something to our understanding of who these writers are and how they created works which are as varied as they are compelling.

For would-be writers there are exemplary tales. Some of the authors on the pages that follow had immediate success. Others suffered multiple rejections until, suddenly, a first book was placed and a career launched. All those interviewed spoke freely of their lives and of their approach to their craft. What is the attraction of first as opposed to third person narration? Is there an ethics to the appropriation of others' experience and, indeed, lives? What is the attraction of history to the novelist? What is the distinction between biography and fiction? Why are some drawn to the stage at one moment and the novel at another? Do some countries offer the writer a greater freedom for the imagination than others?

For the most part those included in this book spoke to an audience of 500 or more (sometimes those turned away watched on large television screens in an adjoining lecture theatre). It is the essence of interviews, however, that they have an intimacy belied by their public circumstance and to me that has always been part of their fascination. And when the event is over I am as anxious as anyone else to have my books signed. Why? For the same reason that I would have treasured Charles Dickens's signature or Jane Austen's or Thomas Hardy's. I know that on some level the sense of connection forged by that signature is factitious but I feel it nonetheless. Once, in a Salzburg bookstore, I found a copy of the life of Nathaniel Hawthorne written by his daughter. It was signed by a Catholic nun. I subsequently discovered that that nun was his daughter. I gave the book to Arthur Miller on the grounds that Hawthorne's forebear was Judge Hathorne who had presided over the trials in Salem in 1692 which he dramatised in *The Crucible*. It was no doubt a sentimentality but that signature itself contained a story even as it introduced one. Sometimes books do not belong to the person who possesses them.

If you were not at the festival at which these writers appeared you missed the party but I still think you can hear the voices of those who make their appearance on the pages that follow. You cannot now get your book signed, but there is a signature of sorts in their words and words, of course, are their stock in trade and the source of their unique identities.

- Christopher Bigsby -
Director of the Arthur Miller Centre for American Studies and Professor of American Studies, University of East Anglia.

In Conversation With Martin Amis

- 18th October 2006 -

Martin Amis was born in Swansea in 1949, son of the novelist Kingsley Amis. He is the author of thirteen novels, including *Success* (1978), *Money* (1984), *London Fields* (1989), *Time's Arrow: Or the Nature of the Offence* (1991), *The Information* (1995), *Yellow Dog* (2003), and *The Pregnant Widow* (2010). He is also the author of 7 collections of short stories and 7 books of non-fiction.

Bigsby: It seems that you have moved from those novels which were very much London-focused, and looking at the mood and spirit of the times – *Money, Success, London Fields* – into the world-historical arena, with *Einstein's Monsters, Time's Arrow, Koba the Dread*. Do you recognise that description of yourself?

Amis: I don't see it as a straight line. It is more that there is the London-based satirical, largely comic stuff about painful things, but that every ten years or so something else pops up. The books you mentioned are a side street in me rather than a road I have been heading towards.

Bigsby: I remember you saying of *Time's Arrow* that it was a digression, but if that is a digression there have been a lot of them.

Amis: Yes, there have been three. I once remember asking Updike about the Bech books. I said, 'I love those books. It is the only bit of you where you allow yourself to be mean,' and he said, 'Yes, I have an uncanny equilibrium, but when I start that mean stuff I don't know where it comes from, but it comes.' And it is the same compartmental thing with me in that it is there, but it is not quite the main thing.

Bigsby: How far is there a private, personal springboard into these larger issues? Thinking of that sense of living in a nuclear age that you address in *Einstein's Monsters*, were you prompted to write that by your own feeling of vulnerability or was it the vulnerability of others that made you suddenly focus on this?

Amis: I was twelve or thirteen and I remember feeling very terrible for about a week, numb and slow in my movements. Thereafter I used to bolt from the room very frequently. They would have a target map of England and London was the bullseye. I was living in Cambridge then and we were in a twenty-five per cent fatality ring on the target. I couldn't bear to watch it. I think it was the absurdity of it. It seemed humiliatingly absurd that we should all be cringing from this. Then that feeling went to sleep, as these things so often do.

I think *Time's Arrow* dates from a moment in my childhood when I had seen some images of the smoke-stacks and the railtracks, the iconic stuff from the Holocaust. I asked my mother very uneasily, 'Who was Hitler? and she said, 'Oh, don't worry about Hitler. He would have loved you.' I was like one of the children in *The Village of the Damned*. I had white hair and piercing blue eyes. I think that is why I wrote that book, because I wanted Hitler to hate me, not love me.

So the nuclear fear went to sleep and then when I had children myself I started to read about it, to find out more. It was Jonathan Schell's book, *The Fate of the Earth*, a book about nuclear weapons, which led me to start feeling tremendously indignant about it. Then I found myself writing a long essay and short stories that were all to do with it. Again it was the absurdity, the thought that this was no way for a species to live, under a system candidly called MAD, mutually assured destruction. When the Soviet Union collapsed officially in 1991 I remember saying to my sons, who were six and seven, 'I am so glad you are not going to live under what I lived under. I am thrilled for you that you don't have to do that.' Then we had ten years off and it all started again.

Bigsby: Elie Wiesel said that there couldn't be a Holocaust novel because either it wasn't a novel or it wasn't about the Holocaust. Now plainly you don't believe that but it was very fraught territory to enter. Did your heart skip a beat when you considered writing the book?

Amis: It did a bit, and I would have said of myself that I was the writer least likely in my generation to go anywhere near this subject. In fact it was much less of a struggle to write about the Holocaust than it was to write *House of Meetings* for the simple reason that I was writing about a perpetrator, in the Holocaust book, and this time I am writing about a victim. There is an enormous moral difference. My racial identity is with the Aryans and with the perpetrators. I am married to a Jew and my two daughters are Jewish.

Bigsby: But not at the time you wrote *Time's Arrow*.

Amis: No. I perhaps might have ventured there now that I am connected in that way to Jewishness, but I wasn't then. I couldn't have written about a victim of the Holocaust. The victims are there en masse. The way I did it was to run it all backwards in time so that it was not about genocide so much as genogenesis. My innocent narrator, who is trapped in this old body that is getting younger, the old Nazi doctor, is reading these events with an innocent eye, so it looks like an enormous, if very messy, act of creation. The smoke from the chimney runs the other way and the ovens and then the gas chambers produce these vivid living people. Then they take them on the trains and put them back in their villages. So the moral burden is with the reader, not with the writer, in that book, because you are describing disgusting things but quite happily and it is when he is describing ordinary life in a regular city hospital that it sounds like the Holocaust. If you run a hospital back in time then it is just completely savage, as indeed was the Holocaust. The Holocaust itself comes over as a benign event.

I had a few rules. I would not make anything up about the Holocaust and the imagination stays completely flat here. There is no ingenuity, no invention, because you have such a horror of adding to what you are describing. That didn't apply in *House of Meetings*. It just is the case that the story of Soviet Russia and of the gulag doesn't have that sepulchral glow that the Holocaust does. But on the other hand I was writing about a victim, two victims, three victims, and I was doing so in a picturesque setting in Uruguay where I could see and hear the sea from my study with my beautiful wife and embarrassingly adorable daughters, leading a completely stress-less existence. Uruguay is a haven of civility and sanity in a mostly insane continent, and I was writing about penal servitude above the Arctic Circle.

I have been reproached by some journalists for not having done ten years of slave labour in preparation for writing this novel and I see what they mean. That is what I was feeling, too. I couldn't do the ten years of slave labour. All I could do was suffer in the study, and all writers know what that is. It was very intense for what it is. You just go to write the next scene with a sense of dread and you have to lift it up over your shoulders.

Bigsby: With *Time's Arrow*, even when you describe the mechanism that you employed, which was a distancing mechanism, a controlled mechanism, you can see that someone could say, 'But you are playing a game and you are playing a game with the last thing in this world that anyone should ever play a game with.'

Amis: Yes, and I felt twinges about that but I was convinced that this was legitimate because *Time's Arrow's* subtitle is *The Nature of the Offence*. I kept on thinking, every day, that this is right for the Holocaust to be what its perpetrators said it was – which was a biomedical vision of Germany where, as they said frequently, you cut out the cancer of Jewry and make the body strong. That is in fact what happens in my book when the story moves backwards in time. Then the Holocaust would have been what it was said to have been, a curative operation. It could only be this, though, if the hour of time ran the other way. In other words, that is the nature of the offence, that is the extent of the offence, that is what you would need to fix for it to be what they said it was. I was aware that I was doing something tricksy with the terminal point of human morality, but I was very strongly convinced that it answered that challenge.

Bigsby: That was 1991, forty-six years after the end of the war. What was the trigger for that book?

Amis: It was a coincidence, really. I was toying with the idea of a short story about doing time backwards. It had been done before by Scott Fitzgerald, in *The Life of Benjamin Button*, and by Philip K. Dick, the writer of *Blade Runner* and many other science fiction classics. I looked at them later and they didn't do it as I did it. They had different strategies. Anyway, I was aware that there was this short story, probably quite a short short story, that I wanted to write which would be about a life lived backwards, which is a much better way to live. You may feel pretty rough when it begins but then you feel better and better, and stronger and stronger, and by the time you get to youth, you know what it is for. It is not wasted on you. And along with this there is a rather sad poetic shrinking, your thoughts getting more and more innocent before you then fold up into the mother, a much better arrangement than the one we are saddled with.

I was in Cape Cod and the man I play tennis with there, Robert Jay Lifton, a very celebrated psycho-historian who has written books on all the shittiest things that have happened in this century from Hiroshima to China and Vietnam, had also written a book called *The Nazi Doctors*. He gave me a copy to read. It was a terrific breakthrough in historiography. He went and talked to prisoner doctors, Nazi doctors, victims all over the world. It is incredible. He is a doctor himself. I read it and I thought of telling this story backwards in time. I asked his permission. It was a case of opportunism, I have to say.

In the context of *House of Meetings* the question arises as to which was worse, the Nazi system or the hard Bolshevik system of 1917-53. There are huge differences and the German example is much more disgusting than the Russian, in my view. I think we all feel this up to a point, and sense that it is worse. There are reasons for that. For instance, with Nazism there was another magnitude of aggression. It was worse than Communism. The Communists sent out propaganda, tried to develop fifth columns in other countries, did a bit of espionage. But there is a difference between that and a two million strong army rampaging across the border to fight a war of extermination against Russia. Also the gulag system, and the terror system, in the Soviet Union wasn't entirely irrational, as the Nazi idea was. It wasn't a frenzy of race hatred. It was a mistaken experiment and the gulag was meant to benefit the state. It was meant to earn money for the state. It didn't. Its other function was to keep everyone terrorised, which they were already. In fact it lost money and the only person in the government who didn't know that was Stalin. No one dared tell him, so it went on until he died but the minute he died the Jewish doctors were instantly released from jail. The gulag lingered on as long as the system did but it was no longer a part of the industrial base of the Soviet Union. You can't point to a rationale of any kind for the Holocaust. It is all nuts. So that is another difference.

Bigsby: Your father had been a member of the Communist party. There is nothing unique about that, of course. What is surprising is the sustained enthusiasm of some of them long after the Moscow trials and the Hitler/Stalin pact.

Amis: Hugh MacDiarmid got fired from the Communist party for being so extreme and then, after 1956, when a lot of people left because of Hungary, including my father, the ranks got so thin that MacDiarmid eagerly joined again. I think the great historian Eric Hobsbawm continues to be a member, even though the whole system is wiped off the face of the earth. I am not an ideologue. In fact my ideology is the ideology of no ideology. Don't have one. Do not do anything for the crowd or with the crowd. But my father – who didn't give a bugger what anyone thought of him and liked to excite hostility and derision – still needed this community of like-minded people. When he ditched Communism in 1956 the ideology was instantly replaced by anti-Communism, which is an ideology, too. It leads you into something like Vietnam, and he went to his death saying that it was a tragedy that we didn't show the willpower to win in Vietnam. You are always having an argument with your father even when he is dead, and that was my argument with him.

Bigsby: Why, having written *Koba the Dread*, which is dense with facts about the failed experiment and its terrors, write a novel – *House of Meetings?* Was there something you could not get at in writing *Koba the Dread?*

Amis: This has happened to me a few times. I wrote a very long piece about pornography, American pornography, and then I came to do it in fiction a little in *Yellow Dog*. After a couple of years gathering information and writing the odd discursive response to a phenomenon, you expect, a couple of years later, for it to trickle down into your subconscious and have further things to say. That is what happened with this book. It just takes something to spark it off and in my case it was reading in Anne Applebaum's book *Gulag: A History* that they had, ridiculously but somehow very typically, allowed conjugal visits in the Gulag. These intrepid women would travel for weeks and sometimes months in freezing railcars, or bouncing around on the back of trucks, or hitching, and would get to these incredibly remote slave camps and spend one night with their husband. Perhaps they wouldn't even get that. They would just be turned away with a taunt, or have half an hour alone with a guard sitting in between them, picking his teeth. That happened often enough. But whenever they did have a night together the result was almost always tragic. When they came staggering out of the house of meetings it was always a disaster. At the very best it was a virtuoso display of impotence because, after being starved like that, the hormones are no longer there and you are anaemic. But there were also terrible revelations about the sufferings of your family because they would have been persecuted as members of the family of an enemy of the people. When these poor bastards came staggering out of the house of meetings, which is also always a house of partings, the other men never ridiculed them. They showed a quiet respect for this suffering. In an atmosphere where there is otherwise no empathy everyone respected that and would help with the work norms.

Bigsby: Why did you choose to make your narrator a murderer and a rapist?

Amis: The real point about him is, as he says at the end, the Gulag memoir is a noble library. It is nothing like the great industrial-sized scholarship about the Holocaust. There are these two or three dozen really brilliant memoirs of the Holocaust. That is not so of the Gulag. And where there are, the narrator says these books are sometimes untypical of the Gulag experience because they are all written by intellectuals, by the politicals. And he says they are untypical in another way, too, because these famous memoirs are written by people with towering souls, amazing spirit, robust, their integrity never challenged, but surely the more typical experience is of someone whose integrity was challenged or destroyed. The whole intention of it was to push you into the most intolerable position and not everyone can write about that. I am sure the typical experience was you come out very damaged morally.

Bigsby: *Koba the Dread* was supposed to come out with two other pieces but you decided not to include them. One was the Mohamed Atta piece, which has appeared, and the other one was about a Saddam double. I can see why you pulled them. I don't think they belonged there, but if the word terror applies to the Holocaust and the Gulag, it also applies to the situation we are in now, though that word means something completely different. The threat of Islamism is surely of a fundamentally different kind from what we have been talking about.

Amis: Yes, except terror is always a confession of hysterical insecurity. It is because you have a vacuum of doubt about your own legitimacy.

Bigsby: Are you sure it is not the opposite: absolute certainty?

Amis: No, it looks like that but in fact the ground is swamped beneath their feet and this is the sort of hysterical overreaction to that. The other weird thing about terror is that it brings with it much boredom. I was going to call this book *Terror and Boredom*. I don't really mean the whole business of taking your shoes off at the airport and answering all those meaningless questions, I mean more the feeling you have when you realise you are going to have dinner alone with a fanatical Christian. Boredom is not really violent enough for this. It is death by inanition.

You realise you are going to have no bloody use for all your higher faculties for the rest of the evening. It is a confrontation with someone who fanatically believes something, though I still think that is rooted in insecurity. It is the impossibility of having any kind of meaningful meeting of universes of discourse which makes your head drop. And I do think they are intimately linked.

The Soviet Union was like an enormous experiment with boredom. The newspapers were full of boring lies, schools were boring. You couldn't show the path of a river without praising the marvellous plenty that Stalin had brought to the USSR. So school was boring, university was boring, all the interesting subjects were so impossibly controversial that they just died. No one dared do them. People couldn't go near history or philosophy. Newspapers were boring, radio was boring, everything you said to each other in public was boring because it was insincere. You couldn't do what came naturally. That, plus a lot of terror, left you punch drunk with boredom and shitting yourself at the same time.

In Conversation With
Alan Ayckbourn

- 21st October 2002 –

Alan Ayckbourn was born in Hampstead, London, in 1939. He left school at 17 to work in the theatre. Following a career as an actor he began to write plays and to date has written 75, more than half of which have made their way to Broadway and the West End where, at one time, three of his works – *The Norman Conquests*, *Absurd Person Singular* and *Absent Friends* – ran simultaneously. He has also worked as a director and was for many years Artistic Director of the Stephen Joseph Theatre in Scarborough.

Bigsby: Let me take you back to the beginning. Your mother was a little larger than life, wasn't she?

Ayckbourn: Yes. My mother was a writer as well. She wrote short stories and had a tumultuous private life, I suppose, of which I was part. We finished up as a single parent family, I think they call it these days. We did not have a dad in those days and she earnt her living by her pen. She kept us, and so the sight of my mother writing with an Underwood typewriter on a kitchen table, banging away with sheets of carbon paper, was something I grew up with. That is the first real memory I have and I always say that if my mother had been a pastry chef, I would probably have done pastry. She bought me a little John Bull typewriter. I remember sitting under the table writing my own stories in vivid purple, so I guess I was writing quite early. It was imitative, to a certain extent. As I grew up, though, it was theatre that I felt passionate about and I really wanted to act, but the writing and the acting remained quite close.

Bigsby: But isn't it right that your mother gave you gin when you were young and set fire to the house? I can see this doesn't bear directly on your career, I am just trying to check my facts.

Ayckbourn: The gin I can't remember but I must have been fairly zonked because there is a story that I was brought up during the Blitz and when I was in London I slept in a cot in Ealing and my mother was in the pub and I was unattended and a bomb went off next door and they ran back. The cot had shot straight across the room and practically through the wall and I was still asleep, so I guess it was gin.

Bigsby: Your father was absent, but he was also in the world of the arts.

Ayckbourn: Yes, he was a violinist. He was deputy leader of the LSO for a long time. Funnily enough he gave up everything at the age of about sixty, ran off with a second violinist who was sitting behind him, rosining her bow, and they had this romantic dream. They bought a cottage in a village called Tacolneston, a cottage with roses around the door. Her name was Daphne, and they called it Daphne Dene. She bred St. Bernard dogs and the house was full of these massive animals. I used to go and visit them and these dogs took me for walks, I remember. That was how he finished his days in Norfolk.

Bigsby: I haven't been asking these questions just out of prurience. I am interested in whether trace elements of this were later going to appear in your plays. But let me defer that for a bit and let you go to school. You went to an all boys school.

Ayckbourn: It isn't now. It was. I wish to God it hadn't been, but it was. Girls were a curiosity. We had one fixture every year called Dance versus Queenswood, which was the girls school. They were also a single sex school and were also rather like a nunnery as opposed to our monastery. They were only let out once a year and they were allowed to wear perfume, which they did in gallons, and evening dresses and makeup. And so they arrived. It was like a whore's bus. You could smell this bus coming and boys in evening dress, dinner jackets. I thought this is not good and then they did this super thing. The girls were made to line up across our dining hall, which was massive, a huge long line, and the Head Boy had the first pick and I remember thinking, even at thirteen, this is not good for these girls, is it. Someone, usually me, got the last one who was standing there, now completely shattered, and then everyone tried to get the Head Boy's girl for the rest of the evening. That was our sexual initiation. It was very creepy.

Bigsby: But you did some writing and acting there?

Ayckbourn: Yes. I wrote plays and things. There is always one in every school if you are lucky, a teacher of some description, who really should have been in the theatre but didn't either get encouraged or didn't quite have the courage and they finished up in school. This guy taught French but he was born to be an entrepreneur. His name was Edgar Matthews and every year he toured a school production of Shakespeare around the place. He started touring England and then, later on, as he got more ambitious, started touring Europe. The first year I was there when I was eligible, when I was sixteen, we went to Holland with *Romeo and Juliet.* The second year was going to be his bow out and we were allowed to go the United States and Canada and we toured there with the Scottish play. That was just like magic. They were rotten shows. We were so drunk, but it was the most wonderful trip. It was like professional touring with none of the responsibilities. You just did the shows. So, when it came time for me to leave, and my housemaster was confidently making sure I got my next step, which was to go to university, I said, 'no, I don't want to go to university. I don't want to go any further. I want to start work in the theatre on Monday.' He looked appalled. I have never seen a man look so horrified and Edgar, the man who ran these things, got me a job with the great Donald Wolfit.

Bigsby: That must have been a bit of a shock because Donald Wolfit was like a time-tunnel back to the nineteenth century in some ways, wasn't he?

Ayckbourn: I thought all actors were like him and of course he was, as you say, a left over. He was far bigger than life and he ran these wondrous touring companies. *The Dresser,* the famous Ronald Harwood play which Tom Courtney did, is based entirely on this man, but he was a true, true actor, and very generous. We were scruffy ASM boys doing this play called *Strong and Lonely.* It was an all male cast and he took time for us. He auditioned us one afternoon. He sat in the stalls, though there was no real reason why he should, and we all came on and did our bit of Shakespeare for him and he gave advice. That was how it was. But then I went to Leatherhead and joined a real rep and I never saw anything like him again.

Bigsby: Gin comes into the picture with Donald Wolfit, doesn't it?

Ayckbourn: Yes, well I was serving as the call boy, the humblest of people. I had only left school three days before and I banged on the door and said, 'A quarter of an hour please, Mr. Wolfit,' and he said, 'Boy, I

15

need some water to dilute the gin. Never drink undiluted gin before a performance.' I said, 'Yes, right,' and he said, 'Can you get me some water,' and I said, 'No, I can't, because the curtain is up.' He was dressing in a confessional and he said, 'Come on, use your initiative boy!' and he grabbed hold of me and marched me down the passage. He kicked open the door and there we were in the chapel and he saw this barrel with holy water in it and he just went and put it into his gin and I waited for an explosion. He was quite something.

Bigsby: You began as an assistant stage manager, which is a fairly lowly form of life. What was your ambition then? Was it to become a Donald Wolfit, a great actor, or what was it?

Ayckbourn: I really wanted to act. That was my great aim and I think I would probably have finished up being a very unhappy and second-string actor if I had carried on that way.

Bigsby: But you did carry on that way for quite a long while.

Ayckbourn: Eight years, yes, long enough. I did a couple of repertory jobs and then, and it was pure luck, I happened to join a company that was touring up to Scarborough. It did summer seasons there for twelve weeks, and it was run by a man called Stephen Joseph. I think if you are lucky in life you meet the right people. They are my guardian aunts and uncles who have been in my life at the right time and said, 'Don't do that, do this.' He was one of them, and if you are clever you use their advice, take it and follow it. I was very lucky. I met Stephen.

After about a season there he gently suggested that maybe I would like to do some writing and that I should start with writing for myself as an actor. This was attractive since nobody else was, so I started writing shameless vehicles for myself. I wrote wondrous, large, vast parts. The first play was a three-act play. I came on at the end of the first act, everybody else having worked very hard to establish what a great character I was. I then stayed on for two acts with all the lines, really, as they stood around listening, which made me very unpopular in the dressing room. But it was a great learning curve because once you have that freedom you tend to get a little drunk with it. This was just the beginning of the pop scene, skiffle was in, and all that. The beginning of rock 'n roll in this country, early Adam Faith, and I wrote myself the role of a pop singer with a shy private life so I could play two characters, one with glasses and one without. It was so I could show a certain versatility in my performance. When he didn't have his glasses on he was a real rocker – it was before Buddy Holly – and I played the guitar and I sang and danced. It was only when I got to the actual rehearsals that I realised I could do none of these things. I certainly couldn't play the guitar and I had two left feet and I couldn't sing. So I went off to find a boy called Donny, who was giving guitar lessons, and who had advertised in the *Scarborough Evening News*. A sweet boy opened the door and I said, 'Hello, I hear you give guitar lessons,' and he said, 'Yes, where's your guitar?' I said, 'I don't have one.' He said, 'So how long have you got to learn?' and I said, 'Well, two weeks,' and he said, 'I can teach you two chords,' and so I just played the two chords and sang and that was my debut in theatre.

Bigsby: You nearly got derailed early on because of something which does not now exist, namely National Service, into which you went under slightly bizarre circumstances, and left under even more bizarre circumstances?

Ayckbourn: Yes, National Service, where they are supposed to make a man of you. I had been dodging them so I got in around the age of nineteen, by which time I was married and had one son. I got married quickly, because after all those years of no women I had to make up for it. As soon as I left school I proposed to the first girl I met and she was stupid enough to say yes. Anyway, I got called up and we did the tests and I opted to go into the RAF because they seemed to wear nicer shoes. The Army had boots and the Navy made you sign for twelve years or something, so I went into the RAF in a place called Cardington in Bedfordshire. These places only exist on army maps. You can never find them if you look. They were strange places.

When I arrived I was the only National Serviceman to have been called up. The rest were regulars and there had been a slight army cock-up. So I was put in a hut with forty-eight beds on my own and they said, 'You'll be alright, son. We'll get you some more people in the morning, but just make yourself comfortable.' It was freezing – January – and I was in this hut. There was a stove that wasn't working, and there were forty-eight beds with blankets all folded. I looked at the notice-board and it said, 'People are expected to be on the parade ground at 6 a.m. Latecomers will be severely reprimanded,' and I thought, 'God almighty', I haven't even got an alarm clock so I hope somebody is going to wake me. So I got into bed and I couldn't sleep so I stripped off six or seven other beds and piled the stuff on me and I went to sleep. The next thing I knew, it was broad daylight, and there were people shouting and I looked out of the window and it was bright sunshine and blokes were polishing coal and all the sort of things you do in National Service, and bashing about the parade ground, and I looked at my watch and it was 8 o'clock. Then I looked at the notice board and it said, 'Folding of blankets, two centimetres,' and I looked at the debris in there and started to try and fold these things up.

The corporal stuck his head around the door and said, 'Good morning, sir,' and I said, 'Good morning, I am terribly sorry, I didn't hear the bugle.' He said, 'That's alright, I had a look in at six and you looked very peaceful so I left you.' I said, 'Thank you very much.' He said, 'Don't bother with all that, somebody else will do that. Why don't you go to the NAFI, have a cup of tea, have a breakfast and be back here at twelve and we will get some lads for you, so you won't be on your own.' So I went and had a large breakfast and came back and sat in the hut and he came in again and said, 'Hello, they have all been delayed. Why don't you go to the NAFI, have lunch, come back here at 2 o'clock and we'll have some lads.' So I had another large meal, came back and sat on the bed and he came in and said, 'Good news, forty-eight Glaswegians just arriving.' I said, 'Forty-eight?' He said, 'No, probably not. Listen, I'll get you another hut. You won't survive, will you?' I said, 'Well, I am public school.' He said, 'Yes.' So I got another hut and the sergeant said, 'We have got a very dodgy customer in here. He said he was in the Maltese Air Force and was a Pilot Officer and he has come over here and thinks he is going to be a Pilot Officer. He is not. He is going to have to work from the bottom up and he is very, very angry, in fact he has had a go at someone with a knife, but we have overlooked it.' He said, 'I am giving you the bed next to him. Can you keep an eye on him?'

There was this guy trembling. He was burning with anger. I said, 'Hello,' and he went, 'Um,' and then I tried to make friends with him. He showed me a picture of his girlfriend and I said, 'Yes, oh.' He said, 'Awful looking slapper.' She looked terrible. I said, 'She's lovely.' He said, 'I met her in Soho.' I said, 'Oh, right.' He said, 'She said she'd wait for me.' I said, 'Yes, yes.' The following morning we had a medical. They took a blood sample first of all. I faint at the sight of blood, which is not a good quality to have when you are joining a fighting unit. They stuck a pin in my ear and pulled the blood and I hit the deck, bang. He said, 'Do you do a lot of that sort of thing?' and I said, 'Only when people take my blood.' He said, 'What about other people's blood?' I said, 'I'm not worried about that, just mine.' So I got to the doctor and he said, 'You want to do this?' because I had told him I had a wife and a baby, and I said, 'No.' He said, 'It is a terrible waste of your time, isn't it? I am sure there is something wrong with you.' I said, 'Well, probably.' He said, 'What's this knee injury?' I said, 'Well, I got that in cricket, actually, years ago, pulled it.' He said, 'Well, I don't like the look of this. Could you walk to that wall and back?' He said, 'No, don't try. Could you do it?' I said, 'Well, with difficulty,' and he said, 'And then what would happen?' I said, 'Well, I would probably have to lie down for the rest of the day' He said, 'I've got bad news for you. I'm afraid we are not going to be able to take you.' And I went, 'Damn!' He said, 'And I will expect my cheque in the morning.' And I left.

I did two days in the RAF and I got home to my wife and baby who didn't expect me – fortunately nothing was going on – and a week later I got a letter from the RAF. It was one of those roneo things saying, 'Dear Ayckbourn, following your long and faithful service in the RAF, we invite you to join the RAF Club.' And I thought, no I can't, I can't in all honesty stand there with a lot of seasoned fighter pilots saying, 'Well.' So I served my country for two days.

Bigsby: Let me take you back to the plays. You were now in Scarborough and had largely stopped acting. You were writing plays for a particular kind of theatre, a theatre-in-the-round. Are there any plays that cannot be done in the round?

Ayckbourn: Oh, yes. Plays over two floors are difficult. When I went to the National Theatre, which I did at the end of the eighties, Peter Hall asked me to direct three plays there and he said there would be one in the Olivier, one in the Cottesloe and one in the Lyttelton. His proviso was that the one in the Olivier would be mine. It would be a new one of mine. He was obviously working on the presumption that if I buggered up the other two, the Olivier, being the biggest house, would perhaps recoup some of the money. I looked at this big, big, theatre and I wrote *Small Family Business*, which was one of the few opportunities I had to write such a play, and I set it on two floors. I had always wanted to write a play where the set was actually the front of a doll's house when you had taken the front off and the rooms were exposed, with activity happening all over. I had a theme behind that. *Things We Do For Love*, another play of mine, is very much to do with levels. It is mostly levels that stop you writing for the round because they are difficult, but a lot of the time, no, you can find solutions.

Bigsby: But acting in the round can be a challenge for some. I was reading a biography of you and there is a story there about Michael Gambon which seemed a little cruel in some ways, although the very essence of the theatre.

Ayckbourn: Well, Mike, like a lot of actors, is essentially a proscenium arch actor and mistrusts theatre-in-the-round, partly because a lot of Michael's acting is about seeing what else he can do when he is not acting. The jokes he plays on stage are extraordinary. Anyway, he agreed to come up and do Othello for me in Scarborough. He was probably the last white Othello. He looked around and I said, 'Well, you will not be able to muck around in this very much, because they are all three feet away from you and all round you.' So, all his usual gags were out of the window. Ken Stott played Iago and we had a fountain on the stage, which was rather nice. In one of the scenes it spouted gently. There was a lot of water in the bottom of it. At one point we blocked it so that Mike in his jealous fury – it was quite frightening – grabbed hold of Ken by the neck and pushed him under the water and held him under for a second and then pulled him up again. Mike always claimed you could say anything in Shakespeare and no one would ever hear it, and I came in one night and he was pushing Ken under, saying, 'Shampoo and set, shampoo and set,' and Ken was coming up saying, 'Short back and sides, short back and sides.' There were a few students looking through their books as though we were working from another text, an earlier one.

The round in general is a terrific medium for companies, for actors who don't want to score, but actually want to play. I think when Stephen introduced it, it was a great medium for new work because it almost insisted that the text be taken quite seriously, quite intimately and intricately. I have always loved working in it. I do work with a proscenium arch a lot because there aren't a lot of round theatres, but theatre-in-the-round is a terrific medium. If you are playing Rosencrantz in the round you are very important indeed. If you are playing Rosencrantz in a proscenium arch theatre you are less important because you are probably down stage of Hamlet most of the time, but Hamlet, in the round, knows that Rosencrantz and Guildenstern are sharing the scene with him. They may only be listening a lot of the time but the quality of their listening is informing the audience that can no longer see Hamlet for a second. It becomes a great medium for support and for interplay.

Bigsby: But you are very exposed as an actor. On one occasion you asked Michael Gambon to cry, which is something that in the proscenium arch he has ways of handling.

Ayckbourn: That was quite interesting. At his best, of course, he is extraordinary. He always has enormous potential in him. I have never reached the top of his potential, which is saying something for actors. With some actors it is as though somebody has lent you a really fast car. You keep putting your foot down and going faster and faster until your nerve breaks eventually. There are some you can barely get up the hill, by a lot of subtle gear changing and they are worthy, but not quite roadsters. Gambon is a highly tuned car.

We are talking about *A View from the Bridge*, which he made a tremendous impact in, and in rehearsal he did what English actors do. Eddie cries at one point, he cries because he has lost his girl, lost his daughter, really, though in fact she is his niece, and realises he has blown the whole thing. He turned upstage and buried his head in the back wall and cried. It was very moving and I said to him in the next rehearsal, 'Mike, could you do something for me?' And he said, 'What?' I said, 'Could you just cry without the hands on the face, just straight out,' and he said, 'What, just cry?' I said, 'Yes, when you feel it, could you just do it for me?' After a long pause he said, 'You bastard.' I said, 'Well, don't do it now, do it in the run.' When it came to the run he stood there and he did it and everybody cried, everybody watching, everybody just wept. It was an absolute knock-out and he knew that was right.

But on another level, and this is what I love about an actor like that, I said to him, 'At the end of the show, you have got the big moment with the knife when you confront Marco at the very end and it is very important that I have a clear stage. Up to that point this has been the kitchen but I just want to get rid of the furniture and what I don't want is a load of burglars coming on in black shirts taking it all away. Who stole this furniture, because up to now we have had no stagehands in sight?' And he said, 'What do you want me to do?' I said, 'Well if you could get rid of the furniture upstage it would be brilliant, when you are pacing up and down doing the big angry bit on your own before the girls arrive.' He said, 'Yes, I'll have a go.' So we ran it and he walked up the stage and there was a rocking chair down left and he kicked it with his huge boot, and it arced up and landed. Then he walked across the other way and did it to all the other three chairs. They just smashed and by now everybody is going, 'What is he doing? He has freaked.' So I thought, what is he going to do with the table? The girls by now had arrived in the doorway.

They have just come back from church and he sees them and he picks the table up. He is an engineer so he judges things pretty accurately and he ran at them with these four table legs and the legs are just wider than the door frame so they go bang, and they both screamed. He drops the table and there is this terrible silence and he looked at me and said, 'Something like that?' That was done every night and every night the audience went, 'Wow!' and we knew it was a scene change.

Bigsby: You direct your own plays and have directed other people's, in that case Arthur Miller's. It is a curious thing being a director, isn't it. Back in the nineteenth century there really wasn't such a thing and there's no real training for it now. People tumble out of Oxbridge and simply do it and their style is totally different. I sat in on some of the rehearsals for *A View From the Bridge* and you seemed to have a very withdrawn style of directing. You would make a suggestion and then say, 'Oh, but I don't suppose that would be of any interest, would it?' There are other people who are extremely directive. They take the play over. Where do you locate yourself in terms of directing?

Ayckbourn: Well, as you say, I do structure productions quite carefully but I was brought up by Stephen to feel that in the modern theatre the director was a necessary evil rather than someone of great importance. Ideally, the author should direct from the keyboard but a lot of authors are unable to do that, or are reluctant to do that, or, indeed, would be very ill-judged if they did so. I have always worked on the principle that any idea the actors have for themselves are worth ten that I give them. Now, how they come to that idea can often be by gentle leading, by gentle suggestion. There are actors, like Mike, who if you ever said anything to him directly, would never do it. He would just look at you and then, two days later, one in three would turn up and you would say, 'Nice idea, Mike, good.' Half the time I don't think he realised where he got it from and that is alright. I don't have much ego as a director because I get all my ego kicks from writing, so all I am there for really is to deliver the play via the actors to the audience. To that extent, yes, occasionally, you do have to be a little strong but most of the time, with the right shows, everything runs for you and all you are actually doing is just editing, helping, shaping, keeping an eye on things that individual actors can't, like the pacing of different scenes, the contrast between them.

I don't have a great joy in tramping over other people's work. I always feel that they have written it, my job is to deliver it, maybe visually a little differently occasionally but most plays that I do I have no wish to do that. *A View from the Bridge* as an all singing or dancing show? It is a powerful piece and all I wanted to do was to make sure it came across and I think some of the decisions we made were quite interesting, certainly to Arthur Miller when he came to see it. For example, it was terribly fast. He told me that the production they had just done in New York was about forty minutes longer than ours. It was massively long. I can see how you can play it like that and maybe in New York they liked it that way, but I said this is one of the most heartbreaking plays we are ever going to do. The end just cuts me in half. We have got to start finding comedy at the beginning. I don't mean we are going to put laughs into it, but let us find the laughter within this family. It is very short-lived, because very soon events catch up with them, but let us have at least one scene where they are laughing together and having fun because if they are having fun we begin to like them, we may begin to love them, and therefore we care about them and thereby, by the end of the play, we cry for them. If we think, 'What a glum bunch of Italians, what an awful, gloomy bunch,' we don't want to know about them. We are not going to cry quite as deeply at the end. We may academically, but I wanted people to be really involved and so we worked on making what was there. We didn't change anything.

Mike played around frightening his wife and the daughter doing spooks with spiders and things and got a lot of good laughs and that I think was me suggesting it. They then went on to discover it and I think that is directing, really. I think what happens is that quite a lot of modern writers have lost one of the things that they really own, which is the visual content of the play. I am very insistent that a lot of my plays are fifty per cent visual. That is what I am writing. It does not mean I have made all the decisions, how people look and so on, but I put enough visual into it that I have control over it to a certain extent. A lot of them just leave it to the director and therefore they are surprised when they turn up and it is set in an igloo. They say, 'Oh, I didn't intend that,' and they say, 'Well, what did you intend, because there is absolutely nothing here to say what's happening while they are talking.' And you confront a lot of writers and say, 'Have you any ideas of what they should be doing while they are talking, because you have just got these big lights, this stage and everything and a couple of blokes standing here saying interesting things to each other, but do you have any idea what they should be doing apart from that?' They say, 'No, not really.' And then you think, 'Well, why aren't we doing it as a radio play because it would be cheaper and we wouldn't have wasted all these wonderful doors and windows and things that we've put in.'

But a good play informs with movement as well as with dialogue and sometimes I think we are just dialogue obsessed really. There is no room to act, we are too busy talking. What are we doing in theatre except watching acting. Sometimes actors can say so much with what they don't say. One of my very first experiences was being directed by Harold Pinter, who then was quite strange. Nobody had seen the like of him before and we looked at him like he was balmy, but we followed him because he was directing us and he had a sort of frightening obsession with getting the play right so we followed him, being working actors. I am so glad we did because I was in the second production ever of *The Birthday Party* and it was quite extraordinary.

Bigsby: You have said you had no idea what it was about while you were in it.

Ayckbourn: Well, he wouldn't tell us much. I said, 'Harold, sorry can I ask you, I am playing Stanley and he is the pianist and then these two blokes arrive, McCann and Goldberg, and they do him over and then they take him away in a van.' He said, 'Yes you have got the general gist of the play.' I said, 'I just wanted to know, for me really, where does he come from, Stanley, and where does he go to in the van?' Harold looked at me for a long time and he said, 'Mind your own fucking business.' I said, 'Okay fair enough.' I have always wanted to say that to an actor but never dared.

Bigsby: I would like to take you back to your own plays. You have a very high wire act, that is to say you have been known to announce a play, along with its title, before you have written a word of it. Is that part of how you write a play, by putting pressure on yourself so that you have to write that play?

Ayckbourn: You need some sort of pressure. When I was younger, actors literally didn't get the script until the first read-through, but then I had a permanent company and you could see them picking up the script and trying to look cool about it and seeing if they died on page three, whether I am still on in page fifty-eight. The funny thing is they were often titles which were so vague and would therefore fit anything I was likely to write. A quite well known early one was called *Absurd Person Singular* and I got a very long document from a university student in Canada who researched the title and had worked out how it did have relevance to the play and had cracked the code. I didn't have the heart to write back to say, well, actually the play has nothing to do with the title. It was a hand-me-down title and I just used it. I have been a little bit more cautious in the last decade. I tend to write the play, sit on it for a week, and then we cast it.

Bigsby: That is terrifying and I think a little dismaying because you write plays in between two and four weeks and then they are on. But you can't do that, that is not possible. How can anyone do that? These can't be real plays. Real plays are what people spend two or three years writing. How on earth do you have this facility?

Ayckbourn: The way I work, and the way I suggest people do approach it, is that a lot of it has to happen in the planning stage. I think the big mistake people often make is to start cracking in with the dialogue. Enter Horatio and off they go and then they are a bit surprised when on page eight they really do hit a brick wall and think, 'Oh, hell, what happens now?' My plays all start from an idea, but I am usually rolling that idea around in my head for about a year, nine months, until at a certain point, when I bow out of my directorial artistic director duties for a brief period, I say, 'Look, please, unless the theatre burns down, don't get in touch.' Then, probably for a week or so, I just walk around, clear everything and marshal all those little ideas I have had. Hopefully, there is enough there to write and that is a week to ten days. Often it is like a picture and I have to get everything down fast because everything in a good play relates in some way. It is not all tidy. There must be loose ends otherwise it would become trite but quite often that is happening there and then and you think oh, no, that is because that relates with that and you put it together. It does take practice and does take technique. The first time I wrote I story-boarded and I made sure I knew this picture was where they had the argument, and that picture is where she walks out of the door, and so I knew where the story was going, but now I suppose I am experienced enough. You still need the idea and you still need the inspiration.

Bigsby: When you say the idea, how far are you sometimes fired by the challenge of staging in a particular way, as in *Way Up Stream*, with a boat, or *House and Garden*. Is that where those things started? What if we did this?

Ayckbourn: No. I have ideas. I wanted to write a play set on the river because I thought, great, that would be wonderful, put a cabin cruiser on stage, what a challenge. But I couldn't just write a play about cruising today. It had hung around, that idea, and then I got really interested. I said, as a lot of us do, I wonder who it is who decides that they are going to stand for parliament or for council, who believe they are qualified to run things. Certain people feel they are and they put themselves forward as mayors, MPs. The converse of that is that the majority of them aren't qualified to run anything. The very people who should be running things never get up, and the people who do get up should never have been asked. Of course there are a lot of exceptions to that but of some you say, how the hell did he get into parliament? He must have been the only person who said, 'I am willing to do it.' So I thought of a play about the nature of leadership, but that is a very dry subject if you are not careful so I thought, gosh, where do people lead most. I ran many a boat aground near here in Norfolk. I thought I was Lord Nelson. I would shout at my family and I thought, I am just one of hundreds of Englishmen who really believe that they are direct descendants of Nelson, and there's the leadership, there's the person who does stand up. The people who should be steering the boat are down in the galley cooking boiled eggs.

Bigsby: Your plays are staged at Scarborough but then, almost invariably, transfer to London where they come up against a different system. That is to say they are not going to take your Scarborough cast. They are going to want to put other people into it. Is the play that people see in London the same play that they would have seen at Scarborough or does the star system create something else?

Ayckbourn: I could say honestly that the first few were unrecognisable as my plays. Robert Morley, in *How the Other Half Loves,* was the Robert Morley show with full supporting cast and then it was done a few years later by the Actor's company, when it was done by actors, and the critics came to see it again and said, 'Hey, this is quite a good play.' Slowly, over the years, by the time I got to the National, there were more and more people coming. That whole National company, give or take the Gambons and a few others, were all Scarborough people, ex-Scarborough, and I was beginning to formulate my own people. This year, for the very, very first time ever, *Damsels in Distress,* which is running at the moment, has an entire one hundred per cent Scarborough cast in it and I have done it at last. It has taken me years and they are very unhappy about it because we are celebrity fixated now. Everything has got to have something off a cornflake packet or has to have a star from America. Sometimes it is good and sometimes it isn't, but the fact is it does us no favours to go and see Madonna doing a rather indifferent play. I think it would be much more useful if she had sat having dinner at the table with a red rope round her and people could walk round and have a look at her. All that happened was, yes, it brought a new audience into the theatre and hooray, but apparently the evening was a such a disaster that you couldn't hear it beyond row D and it was a pretty boring old play. For people who came for the first time it was probably the last time they came. They said, 'Well, that was very boring theatre, I'm not going again.' This is instead of coming to see a really exciting performance by stage actors. The Royal Court and the National Theatre, and occasionally the Royal Shakespeare Company are the only companies that are now producing and they are not producing their own stuff.

In Conversation With
John Banville

- 20th October 2010 -

John Banville, novelist and playwright, was born in Wexford, Ireland, in 1945, the youngest of three children. His brother and sister have also published novels. His own novels include *Birchwood* (1973), *The Book of Evidence* (1989), *The Untouchable* (1997), *The Sea* (2005) and *The Infinities* (2009). He also publishes crime novels under the name Benjamin Black. He has won the James Tait Black Memorial Prize, the Booker Prize and the Irish Book Awards Novel of the Year.

Bigsby: You were born and raised in Wexford, which is not a very big place.

Banville: It is a small town in the southeast corner of Ireland which I hated. I loathed it. I was so bored I never even learned the names of the streets and I couldn't wait to get out. I stayed there chafing for seventeen years and then I escaped. Now I see how beautiful the town was and how much I missed it and how foolish I was not to value what was there while it was there.

Bigsby: Like all Irish places, it is heavy with history.

Banville: When you are young you hate history. I was turned completely towards the future, towards what was going to happen, the history that I was going to make, so I wanted out. I was thinking recently that when I was about fourteen I had a friend who was about sixteen, or maybe seventeen, and he was very sophisticated. He used to wear a three-piece suit and a watch chain. He smoked cigarettes and had a tremor in his hand, which was terribly impressive, and he used to tell me about wife-swapping parties and I never believed this. I thought this was all fantasy. Now I look back on it and I think there probably were wife-swapping parties and I missed them. I left before I had time to get invited.

31

Bigsby: Not long ago I was talking to Colm Toíbín. He went to a Christian Brothers school and then to St. Peter's College and as a matter of fact you went to a Christian Brothers school and on to St. Peter's College.

Banville: Yes, and St. Peters is now famous. It was a real hot-bed, in all senses of the word, for paedophilia.

Bigsby: Were you aware of that when you were there?

Banville: Oh yes, of course. We all were. Everybody knew. We thought it was slightly funny but of course what we didn't realise, what we didn't acknowledge, was that it was always the weak kids, the boys at the back of the class who didn't speak and who couldn't do their sums, that were the ones who were picked on. That is a source of real sorrow now for people like me. We should have taken care of them, the little boys at the back of the class, but it was a great centre of homosexuality. It was also the Diocesan college so that students would go from here to there and it was always the gay students who went on to become priests. So as far as I can see the entire Catholic church is run by homosexual priests, which is not a bad thing. I don't see why it shouldn't be the case.

Bigsby: I have a tendency, when I hear people went to a Christian Brothers school, to ask whether they have still got the bruises. Do you have any?

Banville: Well, curiously I was beaten more at St. Peters than I was at Christian Brothers. I was lucky that I was top of the class. I was one of the bright boys. I was in a way untouchable. As I say, the people at the front of the class were not victimised so I did get beaten but we accepted it. That was what happened and one never spoke at home, one never told one's parents, and one's parents didn't want to hear about this. If you were beaten you must have deserved it and probably did. We were little boys. We deserved it.

Bigsby: You started writing very early.

Banville: I think I started when I was about twelve. I may be romanticising, but certainly it was very early. It is a classic thing. Joyce's *Dubliners* was a great revelation to me, that writing could be about life as I knew it, because the Dublin in Joyce's writing, the Ireland in Joyce's writing, was very like the Ireland that I grew up in. Nothing much had changed in fifty or sixty years and here was evidence that one could write about life itself, the thing itself. So I immediately started writing really bad pastiches of Joyce's *Dubliners*. I threw them all away, to the great dismay of various librarians who keep these manuscripts, but I do remember the opening of one of the stories, and this was written when I was twelve, thirteen, fourteen. The first sentence was "The white May blossomed, spiralled into the open mouth of the grave". I knew nothing about life. I certainly knew nothing about death, but I knew that I wanted to deal with words and Joyce was the great leader there.

Bigsby: But you were also interested in painting.

Banville: Oh, yes. I tried for a couple of years, when I was about fifteen or sixteen, to paint. I couldn't draw. I had no sense of draftsmanship. I had no colour sense. All of which are distinct disadvantages if you want to be a painter. I thought at the time that it was a useless and frustrating exercise but looking back on it I can see that it taught me to look at the world in a very particular way. I write in a very high style, as did Nabokov and Updike. Nabokov said he should have been a painter. Updike claimed that he studied drawing in London. It does teach you to look at the world in a very particular way, or maybe we are predisposed to look at the world in that way anyway and therefore the art of painting attracts us.

Bigsby: Is that why art recurs in your novels?

Banville: Partly, but I am not a psychologist. One of my favourite things from Kafka is a little line from his diaries that went, 'Never again psychology.' To me, art is evidence. It is a surface to the world, a surface to people. It is all we can see. I can't know anything more than what I see from the outside, but the surface is where the real depth is. So my interest in painting, as in writing, has to do with the spectacular aspect of painting.

Bigsby: I think anyone who reads your work would assume that you went to university and read a great deal in literature, classics, science, but you didn't go to university. So where did this education come from?

Banville: We all educate ourselves. I now deeply regret not going to university. It was very stupid. It was part of my strategy to get away from my family, be free. Now I am sorry that I didn't indulge myself for those three or four years of drunkenness and carousing. I suppose it was the height of arrogance to think that I could do it myself and now I have to display my little bits of knowledge in the most pathetic way, trying to impress people. But I have a curiosity. I am interested in things, in painting and physics, and they feed into the work. I find it absolutely extraordinary that a writer or a painter or a musician will say blithely that he knows nothing about physics or astronomy or any of these things. If a scientist said he didn't know anything about Shakespeare or Beethoven we would consider him to be a barbarian. I think that physics, for instance, is one of the most interesting disciplines of the twentieth century. I think that the ideas and even the images that physics threw up from Einstein onwards are absolutely fascinating and in many ways more interesting than twentieth century philosophy.

Bigsby: Did you have a mentor or a guide at any stage or did you just go into libraries and follow your whim?

Banville: No, as I said, arrogance was a great guide for me. I felt that I could do it all myself. There was nobody who could be a mentor to me because nobody was as clever as I was. I am being largely facetious but I think anybody who wants to be an artist needs a good, strong, healthy dose of arrogance.

Bigsby: I noticed that when you won the Booker Prize you said, 'Thank heavens a literary book has won it at last.'

Banville: What I said was it is very good to see a work of art winning it. I was being largely mischievous, but again I was being partly serious. I think it is right that a prize like that should go to my kind of book, though not all the time because the poor prize would wither on the vine. You need strong middle brow books to win prizes, to sell lots of copies and keep people interested in fiction with these stories on the front pages of newspapers. Now and then it is good. I am not saying that mine is a successful work of art. It is, but I am not saying that. What I set out to do was what I have been trying to do since I started to write, that is to turn the novel towards a more poetic form. It is perfectly reasonable to argue against that, especially here in England where you have such an extraordinary tradition. Henry James spoke disparagingly of the 19th century novel as a loose baggy monster, but in many ways it is arguable that the novel should be a loose baggy monster and should not be this carefully fashioned closed object. It should be open.

Bigsby: You have also said that you are not really content with the novel as a form and that in some sense a poem can do more.

Banville: I don't like fiction. I don't like the novel. It is not a very interesting form.

Bigsby: So why have you written fifteen of them?

Banville: Well, what else can I do but what I am trying to do, to make the novel a poetic form, to give it the weight and the denseness of poetry and to be as demanding. Auden said that the poem is the only work of art that you either take or leave. You can listen to a piece of music and no matter how hard you concentrate you can, for a little while, think about what you are having for dinner. You can look at a painting and think about that very pretty girl walking past. You can't do that with a poem. You read it or you don't read it. I want my prose to be at that level, to be as demanding as that, so that you either read it or you don't read it. Many people, when I offer them a take-it-or-leave-it choice, to my amazement decide to leave it.

Bigsby: There is a sense in which you can taste some of the words in your work.

Banville: For me there is no point in writing discursive fiction unless that is true. There are five senses. You should be able to smell, hear, taste the thing. I am particularly interested in smells. It fascinates me that the novelist almost never talks about smells. We are brought back to the past by smells. We are disgusted by smells, we fall in love because of smells, so all the senses have to be involved in this to give a feeling of that squashy sense of the world in all its awfulness, in all its beauty. I have a friend who said to me, look, I admire your books but I can't read them because your prose does too much work. You don't need me. You don't need my imagination. I can understand that but I like to feel that if you do manage to get onto the wave-length of this prose the rewards will be high.

Bigsby: You were suggesting just now that there is a playful arrogance in what you were saying but there is no fiercer critic of John Banville than John Banville. You have actually talked about abhorring some John Banville work. Is that because it will always fall short of what it is you want to do?

Banville: Yes, all my books stand behind me like mortal sins. They are all wrong. They are all failures. There is a wonderful cartoon by Gary Larson and it is in two parts. The top half is a flowerbed and the flowers are all very pretty. In the bottom half the flowers all have crossed eyes and snaggled teeth and the caption is, 'The top is how people see flowers and the bottom one is how flowers see themselves.' That is how I feel about these books of mine. Of course I suppose on some level I am proud of them, don't get me wrong. I think they are better than everybody else's. It is just that they are not good enough for me, but that is the condition. As Beckett says, all you can do is fail again but fail better. I keep trying to fail better.

Bigsby: That is very Beckett, and if you are an Irish writer you have these two huge figures looming above you. You have mentioned both – Joyce and Beckett. Has Joyce given way to Beckett as far as you are concerned?

Banville: I don't think so. Irish prose has a certain tone, a tone of high rhetoric and high comedy which, when successful, is a wonderful heady blend. If I were to pick a writer who has influenced me, certainly as I get older, it would be Yeats. The difference between Yeats and me is that he had absolutely no sense of humour, which allowed him to be great. He wouldn't be great having a sense of humour and a sense of the ridiculous and a sense of one's own absurdity. These are very grave misfortunes.

Bigsby: You said just now that you wanted to get away from your parents. Specifically from your parents?

Banville: No, everything that my parents represented, their world, though I look back on it now with a great deal of grief and regret.

Bigsby: What did they represent?

Banville: Oh, they represented narrowness. I speak of my parents, though my parents were splendid people. I loved them dearly.

Bigsby: On the other hand, when they died, when you were in your thirties, you said that you felt released.

Banville: Of course. I forget who it was that said it is the best gift a man can give to his son to die young. I think it is true. Don't we all feel that? Along with the grief at loss of a parent there is a sense of suddenly becoming one's own man or own woman. Some people's parents live to be very old. I can only speak for myself but I didn't feel that I became an individual until my parents had gone, taking with them all that world that I grew up in, because once they were gone I wasn't tied to the place I had come from in any way.

Bigsby: Your first novel wasn't set in Ireland. Indeed was it set where it was in order not to be set in Ireland?

Banville: Oh yes, of course. I was young and reading all the wrong books. I was reading people like Lawrence Durrell and I wanted to be a dashing cosmopolitan writer, so I set the book in Greece having been there for a few weeks. But I always feel that the Hemingway advice to write of what you know is not quite right. I would encourage writers to write about what they don't know and then they might find out a lot of things both about the thing they don't know anything about and also about themselves, about which they know less.

Bigsby: But you struggled in the writing of that book. You had several cracks at it.

Banville: Yes, of course. It was my first novel. It used to pile up in the corner, each of the drafts, each of them wrong. My poor wife. We were living together in London then and she was working while I was at home. She would come home in the evening and say, 'How's the novel?' and I would say, 'Oh, it's alright,' or if I had said it has collapsed she would say, 'I think I'll go out again and come back later.' The people who sustain artists never get enough acknowledgment. How she put up with it, how my family and various people that I have lived with and am living with at the moment, how they put up with it I don't know. I wouldn't put up with it.

Bigsby: One thing you did in writing that novel was to change it from third person to first person.

Banville: Yes, I did. Really all my books, even third person books, are in the first person. If all my books were put together into one huge volume, hideous thought, it could be called *The Book of Evidence* because I think that is what art is. It is the record of one man. I was here. This is what I saw. This is what I record. That is what art is for me. I don't think it is anything other than that. I think that is a great deal but I think claims to psychological insights are foolish.

Bigsby: So, as a writer, you have a distrust of psychology.

Banville: Yes. I think Freud was a great novelist in his way. He didn't have a very good style but yes, he was. He and Conan Doyle were first cousins. We are such complex creatures that psychology really doesn't go very deeply into us. One of the aims of the artist is to make the object blush, whether it is a human being or a tree or whatever is being described. You have to describe it in such a way, in such detail, with such concentration, that the thing which didn't expect to be concentrated on at this level begins to blush. When we blush, or when the object blushes, it is at its most vulnerable but it is also at its most sensitive and it gives up something of itself that otherwise would be held inside. So I think that is the chief aim of the kind of art I do, to make the world blush.

Bigsby: The first one of your books that won a prize was *Birchwood* in which you threw yourself into Ireland, its politics, its violence. But it is also a book with a sense of the carnivalesque. There is even an act of spontaneous combustion.

Banville: Well, there was a case of it in Dublin. In fact I came across the cutting from the *Irish Times* the other day. An old lady was watching television when she blew up and all that was left were her boots, button boots. She was an old-fashioned lady and there was the armchair and this charred thing, the boots and also the screen. The television had melted but otherwise the room was unharmed, though with a certain amount of soot around.

Bigsby: So not Dickens.

Banville: I didn't even know there was combustion in Dickens, not until afterwards when people started asking me about it.

Bigsby: Is it right that after you had published that book you had a moment of pause as to whether to go on or not?

Banville: Yes, I was going to give up fiction. I was going to do something else and I started to write a book about the Norman invasion of Ireland in the twelfth century but somehow that changed, by a process that I don't understand and don't remember, into a book about Copernicus. Fiction's a very funny business, but I did the Copernicus book because I felt that *Birchwood* was my Irish book and I wanted to get away. I thought, what can I do? I can't keep writing Irish books for the rest of my life and also I wanted to be a great European novelist who was up there with Thomas Mann and so on. I was very young.

Bigsby: You wrote a novel about Copernicus and one about Kepler.

Banville: When I finished *Copernicus* I thought, my God, I will never do this kind of thing again because I was half way through *Copernicus* before I realised it would be regarded as a historical novel. I didn't want to do that at all. I had wasted so much time reading the background to it but then when I finished it I looked again at the life of Kepler and I couldn't resist it because he is such an attractive character. So I was stuck with doing Kepler. Looking back now I suspect that it was probably a wrong direction but we take the directions we take. There is no point in saying this is right or this is wrong, but I think I wasted a certain number of years. I became fascinated by fact and all novelists want to be factual.

Bigsby: Is there a sense in which you were interested in whether science can get closer to reality, to truth, than fiction?

Banville: No, I know what you mean but I think it was the opposite. I think it was that I realised in the little bit of reading that I had done about the early astronomers, and then about modern physics, that science and art came from the same source, that it is the same creative spark for science and for art. Once it has been made it becomes entirely different. Science has a rigour, or it claims to have a rigour, that art has not, but I think it is the same process and the same desire. The desire of the scientist is to impose a system on the world and I think the same is true of art.

Bigsby: You have said that it wasn't the exotic you were after but the ordinary. That seems to me a key to your work, that interest that you referred to earlier in the surface of things as they present themselves to you.

Banville: I think that would be true of all artists. We have nothing other than the ordinary. The transcendent we may aspire to but all we have is the rather confused and grubby world that we live in, which is also transcendently beautiful, of course, but I don't know what else one could write about except the ordinary. Artists get carried away with themselves and think that they are part of a priesthood aiming for something beyond life, but we are not. I, at least, am trying to describe this world and what it is like to be here, the sense of being alive, this very, very strange phenomenon. I never ever get used to being alive. I never get used to being on this earth. I look at the sky and think, I am standing here on this ball rolling through space and I am looking up into space. I never ever get used to it. It just seems too baffling. I suppose that is the reason I keep plugging away trying to describe it as accurately as I can, the experience of being here.

Bigsby: You have a fascination with words. Of course all writers do, but you have a special fascination with words. You like words which are not part of the common vocabulary but which have a kind of glow to them which people, when they read, do not necessarily understand.

Banville: Well, I try to be accurate. I don't use words like screwdriver and marmalade lightly. I try to be as accurate as I can. The English language is so rich, so phenomenally rich. There is a word for everything. I discovered one day in the dictionary that when you get up in the morning and stretch and yawn there is a word for that, though not a word that trips lightly off the pen. It is pandiculation, so when you get up tomorrow morning and you stretch and yawn you will be pandiculating. The ingenuity of human beings in inventing a word for stretching and yawning is what fascinates me about language.

Bigsby: Can you recapture for us the moment when you decided to write under the name of Benjamin Black, because you write in a different way in the Benjamin Black books?

Banville: I was driving from my home to the city and about half way in it suddenly struck me that I had a television script that wasn't going to be filmed and I thought, I know what I will do. I will turn it into a novel. I had been reading George Simenon for the first time. I hadn't read him before and I was absolutely bowled over by what he achieved in what he called his hard novels, not the Maigret books, which I have never succeeded in finishing. His hard novels are astonishing. At the time it seemed a little adventure, a little frolic that I was going off on, but, looking back, I think it was more than that. I think I needed to take a different direction and give myself a kick, and it has been a fascinating adventure. It may not succeed, I don't know, and maybe I will make a fool of myself, but one does what one does.

Bigsby: But you write them differently. You write more words a day as Benjamin Black than you ever would as John Banville.

Banville: Oh yes. I write them very quickly indeed. I write a Benjamin Black novel in three or four months. A Banville novel would take three, four, five years. It is an entirely different process. I don't know why crime writers get so annoyed with me when I say that because Simenon used to do his books in a couple of weeks. It is just a different way of doing things. It is analogous to writing film scripts. If I could type fast enough I could do a film script in real time. I could write a film script in an hour and a half because I would roll it in my head. It is somewhat the same with these books. I see it in my head and I write down what I see. I stop myself from getting interested in sentences and I say, keep on, keep on, keep on, because I am trying for spontaneity and fluency and fluidity. That is what Black does best.

Bigsby: Why do you set those novels in the nineteen fifties?

Banville: I had set the television script in the nineteen fifties and as I wrote that novel, and subsequent novels, I realised that the fifties were an absolutely perfect time for noire fiction, especially the fifties in Ireland. It was such a dark time. It was a stricken time, both financially and spiritually. It was stricken, rife with dark and dirty secrets. There was lots of fog, lots of cigarette smoke, gallons of drink.

Bigsby: You have said that you find it difficult to read aloud from a Benjamin Black novel.

Banville: I can't find a voice for Black. I find it very hard to read these books in public. I don't know why. It is like trying to find a place to stand on. I can't find a solid place.

Bigsby: But surely the voice is in the prose. It is on the page, isn't it?

Banville: Yes, it is, but whenever you read in public you have to perform. When someone asked Philip Larkin why he wouldn't do poetry readings he said he wasn't prepared to go around the country pretending to be himself. When you do a reading first of all you have to overcome the shyness. We are all afflicted by shyness to a greater or lesser degree. Yeats's wife said about him that he was terribly shy but he developed a patter, and that is what one does. For reading in public one develops a voice and I haven't developed a voice for Benjamin Black and I don't think I will because I can't think what it would be. Would I put on a different accent? I don't know.

Bigsby: When you are writing a John Banville novel do you know the whole thing before you start or does the writing generate the novel, as opposed to a Benjamin Black novel where presumably, as crime fiction, you almost have to write backwards, to know where you are going?

Banville: Yes, that's true. I would have to have the plot of a Benjamin Black novel much more clearly before I started. I would have a general outline of the plot I suppose for a Banville book but the thing about Banville books is that one has to let things happen, one has to allow instinct to have its way when it is very strong. One of the things I notice about writing crime fiction is that it is very difficult to be humorous. It is very difficult to be ironic. The form somehow won't allow for that. The people who do try to be funny, Raymond Chandler and others, can be witty but they can't be funny. I can't imagine laughing out loud in a detective novel. As I say, I have no explanation for that. It is just entirely different. For me, there is good writing and bad writing, but it is certainly an entirely different way of working, an entirely different voice.

Bigsby: Were you tempted to hide behind the pseudonym, and try to keep it secret?

Banville: No, from the start I intended that it would be an open secret. I simply took a pseudonym to let my readers know that this was something different that I was doing, that I was going in a different direction. I didn't want people to be cudgelling their brain and saying that this was obviously a postmodernist literary joke. I wanted people to realise that this was straightforward so, to be helpful, and to be playful I suppose, I chose a pseudonym. But no, I didn't want to conceal myself. It would have come out. Nowadays with Google and the internet nobody has any secrets any more.

Bigsby: What is the difference between allowing instinct to have its way as against a closely plotted book like a Benjamin Black novel?

Banville: It is all very well for me to say I don't believe in genre but these are entirely different kinds of books so if they are not genre, what are they? It is just that I think the reason I am against using the word genre, or the notion of genre, is that it somehow implies that these are lesser works than the Banville books. They may be lesser works, I don't know, but they *are* different. There is a lovely marginal note in one of Darwin's notebooks when he just says, never say higher or lower, and I like that. It is one of the things that endears Darwin to me and I try, with these, not to say higher or lower. They are different kinds of work. Benjamin Black is a craftsman. Banville is an artist. I like being Black much more than I like being Banville. It is much easier apart from anything else. I didn't say that. Crime writers will be out to tear my heart out if I say things like that.

Bigsby: You said of Banville's novels that they fail and that the aim is to fail better next time. Do you feel the same way about a Benjamin Black book?

Banville: No, I don't. That is the odd thing. I don't. When I have finished a Benjamin Black book I feel as I think a craftsman would feel when he has done a fine piece of work, a beautifully carpentered and polished table, a wonderfully comfortable elegant armchair. It is a pleasant sensation. I get satisfaction from that. Banville books seem to me such messes. By the time I have finished them they infuriate me, they niggle at me. That is why I have to immediately go on and write another one. Somebody once asked Iris Murdoch why did she write so many books and she said I keep thinking the new one will exonerate me for all the ones that have gone before. I know exactly what she meant.

Bigsby: In *The Infinities* how do you persuade the readers to believe in what is a fantastical world?

Banville: The world that is presented in the most straightforward and supposedly realistic novel is nothing like life. We all know that. Life is not as fiction is but the desire of the reader to suspend disbelief is very strong indeed. We all want to be told a story and we all want to believe in it. We most probably don't grow up at all. We think we do but we just get older and we are still children wanting to be told a story so it is not difficult to foist an entirely invented world on an audience because the world that I present to them in my so-called straightforward novels is just as fantastical as the world in *The Infinities*. You can start speaking as a God in a novel and they would believe in it, and I supposed I believe in it too.

Bigsby: And alternative universes.

Banville: I have just been reading Stephen Hawking's latest book where he is talking about manipulating the infinities, just as I did in my book, so I was there before Hawking. We live in a fantastical world. We see a very tiny spectrum of reality. Dogs and cats see far more than we do. We can't see x-rays. We can't see neutrinos. We express the thoughts we have with the words we have to express them and we see the world according to the rules that will fit the world we see. As we sit here neutrinos are shooting through us and going out the other side of the world in a nanosecond. This is happening to us as we sit here but we have no experience of them so it is a very narrow band.

Bigsby: You have said that you don't like the form of the novel. Why not be a poet?

Banville: I couldn't write poetry. The technique of poetry baffles me. It is almost as baffling to me as music. My old friend John McGahern used to say that there is verse and there is prose and then there is poetry, and poetry can happen in either though it happens far more often in prose than it does in verse. I think to some extent he is right. Poetry is something that is beyond the form. I think of myself really not so much as a novelist as some kind of poet. I don't like to say that because it puts people off and of course I am a novelist. I am stuck with the novel form which, don't get me wrong, is a wonderful form as well. It can encompass all the mess and confusion and loveliness of life. It is an extraordinary form to work in so I have I suppose a love hate relationship with it. When I was an adolescent, of course, I wrote poems. We all did when we were adolescents. I destroyed those too I can tell you.

In Conversation With
Sebastian Barry

- 17th November 2008 -

Sebastian Barry, poet, novelist, playwright, was born in Dublin in 1955, the son of the Irish actress Joan O'Hara. He has published two volumes of poetry while his novels include *The Whereabouts of Eneas McNulty* (1998), *Annie Dunne* (2002), *A Long Long Way* (2005) and *The Secret Scripture* (2008). Among his plays are *Boss Grady's Boys* (1988). *The Steward of Christendom* (1995), *Our Lady of Sligo* (1998) and *The Pride of Parnell Street* (2008). He has won the Costa Book of the Year prize and has twice been short-listed for the Booker Prize.

Bigsby: Your mother is an actress, as is your wife. So is acting in your bloodstream?

Barry: I have only once been on the stage, in Trinity College, Dublin, for a revue in, probably, 1976. I played Tonto and I had no lines. The reason they cast me is because I had long hair down my back, so I had this slightly Indianish look. All I had to do was smoke a cigarette, which you would think would be an easy enough task, but I didn't smoke and was so frightened that my fingers started to tremble and as they did the cigarette started to move up and down faster and faster and then flew off into the audience. So there and then I decided theatre wasn't for me. But I have been in rehearsal rooms all my life, both as a child of an actress and with my own plays, and there is no more wonderful, magical or human place to be. Happy times. My mother actually died last year and when I read *The Secret Scripture* I hear her voice very much in it.

Bigsby: Because she performed in your plays.

Barry: I wrote a play called *Our Lady of Sligo*, which was like an African play because it was composed of the stories she had told me about her mother when I was a child, which was probably not entirely a good thing to do because they were very dark stories. Her mother was an alcoholic.

So I wrote this play, which Sinéad Cusack played in at the National Theatre, very wonderfully and beautifully. Then it came to Dublin and I was wondering would my mother go and see it but of course she certainly wasn't going to waste her time doing that. She did, though, come in to congratulate Sinéad Cusack who was her friend. She came into The Gate and, coming up the stairs was a woman, obviously from Sligo. She said to my mother, 'I don't blame Sebastian. I blame you for writing this terrible play about that poor woman.' And I thought, you would think my mother might be aghast and appalled but she was absolutely delighted. That was all she required to entertain her. She didn't need to see the play itself.

Bigsby: Is it true that you broke off writing *Our Lady of Sligo* to write *The Steward of Christendom*?

Barry: It was such a fierce old play. I thought that in writing *The Steward of Christendom* I would find a traitor in Irish history, who was my great grandfather, that I would find a rather rough and appalling person. In the end, I found somebody quite different. Even that was a rather dark play, though it wasn't as dark as *Our Lady of Sligo*, so I chickened out of writing that for a number of plays, actually, because *Steward* was written fifth. I was always writing a play instead of *Our Lady of Sligo*.

Bigsby: And that play was successful.

Barry: I hear it was successful. I never actually saw both acts together in one theatre because I was so fearful of it still. I was in my forties. You would think I would have learned a bit of courage but I hadn't, really, but, yes, it was successful although I just regarded it as a play about this demon of my childhood. I was very deeply encouraged going over to the National Theatre to a meet-the-audience thing and people, who had been into it a number of times, were admiring this woman and I was reconciled to the play through the responses of the audiences who didn't find her so fearful as I did.

Bigsby: You write novels, plays and poetry but I don't think anyone reading them, or hearing you read from them, would think of them as wholly separate genres.

Barry: Plays are obviously the most ancient form. Drama pre-dates writing. It is an ancient form of activity that we seem to do as the creatures we are. There is something very pure about the form. It goes back to our very primitive ancestors. And the lyric impulse is an incredibly exciting thing that you can devote your life to because it is always miraculous. It is also very ancient and admirable, so I am not sure that words like genre cover it. It was the Greeks who started to try and talk about things separately. All I know is that because I am writing about forgotten or lost memories of my family, or people who have been erased for various reasons, they are sometimes to be found hiding out in a poem. Sometimes they have chosen to hide out in a play. Sometimes they are hiding out in a novel, and sometimes I go looking for them in a play and don't find them there.

Bigsby: I seem to remember you saying once that your work occurs to you first as a play, then you may transmute it into something else. Is that right?

Barry: Usually there is a little whistle tune. In a way language, at its most magical, is a considered language. If you are listening to people talking you are obviously not thinking of the next line to say. You haven't learnt your lines and yet you are talking so brilliantly and spontaneously and in such a human fashion. I do regard language in that sense, in a praising way, as the bird song of an individual and most often for me the whistle tune I hear, or the bird tune I hear, is a poem, maybe a short poem, and that can sit there for maybe ten or fifteen years.

I remember when I did my first play for the Bush Theatre, in 1991 or so, I brought in a book of poems that I had published recently and I said, 'you could choose one of those and maybe I could write a play.' It was like a tailor's samples. 'And then it will choose to be what it is.' But the older I get the more I just allow those things to be the mysterious things that they are.

Somebody was asking me about this recently. They said, 'of course, you obviously write aloud. You speak aloud.' But I never speak anything aloud. When a book comes out, and when I am bringing it in for a reading, I am always genuinely fearful and worried that there won't be anyone hiding in the syntax. I couldn't read or write until I was nine. My world of language was in the mouths of people I loved, and in my family members, and I think, when I read it, is their syntactical apprehension of things that is in me and this translates somehow into how the thing has been written. It belongs to it but is independent of it, I think, for readers.

Sometimes people say, 'Can you do the audio books?' But I think that would be unfair because I am more interested in the person that the reader brings back to life, because the whole purpose of them, if they work, is to try, and even by magic, even by foolishness, to bring them back for a moment into the living world so that they can be seen and appreciated and in some instances thanked for the ordeals they suffered. This woman particularly, in *The Secret Scripture*, suffered at the hands of my family. A previous book, called *A Long Long Way*, was about a great uncle who went to the First World War and died in the war, but if he had come back he certainly wouldn't have been particularly thanked. The reader is complicit in that fact of thanking, so I don't want to contaminate the book with an audio book and risk losing whatever that voice is. But I am always very grateful when I start to read and she is there because I couldn't do it on my own.

Bigsby: I am interested in the boy who couldn't read or write until he was nine. Does that mean that you were simply listening? Have you any idea why it was so long delayed?

Barry: It was the very early sixties. I was four or five and my father was an architect and my mother was an actress but there was no building work going on in Ireland so we all came over to London and lived in a little flat in Hampstead. I went to a London County Council school in New End. I don't know whether it was because I had been talking with this quite full Wicklow accent when I came to London but it took me a while to learn the London accent, which for a child is partly a survival tactic. I suppose that after a while I was talking like that just to stay alive. Then, after four years, we went back to Ireland which was a real catastrophe because I was older and my fellow people at school were older and could hit you harder. You didn't want to be talking like that in Ireland so I very quickly learned my own accent, which in a way wasn't my own accent because I was learning it for the second time. Maybe learning language to stay alive created such a sense of emergency that there was no time actually to learn how to read or write. I do remember the triumphant day when I wrote my name – and I was probably nine in all honesty – the feeling of accomplishment which is not far from the feeling you get when you finish a book. Merely to write my name was a triumph at the age of nine, so I haven't quite got over that. There is no Booker Prize for being able to write your name. I probably would have been runner up there as well.

Bigsby: When the dam broke and you could read, did you rush to stories?

Barry: It was the unravelling of an enormous mystery because my beautiful grandfather, who was a painter but also very handy with his hands, naturally enough had made a travelling bookcase for my father. So when we were in London one whole wall of the sitting room was this bookcase constructed by my father according to his father's instructions, which in some ways is like a literary tradition. And this bookcase was full of favourite books but mostly red-spined Penguin paperbacks which were an entire mystery to me. I didn't know what this red wall was, really. My sister had penetrated it a little bit and taken out the bricks. I think I made a mistake as a child because when I started to read it seemed to me to be a mechanism where you could put your head into something in privacy, but the language was just like my relatives with language coming out of their mouths like ticker tape. The people on the page were the same. They were just as living so, if it was *Treasure Island*, it was just an absolutely 3D experience and I rest my faith in that mistake.

Yes, it was an astonishment to me and I don't think I ever got over it. When I have to read books for a book, which I try to do, I still find myself reading quite slowly. I went to Trinity College and I did a degree in Latin and English but I read very slowly. I don't think there is any harm in it. Maybe I was slightly dyslexic, I don't know, but in the sixties nobody seemed to bother about these things. My mother was very busy in the theatre and my father was out mostly, so nobody was worrying too much.

Bigsby: Did you go and watch your mother in the theatre?

Barry: I did inevitably because when we went back to Ireland she went back to the Abbey Theatre. In those days the Abbey was the Queen's Theatre which has since been demolished. They were there because the Abbey had burned down. In fact my mother had been a young actress in the production that was about to go on the day the Abbey burned down so they were in exile at the Queens and she would bring me in there when I was about six or seven. She was playing in a Yeats play. These were wonderful, magical people to me as a child. They brought me in and put me in my seat, the lights went down, but nobody had explained what a theatre was. They probably just thought I knew, but I didn't. The lights went down and we were like cattle thrown into the dark, the dark pitch of night. Then the lights went on in this other place and after a while somebody came in that I knew was my mother but she was an extremely old, old woman. My mother was in her twenties still at this time. She came in and she was very old and I remember sitting there in the chair and thinking, 'How are we going to get home now? Can we still get the bus and get home?' Then there was the relief and magic of going backstage and my mother was a young woman again.

It was an error of childhood which I rest my faith in. At the end of *The Steward of Christendom* Donal McCann, our very greatest actor – I mean of all the centuries, really – never looked himself and it was the same feeling that something had occurred. I think there are magics in the theatre. I don't mean foolish magics, but true magics that we, as human beings, by our concentration, create in the theatre. And that is worth trying to get at even if you fail at it five times out of six. That is still worth trying to get hold of, and that comes from childhood.

Bigsby: I remember David Edgar telling a story of going to see *Beauty and the Beast* when he was a child and the beast came on and he screamed. At the interval they took him backstage and he met the person playing the beast. He took the mask off, shook hands and said, 'I hope you enjoy the second half.' David went back out, the beast came on and he screamed. It is that doubleness which is surely a crucial aspect of theatre.

Barry: The atmosphere in the rehearsal room is not dissimilar, actually. When I saw my children, when they were a bit younger, playing in a corner, or heard them walking around the orchard being things, there was the same atmosphere. It is a conspiracy of playfulness and sort of joy and that is what they are doing in the rehearsal room. So in a sense you should scream because it isn't the fellow who was in the dressing room with the mask. It is actually the beast when he comes out on stage.

Bigsby: Is it right that you wrote two plays while you were a student?

Barry: I did. I very generously wrote a couple of plays that Samuel Beckett was too busy to write himself. One of them was called *Samuel's Garden*, a fact which I was very proud of. I thought they were very wonderful plays. I wrote them very quickly in the English library in Trinity. I think I am a fan of writing quickly. I think it is the right way to do it. But a very great friend of mine, then and now, caused me a moment of intense bitterness by saying, 'I think you should put them away in a drawer forever.' I didn't go back to plays then for years and years because I did think it was my mother's territory. It was only when I met my wife, Ali, in 1986, when she was doing *Casualty* for the BBC in Bristol with Brenda Fricker, that I wrote *Boss Grady's Boys*. Lorca said most plays are written in about ten days and if they are not there is probably something wrong with them. I had fourteen days so I wrote

Boss Grady's Boys which eventually the Abbey put on, but it was almost like accidentally falling into the theatre.

As a non-writer for the first nine years of my life I suppose I thought that there was something quite grand about writing and if it is grand it probably should be done very slowly. I probably thought of it as something posh that you did. The terrible example though was Yeats's wife George (Georgie Hyde-Lees), who did the automatic writing. But at the same time it intrigues me. When you get the scent of something, or the tune of something, I literally go into my work room every morning for about seven months beginning to sweat with apprehension. My editor in London waits patiently, smilingly but possibly with the smile drifting a little off the face as the deadline draws nearer, and just thinking would you please start. But when it starts it is quite swift. It is quite river-like, quite fast, quite submerged. It is certainly not written with the top part of my brain, which is supposedly a little bit educated. It is accessing a story, so when people say you write well or you don't write well, the terrifying fact is that sometimes when you read over your book to proof it, to your shame, in a way, you don't remember large sections of it, which is terrifying because maybe I was drugged and my wife came in and wrote it. There is no memory of it at all, which seems to me to mean that it is low in a good sense, that it is low on the evolutionary scale. It is so old that it is not even homo sapiens.

Lorca says ten days or maybe there is something wrong with it. But when the fish are in you have to be there. I have worked on a computer now for the last ten years. It seems to me ideal. It is the most primitive thing because you put it out into this other floating brain. Nothing is printed, nothing exists, and you are transferring this floating thing to this floating thing. It seems to me very perfect. People are fearful of the computer but I think it is a fine thing. That is where the sense of speed comes.

Bigsby: You said in passing that you didn't write plays at first because it was your mother's territory. Did it belong to her just because she was an actress?

Barry: It is a beautiful question and I actually don't know the answer. She died last year in a way very characteristic of herself. She was working up until the last few weeks. She was in her late seventies and was in an Irish soap on the television. She loved doing that and got extremely unwell. She ignored the whole thing, of course, and continued unwell. Then she died. In fact *The Secret Scripture* is completely tied up with that time because it was being written all through her illness, and various things were being presented to me almost for the first time because we had had this relationship. When I did start to write plays she was in a few of them. We worked together and I regret to this day saying to her, on the first day of rehearsal, for the first thing she was in, 'Please don't talk during rehearsals.' My mother was a champion talker and she would just fill the rehearsal periods with talk. I don't know why I said it to her. It was very unfair and wrong and she didn't say a word all through rehearsals, so in a way we worked together but we didn't really work together. Then, for some curious reason, when she died, a few weeks later I had two or three play commissions and I wrote them all back to back as if her majesty and graciousness in stepping away was leaving me a gift from her. I was freer to write plays in a way that I hadn't for a while. I had been a bit stuck. I used to explain this to myself by thinking that it was because I was writing novels, but there was another reason for being stuck. I think maybe in any one family, in a couple of generations, only one should fill the niche in the theatre.

Bigsby: It is not quite true to say that you wrote plays and then started writing novels but nonetheless there seems to have come a moment when you did turn more resolutely to the novel. Can you recall the moment in which you thought, 'Now the novel.'

Barry: I am one of those unique writers, I think, because in the present day people get picked up in their twenties and given money. I spent about six or seven years writing, from 1977 to the early eighties, with nobody publishing me. It was called an apprenticeship. Eventually I started to be published and then had various experiences with that, both good and bad. I wrote the obligatory mad book, in 1988, and then met Ali and settled down in some way. It sounds an awful thing to do, because we were all the children of modernism. We hadn't even heard of postmodernism which said that the audience wasn't important and you shouldn't have any proper structure. History was dead, family was dead, love was dead. Because of the wars it was very understandable, but I wasn't that person. I wasn't a postmodernist, but somehow being with this very wonderful Presbyterian Dublin woman allowed me to calm down rather than settle down.

Then I started to write plays and I wrote a play called *Boss Grady's Boys* which seemed to be about me and my brother. My brother was thirteen years younger than me, a very great genius. In every family there has to be a genius to balance out the idiot in the family, but he was a great genius and he went to Harvard at seventeen with a scholarship. My poor brother has been ill recently, but anyway I wrote that play and it seemed to be about him, so it was a family play to some degree.

Then I wrote a second play called *Prayers of Sherkin*, which was about a great-grandmother who had been a Quaker on an island in West Cork. They had come from Manchester to wait for the new millennium. There was no one left for her to marry so she crossed to the mainland and married a poor Catholic man from Cork city. Then I began to think, well, maybe there are one or two more of these people who I should be going to look for because it was at a time in Ireland when there was the war in the north and actually the sort of Irishman that I was trying to be wasn't considered very Irish. I didn't have enough adjectives of Irishness attached to me, so I was inclined to include a few more adjectives, to include myself and be a citizen and make up an Ireland. I thought, well one or two more and I wrote a play called *White Woman Street*, which was about an ancestor who went off to the Indian wars to fight in America. Then I wrote a play about a musical dancer called Lizzie Finn. Then I wrote *The Steward of Christendom* and before I knew where I was I was doing an interview on the BBC and the interviewer asked, 'How many of these plays are there?' I panicked for a moment, because this is the radio and there is a microphone, and I said, 'Seven.' It just came out of my mouth – seven – so I thought I will have to write seven. So I wrote seven. Then, when I got to the eighth play I was panicking and I rang my friend Roy Foster, who is professor of history at Oxford, and said, 'What am I going to do? I said I would write seven.' He said, 'Just do the eighth play and stop worrying about things like that.'

And then I wrote *The Whereabouts of Eneas McNulty*. I wrote a play about him called *Freedom for Nigeria*. It was about him and his Nigerian friend in Lagos. This was based on a great-uncle who was given a death threat and had to leave Ireland, but it didn't work as a play because Eneas was a completely introspective person who wouldn't say a word, which isn't very helpful in a play. This was for Max Stafford Clark, so that was a bit frightening, but I rang Max finally and said, 'I don't think there is a play there.' I started to write it as a book, absolutely not knowing what I was doing. I would send bits of it to the editor at Picador. Finally he wrote to me and said, 'Are you really serious about this?' I said, 'I only want to do it if it is good,' and he said, 'Alright, we will make a contract for it.' He said, 'How much money do you want?' I said, 'Just talk to my theatrical agent and she will deal with it.' I didn't even have a literary agent. She had never done a book deal before and I said to her, 'Look, I don't want any money because this is about a very poor man and I just don't want any money.' So she said to Picador, 'He doesn't want any money,' which they interpreted as I wanted more money. So they came back with more money. So I gave up then, and we did it.

It has surprised me because it started to be bought in Europe and it just surprised me the way writing plays had surprised me ten years before that. And then somehow I was writing another book, *A Long Long Way*. I was at Faber and we were talking about the First World War. I wrote that book and I have a magical editor at Faber now, called Angus Cargill, who has sort of shimmied out *The Secret Scripture*. In a way editors are responsible because editors are often very like salmon fishermen. You are in the dark water and are trying to hide and write plays, but they can somehow sense. If you are fishing for salmon, as you may know, if you see the salmon you can go home because you are not going to catch it. On the other hand if you can't see them how do you know they are there? So editing is a profoundly interesting profession because they have to throw out the fly when they sense you are there, which is a different thing to knowing you are there. Then they pull out this thing and it is a book.

The only time I have had trouble in the theatre was when I haven't worked with people I have genuinely loved as people. Sometimes you find yourself inevitably in that situation but this other little play, *The Pride of Parnell Street*, was done with these two magical actors and this beautiful director and it restored my faith. That is a large part of it. I am sure you feel the same whatever profession you are in. Nothing is worth the candle without that basic fact. You have to be in love with the people you are working with and in awe of them, in reverence even, as they drag you out of the water with a hook in your mouth.

Bigsby: A character in a William Faulkner novel says that the past is not dead it is not even the past, and that is surely true of Ireland. The past is not dead but there are different versions of that past. In *The Secret Scripture* there are competing stories. History is not a fact. It is a contested area.

Barry: Yes, it is many things. You remember, and then you choose what you wish to remember sometimes. That is often out of a sense of guilt, but also things of their nature assemble themselves in your memory and become enabling narratives, become myths. You build yourself upon those myths and their truth or untruth becomes irrelevant, in fact becomes unassailable and shouldn't possibly be interfered with. Her psychiatrist, Dr. Greene, knows towards the end of the book that the woman at the centre, and whose story this is, is probably not telling the factual truth always, but he says he prefers her untruth because it radiates health even though she is supposed to be a mental patient in the asylum. It is a far greater health than he has access to. And I have to say that happened quite accidentally, or just as the book was going on. I didn't quite know what was going on and you don't want to know quite what's going on in a book because if you knew what was going on you probably wouldn't have the energy to write it.

The book is called *The Secret Scripture* because she is writing it in secret, this account of her life. When my mother became ill she told me, to my astonishment, that she had been writing her own secret account of her childhood, really the same people I was writing about, in her car in the dark. It was called *Dear Mr. Bergman*, because her great dream was to work with Ingmar Bergman. She was always waiting for the call and this was a magical account of her childhood which I did eventually have the courage to read. In the week she died Bergman died the following day, which was very curious. She didn't know him from Adam. Even a few months ago, talking about the interconnectedness of things which is really what writing is, I think, I got a note from my American publisher that one of the great Bergman actresses had bought ten copies of my book in Wyoming, or somewhere where she was living. It all seemed very strange but also very enabling. We look for accreditation from people, don't we? We want critics to admire us, or if they don't admire us we want them to not admire us in a gentle sort of way.

You talk about history. I loved history at school but I never could remember any dates because I think, to my mind, as a child and even now, history is not the past and has not even happened yet. There is that sense that everything is always happening at the same time for me. If you narrate a book in the past tense somehow it is still in the present. It doesn't have to be in the present tense.

We grew up in this binary country, north and south, Catholic and Protestant, but the truth of the matter, or the healthy untruth of the matter, is that any Irish family is woven of all these things. There was this big debate in Ireland the day before yesterday about should you wear the poppy in Ireland. I am not saying you should wear the poppy and not wear the lily. I am saying let us do all these things as we wish, as artists of our past, to create this present.

It can seem that this thing that we call history is sometimes unattached to people, but it never is. We all endure our histories, and we all endure the sorrows and few joys of our histories. The great net we are all caught up in, the tangled broken trawler man's net in the deep sea, is our history and we are the fish in the net. So when they drag us up from the depths, when you drag somebody up from the depths of being forgotten, inevitably this other thing comes up with them. It gives me a sense of joy to greet history as if for the first time, to be writing about the Irish Civil War as if I were there. At the end of writing *A Long, Long Way* I felt as if I were returning from the front, entirely safe, unscathed, never in any danger, but the experience of allowing oneself to be tangled up in the same net of history that these characters had been tangled up in gave me an enormous physical sense of having been there. I suppose that is what I was trying to do in the book, so if people wanted to call them traitors or heroes or fools, whatever they wanted to say about them, they would at least have had the experience of being there so we would literally know what we were talking about, which is not always the case.

In Conversation With
Cherie Blair

- 29th September 2008 -

Cherie Booth was born in Bury in 1954 and brought up in Waterloo, Liverpool. She studied law at the London School of Economics and became a barrister in 1976, subsequently becoming a Queen's Counsel in 1995 and a Recorder (part-time judge) in 1999. Earlier she had run, unsuccessfully, for parliament and in 1980 married Tony Blair who served as Prime Minister for ten years from 1997. She is a founding member of Matrix Chambers where she continues to practise as a barrister.

Bigsby: What made you decide to write your autobiography?

Blair : I think two reasons. Firstly, as anyone who has read the book will know, I am a mad reader. I love reading. I cannot travel without several books. I have one now. I have also acquired a Sony book reader on which I have one hundred and thirty books just in case I run out of anything to read. So, being such a reader myself the idea of writing a book which I hoped would be a good read appealed to me. But the other reason, and why it is called *Speaking For Myself*, is because for thirteen years, although I am used to speaking for my clients in court, I had not been able to speak for myself. As a result of which the *Daily Mail* had tended to speak for me and, as some of you may understand, the *Daily Mail* and I had very little in common and therefore the image they projected of me wasn't necessarily the one that anyone, certainly not me, would recognise, and I rather hoped that people who knew me wouldn't recognise it either.

Bigsby: Rainer Maria Rilke once said that fame is the sum of all the misunderstandings that gather about a name and I imagine that is part of this venture.

Blair : It is a very odd thing. We are all brought up, and I was brought up, to think that when you go into a room with strangers you don't thrust yourselves in front of them, but when you become the wife of the Prime Minister and are thrust into the public limelight you walk into a room and are expected to put your hand out and speak to people. So you do get into this rather odd position where people think they know you because they have seen you and yet of course they don't.

Bigsby: Were you ever tempted to call it *Cherie Booth, Speaking for Myself?*

Blair : There was a complete debate about that because when I first went into Downing Street I was very insistent that I wanted to preserve the Cherie Booth QC. That was partly because it was a tradition of the bar, almost certainly when I was coming up as a lady barrister, that many women actually left the bar when they got married or had children. But Cherie Booth was my trading name, if you like, so when I got married I didn't want to change my trading name. When I went into Downing Street I was more used to calling myself Cherie Booth than Cherie Blair except when I was at my children's school. There I am the mother of my children, so that obviously is Blair.

  Number Ten found that very difficult. They said, 'No one will know who you are' and there was a discussion about what we should say on the notepaper. There was a discussion about whether I should have any notepaper at all, which is all to do with budgets because lots of people started writing to me. When Tony came in, in 1997, the number of letters went from approximately seven thousand a week to about twelve thousand. So the Number Ten correspondence unit was being overwhelmed by letters and when they started getting letters for me – and I would get two hundred or two hundred and fifty letters a week plus as the years went by, apart from e-mails – they all had to be responded to. There hadn't been such a volume of letters before but there was no budget even for the notepaper. Then we had this absurd discussion about what should be on the notepaper. A lot of people wrote to me in Chambers and that mail would come to Cherie Booth but Downing Street said that if I had Cherie Booth on the notepaper then obviously that couldn't be paid for by the government. Then they wanted to put Cherie Blair QC on it but I said, 'Cherie Blair isn't a QC. Cherie Booth is the QC,' so we had this ridiculous discussion.

Bigsby: On the other hand, Cherie is not even your baptismal name. Cherie is on the birth certificate but not on the baptismal one on the grounds that there aren't any saints called Cherie.

Blair : No. My grandma's cousin was our parish priest and in the 1950s, as every good Catholic knew, you had to have a saint's name and there is no Saint Cherie – I am working on a sainthood but I think it is definitely work in progress. So he changed it to Latin, which was Cara, and I was actually baptised Cara Theresa, the little flower being regarded as a suitable saint for a young Catholic girl.

Bigsby: Your parents were both actors and aspiring actors, early in their career, and as a result had to move around the country. So they left you with your paternal grandparents in Waterloo, a suburb of Liverpool, and in a Road called Ferndale Road, which just happens to be where my wife was born and raised. Can you describe what sort of a road Ferndale Road was? Would you characterise it as a working class street?

Blair : Yes, a working class street but there are hierarchies in that. It came off St. John's road which was a typical 1950s shopping street so at the bottom of our street was the chemist and along the road there was a cobblers and a chandlers, all the things that my children have no idea what I am talking about when I say those names. We even had a pawnbrokers and, of course, the fish and chip shop and grocers etc. Then there was the railway line and beyond the railway line were the streets which led up to my school and which were called Little Scandinavia. They were literally two up, two down, with outside toilets so we were definitely one above Little Scandinavia. The houses that we had later on I learned had a particular form of freehold/leasehold that was developed in the northwest and my grandparents had one of these. So they were able slowly to buy their house, but it was a terrace house. It had a small front garden and small back garden with an Anderson shelter.

Bigsby: You were raised there because although your parents had another daughter and briefly went down to London you yourself lived in Ferndale Road, as did your mother when she eventually gave up the stage.

Blair : The extraordinary thing was that normally speaking you would have expected me to have been brought up by my mother's parents but because her mother died when she was fourteen, my mother then had to leave school at fourteen because her father was a miner. She left school because she was then expected to look after father and her ten-year-old brother. Her father, without telling her, just announced one day that he was about to remarry and the day he brought his new wife into the front door of the house my mother left by the back door and went down to take up a place at RADA, so she didn't really have a mother to take her baby to. That is how I ended up being brought up by my father's mother and father and my mother spending the next eighteen years of her life there. She was formally separated from my father, though not divorced. She became more a part of his family than he was.

Bigsby: You were effectively abandoned by your father. Did you feel that as you were growing up?

Blair : I have mixed feelings about that because in one sense, of course, yes, he personally abandoned us, but his family did not and I think that made for this slightly unusual dynamic because I was brought up by his mother and father as well my mother and his side of the family were very dominant. He had a large extended family and I was very much part of the Booth family.

Bigsby: But he didn't just abandon you. When he had another child, another daughter by somebody else, he did something pretty strange. He put an advertisement in the *Crosby Herald*, the local paper, to say that he had had this child with another woman: 'half-sister to Cherie' That must have been a scandal in Ferndale Road.

Blair : There was a huge scandal because my father, I think, did that because he thought it would put pressure on my mother to divorce him. We are talking about 1963, which was before the divorce law reform, and you couldn't get a divorce. He certainly couldn't get a divorce, unless she chose to divorce him on the grounds of adultery. In fact, of course, it made my mother all the more determined that she wasn't going to get a divorce and she didn't in fact finally divorce him until I was in my early twenties when she, at one point, thought she might go to Canada and get married to someone else. My father, by this time, was deeply distressed that she chose to divorce him not least because he had no excuse not to marry his latest lady.

Bigsby: The embarrassment did not end there because he was later going to get involved with drugs and drink. Yet you were reconciled with him, as your sister was not.

Blair : Two things affected that. One is because my parents were still actors when I was born. My grandmother was fifty-one when I was born, which I now know is very young, and for her I was almost like her fourth child. I was always very close to my grandmother and my dad was her first born. Though my granddad was very cross with my father for what he did, my grandmother could never quite bring herself to condemn her own. Because of my relationship with my grandma I was never quite sure whether my dad was my dad or my errant big brother and then, in 1979, just before Tony and I got married, he suffered this horrendous accident in which he was seriously burnt. He was in hospital for nearly a year and at that point the only person who went to visit him was me. I went to visit him weekly in the hospital. I would go to the burns unit and you would hear the people screaming. Almost every week somebody would have died and he nearly did twice. I don't think you can see someone like that and still hold grudges against them. He paid for his sins, that's for sure.

Bigsby: At the age of sixteen you joined the Labour Party?

Blair : I did, and I am still a member, still proud to be a member.

Bigsby: Where did that come from? At the age of sixteen life is full of interesting things to do. Joining the Labour Party wouldn't necessarily be high on the list.

Blair : Even though my father was absent he was very much a big supporter of the Party. By that time he was in the television show *Till Death Do Us Part* and was playing the Scouse git, the socialist in the room. Even though he didn't see me very often he used to send me books like *The Female Eunuch* and somehow from that, at fourteen, I told the girls in my class I was going to be the first female Prime Minister of Britain.

Bigsby: Close.

Blair : Close, but not close enough.

Bigsby: Then it was university and you decided to study law. Why law?

Blair : Why law? Why not? As I said, I love literature. I love history but, I think, coming from my background, I wanted to do something that was practical, that was going to ensure that I was going to support myself. I think the one thing I had learnt from my mother and grandmother is that a woman needs her independence. She needs to be able to earn her own living. My mother had that thrust on her. One year she had been a student at RADA with Jackie Collins and then, within five years, she had had to work in a fish and chip shop to support her two children, and that was not glamorous by any means. My grandfather fell down the ship's hole, because he was a merchant seaman, and broke his two hips. She had to go out cleaning to keep the family. My father had to leave school at sixteen because he had to go out and make his contribution to the family. I knew that it was important to have a career that would make sure that I could support myself, though the nuns at school liked to encourage us all to become teachers because then we could be good Catholic mothers and give it all up and have babies. It didn't appeal to me to be a teacher at all, though I think I gained so much from my teachers. I am not sure I would have been a good teacher and so my boyfriend of the time's mother said to me, 'Well, Cherie, you are very good at debating. Clearly you are doing art subjects, not science subjects,' because in those days you could give up the sciences and I did. 'So, why don't you become a lawyer?' In my naivety I thought, 'Oh well, why not?' It never occurred to me that breaking into law in the nineteen-seventies was very much a question of who you knew, and of course I knew nobody.

Bigsby: At that time you managed to go there because you were on a full grant. Those were the days when fees were paid and, as you know, students are concerned with this now because they have to pay fees. One argument is that getting into debt is particularly sensitive for people who come from working class backgrounds, and who have a horror of debt. If you had been charged fees, would you still have gone on do you think?

Blair: I think that my mother and grandmother were so determined that we were going to have a good education that somehow or other I would because of their belief, which is absolutely right, that education is the key. When I went to the bar, of course, though I got a grant for my fee, I had to support myself so that is when I did some teaching. I lectured at what is now the University of Westminster. I was lucky because I came top of the bar finals and was given a loan. So I took out a loan myself, which I was able to pay back. Then, three years after I had become a lawyer, my sister qualified as a solicitor by which time the discretionary grant system, that had paid for me to do my bar final, wasn't available to her. I was just starting as a barrister and I took out a loan in order to pay her fees because, somehow or other, it was really important. I knew I would get it back. So I don't necessarily accept the idea that the fear of debt means that no working class person would go to university. On the other hand every week the man from the Prudential would come along to my grandmother. She had a death benefit because the fear of not being able to be buried was something that I can remember from my grandma even to this day, which I don't think is something that my children, or the children that my children went to school with, and who came from working class families, experienced.

Bigsby: You got a first class degree.

Blair: The reason I got a first class degree is that I absolutely knew that if I didn't get the best degree I could possibly get I might just as well give up then because there was no way that a girl like me, not having gone to Oxbridge and not having a really good degree, could have got anywhere.

Bigsby: But the irony is you did have a chance to go to Oxbridge. You had a place at Oxford or the Inns of Court. Why did you turn down Oxford?

Blair: I turned down Oxford for two reasons. One was that when I went to Oxford for my interview they said to me, 'Cherie, now you are going to become an academic lawyer but you need to have a professional qualification so apply for the bar.' Lincoln's Inn sent me a form which had an entrance scholarship form and to my astonishment they gave me a scholarship. They waived the seventy pounds fee and I suddenly thought, they are paying for me to go to the bar. Why do I want to talk about the law when actually I could make the law, so that is what I did.

Bigsby: But there were aspects of Oxford life that you probably wouldn't have been comfortable with.

Blair: I think that is also true. I felt that the privileged life of Oxford was not for me. I had come from the LSE. When I went to university only eight per cent of working class students went to university at all so I wouldn't say it was full of working class students, but it was in London and it didn't have that aura of privilege about it which when I went to Oxford really struck me.

Bigsby: And you went on being a swot because you came top of the bar exams.

Blair: One of the reasons I wrote this book was because my husband has very successfully told my children that whilst he was going around with his friends – my husband, by the way, got a third in his bar finals –

their mother was holed up in the library eating her sandwiches and reading all the books. The reason for that, of course, was that I knew I had only one chance. I also had a boyfriend in Liverpool at the time and used to go home at the weekend and have my fun so I had to concentrate during the week. I wanted the kids to know that I wasn't this saddo who just spent the whole time in the library, but they still actually seem to think that is what I did.

Bigsby: You then had to look for a Chambers. At the time this was a very male profession. Was that daunting? Did you have the sense that you were against the system in some way?

Blair: That never occurred to me. I can't imagine how naïve I must have been. I was twenty-one. Because I had been put ahead a year I was already younger than everybody else. I had done well at school and then at the LSE. No one had suggested to me that being a girl was a problem at all. The first time I realised that being a girl was a problem was when I went to the bar because suddenly you would try and find a place and they would say, but we don't take women in these Chambers or we have got a woman so we don't want another. It was absolutely perfectly acceptable to say that then. Now fifty per cent of the students qualifying in law school are women. Last year was the first year that the number of women called to the bar reached fifty per cent. It is a completely different world but no one had ever told me, and the nuns certainly hadn't mentioned, that being a girl was a problem. So it hadn't even occurred to me.

Bigsby: You went into Chambers and the name of the person who brought you in would crop up later on because it was Derry Irving, who would become Lord Chancellor under your husband. As it happened, though, he had already promised somebody else who duly turned up but got put in some upper room because he had a third in his bar finals. Tony Blair.

Blair: I have to say he did get a 2:1 at university.

Bigsby: When you first met him, any flicker?

Blair: No, not particularly. When we first met we were both getting ready to go in for this scholarship that Lincoln's Inn were giving. They had given me an entrance scholarship but then they also had what they called major scholarships which were about five hundred pounds I think. I can always remember the first day I went in to start with Derry. He said to me, 'I will waive the hundred pounds fee,' and I said, 'Fee, what fee?' I mean in those days, in 1976, technically you were the pupil barrister. As the apprentice, you had to pay the pupil master and so you certainly didn't get paid as a pupil. The scholarship, then, was really quite important.

He was Blair and I was Booth and so we ended up sitting next to each other in the queue for the scholarship interview because the scholarship was done not on hardship grounds but on merit. Tony was looking quite extraordinary because, as you all know now, he once had long hair but the week before he went for the scholarship interview he had gone to some barbers in Durham and had a pudding basin stuck on his head because that is what it looked like. He had this very short back and sides and had gone to Dunn and Co and bought a very traditional suit with turn-ups and a waistcoat. So he looked like the kind of public school boy that had put me off going to Oxford. He, being Tony, was very charming and said, 'Where are you going? Have you got a pupillage? I have got one with Derry Irvine.' I nearly fell off my chair because I thought Derry had implied to me that I was going to be his only pupil. So I knew from the very beginning that I had a rival.

Bigsby: Later, though, he would propose to you, though in less than romantic circumstances.

Blair : Absolutely. In all those books I read when I was a girl he is supposed to go down on his knees. Somebody obviously hadn't told Tony that because he managed to propose to me after we had been on holiday in Italy, in Sienna, which was very romantic but as the good girl that I was I was doing the cleaning. I was cleaning the bathroom on my hands and knees when he just suddenly appeared behind me and popped the question. However I wasn't stupid enough to hesitate and said, 'Yes' pretty quickly.

Bigsby: What surprises me is that yours was a Protestant marriage, despite the fact that you come from a Catholic background and have become more Catholic over the years. The grandmother we talked about earlier actually turned down the person that she actually was in love with because he was a Protestant.

Blair : Yes. I don't think my grandma wanted to turn him down but in Liverpool, in those days, the idea that the two of them could get married was just impossible but she always used to say that Ed Wilson was the love of her life. She never married him, though.

Bigsby: So now you are both barristers and both in the Labour Party and very interested in what was happening in the Party. Of course these were not good years to be in the Labour Party. In 1983 you ran for parliament in Thanet. The conservative candidate was Roger Gale. You didn't do terribly well. By now there was an SDP party which had spun off from Labour. Why didn't you and Tony go that route because many of the things they were saying surely echoed your own convictions?

Blair : I think for me it is partly tribal, that is for sure, because that is where I come from, but I think the other thing – and Tony felt this very much – was that the Labour Party had its roots in the community and the trade unions and he felt that the most important thing to do was to fight within the Labour Party for the centre-left position that he believed in rather than going off and setting up what was essentially a middle-class niche party of his own.

Bigsby: But in that election the SDP candidate actually got nearly twice the votes that you did.

Blair : It is very gentlemanly of you to point that out but I kept my deposit and was one of the few candidates from the south east of England who did.

Bigsby: Tony, meanwhile, got elected because he was dropped into a safe seat.

Blair : Well he wasn't dropped into it, he wrested that safe seat from the clutches of the hideous Les Huckfield who those old enough to remember know was certainly not of the moderate thinking of the Labour Party.

Bigsby: Were you tempted to run again the next time?

Blair : I think it would be difficult to say what I felt in 1983. By the time 1987 came around two things happened because the thing about that election campaign was that not only did Tony suddenly get elected but he had had nine months when he had been the candidate's husband, an experience that has scarred him for life. As you may have noticed when Hillary Clinton was standing for President, the role of the First Lady, or spouse of the candidate, requires special handling and women seem to be a little bit better at that than some of these alpha males. Tony found it quite difficult to be the candidate's husband. I went to see my agent who came with me and after lunch the agent said to him, 'Tony, do you mind retiring with my wife and doing the washing up while Cherie and I talk politics.' This was a really bad moment for Tony. The election was called and he had no seat. I did, though I wasn't honestly expecting to win, but at least I had a seat. Tony said there was one seat left in the country, in the north east where he came from, and which he wanted to represent. He just went up there and came back as the MP for Sedgefield, an incredibly fortunate stroke of fate.

Suddenly I find myself unexpectedly the wife of an MP in the North East. Then I discovered that the reason I had been feeling a bit sick during the election campaign wasn't nerves. I was actually pregnant and after that we had Euan, and two years later we had Nicholas, and suddenly I found myself earning more money than my husband and therefore becoming the main breadwinner in the family with two children at home who needed my attention. On that basis it became more sensible to concentrate on what I was good at and actually I think I made the right choice. Tony is the consummate politician and I am not always as good at not showing my feelings as he is. I think I am a good lawyer. I know I am a good lawyer.

Bigsby: Over the following years Tony worked his way up through the Party and then suddenly came a complete shock. John Smith, the leader, died and there was a question of who would throw their hat in the ring. Were you instrumental in persuading him to run?

Blair : I think Tony knew from the very beginning that he needed to run, but there was absolutely no doubt in my mind that he was the right person to do that, even though we still had three young children at that stage – Euan was born in 1984 so in 1994 he was only ten, and we had ten, eight and six. Of course at the time I didn't realise it would make such a difference to our family. Rather naively, I knew it would make a difference to Tony. I had no idea that it would also have such an impact on our lives.

Bigsby: You say in your book that Tony and Gordon Brown did, indeed, meet at the Granita Restaurant in Islington, where supposedly they agreed that in time Gordon would take over as Prime Minister, but that in fact everything was already decided. All that does, though, is push that meeting back to another place and another occasion. Your husband must have come back from that meeting and said, 'We have had this discussion and this is what we decided.' What did they decide?

Blair : It wasn't just one discussion. There were a series of explorations between the two of them about who would be the best person to promote what became known as the New Labour Party and from the beginning the truth was it was obvious very early on that Tony had more appeal to the wider electorate than Gordon.

Bigsby: Was there a deal?

Blair : No, there wasn't. I say in the book that there wasn't a deal in that sense. There was, however, an agreement that Tony would go forward and Gordon would not.

Bigsby: To which Gordon responded positively while insisting that he would be expecting, after a certain period of time, to receive the mantle.

Blair : What I say in my book is what he told me at the time, and it is also one of the things that he read very carefully in my book. So you can assume that he will not differ substantially from what I say, though he may well elaborate it more fully. Who knows?

Bigsby: When he read the manuscript did he have a red pen in his hand or was he just admiring?

Blair : He wasn't always admiring and I am sure he must have skipped some of the bits, some of the more romantic bits. I don't think that is going to be in his book but he should be very grateful to me because he doesn't have to say that. It is all in there.

Bigsby: Then came the triumph of 1997. Everything was swept away. You are in Number 10. How used was Number Ten to having a Prime Minister's wife who is not only a barrister but also has children and who intends to live there, or somewhere in that complex? Were they ready for that?

Blair : No, they really were not ready for that and that was the biggest shock to the Number Ten system because there never had been a working wife at Number Ten, working in the sense of working outside the home because Norma Major had done a lot. She wrote books. She did a lot of charity work, as had other spouses, but no one had had the sort of job that I had which involved me with many commitments of my own. I had to appear in court, which was not easily movable, that is for sure. In 1997 they certainly hadn't had a working wife before and they hadn't had children living in Number Ten because the Prime Ministers hadn't ever been as young as Tony was and they certainly didn't have as young children as that. Norma and John Major's children had been in their late teens so his daughter had already left school and his son was still in the sixth form. Norma based herself out of their home in the constituency which was near where the children were. Although they came occasionally it wasn't their main home.

Bigsby: Number Ten isn't like *The West Wing* where when you fancy something to eat there is a chef who will provide everything. You are actually a housewife there.

Blair : Absolutely. When I did my other book, *The Goldfish Bowl*, I interviewed the various spouses of the Prime Minister and I also went to interview Ted Heath and he told me the story of how when he was elected unexpectedly in 1970 he had come in that day and started doing the cabinet reshuffle. They had gone all day and at about nine or ten o'clock at night he suddenly felt hungry and said, 'Should we eat something?' They all looked round and said, 'There are no facilities in Number Ten.' They had to send somebody out to find somewhere with some sandwiches. Eventually they came back with some curled up old sandwiches which they had got from some café somewhere. Number Ten wasn't actually geared to having a bachelor in it let alone a family. Even when Margaret Thatcher was Prime Minister they didn't provide a cook and a chef for her either. That just wasn't the way things were done.

Bigsby: There have been a number of occasions on which stories about you appeared all over the press. One concerned Carole Caplin. I am less interested in the fact that she introduced you to a man who turned out to be a confidence trickster, because she was fooled as much as anybody else, but is it correct that there was a new age element to Carole and a new age element to you?

Blair : It is not correct that there is a new age element to me, that's for sure, except I have to confess I think Arnica is very good for bruising. I don't think I am any more new age than most people. Carole was probably more new age than me but even she I don't think is as wacky as the *Daily Mail* would have you believe.

Bigsby: The other *Daily Mail* issue related to the supposed connection between the MMR vaccine and its alleged connection to autism, which did indeed scare people, which is very dangerous because we rely on herd immunity. At the time you and Tony were asked what you were doing about your own children. There was a period in which your position was that this was private, that you did not want any intrusion into your life. But surely that was not an unreasonable question?

Blair: Looking back on it now I sometimes wonder whether it wouldn't have just been better to say, 'Yes, Leo has had the MMR jab and all his other jabs too,' but at the time we had got to a stage where this whole thing around Leo being born, the first child to be born to a serving Prime Minister for one hundred and fifty years, led me to fear that I would be going into labour and the *Daily Mail* would rush in and take a photograph. The country had already seen the morning after the night before image of me and I really didn't think that they needed to see that again, so I was very concerned. I didn't want to get into a situation where every time Leo sneezed, or if he was ill, there had to be some statement in the press. He is an ordinary child. He may be the son of the Prime Minister but he is not living his life in the public eye and I was always very insistent that the children's privacy be respected. I had been very determined that my children would feel that this was not just something that was imposed on them, but a journey that they were on, too, which is why we had the picture taken outside Number Ten. I wanted to say this is something we are doing together and we had originally come to a deal with the press, or so we thought, that if once a year we gave them a photo opportunity with the children they would leave the children alone. By 2001 that deal had broken down and it got to the stage that we couldn't actually go out with the children without risking them being photographed and because of their privacy issues, because of their protection issues, we didn't want that to happen.

So we had got to a stage already when having made an agreement with the press, they then changed the rules. So I just didn't want to go into this and say, 'Oh well. Okay. We will tell you this one thing about Leo's health, but this is a one-off thing and won't set a precedent' because we were always getting this thing which said, 'Well, you showed your children on your Christmas card therefore we can take a picture whenever we like.' That was the thinking behind that. We had to hold the line with the children. In the end Tony actually went out and said, 'I wouldn't recommend to the public anything I wouldn't to my own children,' which I thought was hint enough but the *Daily Mail*, who after all were the paper that was driving this agenda that the MMR was dangerous, are more responsible for the fact that the uptake of the injection went down rather than my failure to expose my child's medical records to them.

Bigsby: You are not only a barrister, you are a Recorder now, a part-time judge, and you have had a career that is still going. But you don't actually get to pick and choose your cases do you?

Blair : Number Ten found it very hard at first when I took cases that were against the government. Before Labour came into power I had occasionally done cases for the government, which was perfectly alright, but of course once my husband became Prime Minister there was really no question that I could take cases for the government because that would not be a sensible thing to do. So by default, obviously, if I wasn't taking cases for the government, it meant that if I was going to carry on practicing it would be more likely to be against the government.

Bigsby: Did this make breakfast interesting?

Blair : No. I have to tell you that my husband has never spent a lot of time discussing my cases with me, especially when he was Prime Minister, because he was far too busy doing other things than to want to hear a blow-by-blow account of my latest triumph in the High Court. My nanny, on the other hand, who helps look after the children, has become an expert on these issues because if I couldn't bore Tony with them I could certainly bore her with them.

Bigsby: Talking about barristers, you have said that £91 an hour is a derisory sum for somebody to be expected to work for.

Blair : Well, listen, legal aid was actually one of the pillars of the welfare state that was established after the Second World War and I personally believe that access to justice for poor people is as important as them having good health care and a good education. The fact is that we do have a crisis in our legal aid system at the moment and though you say £91 sounds a lot of money barristers are self-employed. From that £91 you have to pay your Chamber's expenses, your Chamber's rent. At least a third goes off automatically. You have to pay your travelling expenses. So it is not the equivalent of your take home pay by any means. I may regret having said that. Many barristers, including me, do legal aid work but I am able to do non legal aid work as well and the fact is my non legal aid rate is a lot more than £91 an hour. So when you do legal aid work you are doing it because of the principle that I believe in, which is you need to have access to justice for everybody in this country otherwise our legal system doesn't work.

Bigsby: When you both left Downing Street would you personally like to have stayed on or did you feel this was, for both your purposes, the right moment?

Blair : Tony's view has always been that in a democracy you need to have a change. The Prime Minister is a job that you can't do forever by any means and two terms or ten years was always the kind of framework he thought was the right time to go. From my point of view, I always preferred the ten years for purely completely selfish reasons that ten years happened to mean that by that time I would have got several of my children through their A levels and from my point of view that was a good time because what I didn't want to do was disrupt them again. That is completely irrelevant to everybody else, and not a good reason to stay on, but as it happened the ten years did mean that all our children had gone through and had left university by then.

Bigsby: What has the role of faith been in your life, perhaps especially more recently since marriage?

Blair : I never thought as a young woman that I was necessarily a very good girl and as you pointed out I actually got married in the Church of England mainly because by this time my mum had moved down to Oxford and we didn't have a local church, so it just seemed easier to do it that way, but actually my faith has always been important to me. It was something that was passed on to me by my grandma, who I have said before was very important, because my mother isn't even a Catholic. It was my father's side of the family who are Catholics. One of the things when Tony and I first met that we had in common was a fascination with belief and what it means to believe in something beyond just the temporal.

Bigsby: But you weren't a regular church attender for quite a while, were you?

Blair : I was a regular attender right up until going to university and then I used to go when I was at home but not particularly when I was at university. Then funnily enough, as I think often happens, it was the birth of my children and my realisation that I wanted to try and pass on my faith to them, that led to me going back to church. I know in fact that my three children have been probably as irregular church goers at university as I was. Certainly when they come home they usually humour me by coming to church with me, or else they stay out on Saturday night so that when it comes to going to church on Sunday they are not actually there.

There is a real paradox about the Catholic church because women are the backbone of the Catholic church but they don't have the full sacramental role, that is for sure. Whether that will ever change is certainly beyond my pay grade, but it is interesting when you think about the role of women in the Catholic church. Mary is a very important part of our whole faith and if you think who was probably the most famous, or one of the most famous Catholics of the twentieth century, it was probably Mother Theresa of Calcutta. Personally I wouldn't have any particular problem with women priests but as I say it is beyond my pay grade.

In Conversation With
William Boyd

- 29th November 2006 -

William Boyd was born in Accra, Ghana, in 1952 and grew up there and in Nigeria. Educated at Gordonstoun School and the universities of Nice, Glasgow and Oxford, he is a novelist and screenwriter. His novels include *A Good Man in Africa* (1981), *An Ice-Cream War (1982)*, *Stars and Bars* (1984), *Brazzaville Beach* (1990), *Any Human Heart* (2002), *Restless* (2006) and *Ordinary Thunderstorms* (2009). He is a winner, among others, of the Whitbread Award, the Somerset Maugham Award, the James Tait Black Memorial Prize and the Prix Jean Monet.

Bigsby: Your most recent book is called *Restless*. It is a spy novel, if also something more than that.

Boyd: *Restless* is a spy novel. I feel I have only got one foot in the genre and the other one is still firmly planted in the world of literary fiction, which I usually inhabit. But I became very interested in spies when I wrote my last novel before this one, *Any Human Heart*. That novel is the story of a man's life in the twentieth century told through his intimate journals. He lives in every decade of the twentieth century. In World War II he is recruited by Ian Fleming, no less, to join the naval intelligence division and he becomes a spy of sorts. He goes to spy on the Duke and Duchess of Windsor in the Bahamas while they endured their exile. His next mission was to be parachuted into Switzerland where he was going to pose as a South American ship broker. So he does parachute in and for a day wanders around Geneva thinking, 'I am a spy.' Then he is immediately arrested and goes to prison. But in the course of researching that World War II spying life I became very intrigued by the psychology of what it takes to be a spy, what it takes to be a good spy. What kind of mindset do you have and can you ever stop being a spy. I was very interested in our famous traitors, our famous Cambridge Five, and particularly Kim Philby, who seems to me to be the most intriguing because he joined the British Secret Service in 1941 and defected to Moscow in 1963. So for twenty-two years he lived a double life, absolutely impeccably.

Everybody seemed to love Kim Philby. He was highly competent. People were desperately shocked when he turned out to have been a double agent. So I got interested in what kind of mind was required to live this life. This is how novels begin, I think, and certainly in my case. They usually start with a question. I asked myself the question, 'What would it be like if you discovered that one of your parents had been a spy, and everything you thought you knew about this person was a fabrication, a fiction, a kind of cover?' What effect would that have on your view of that person, and what effect would it have on your life, because you would be deeply effected by this revelation. I thought, why not have a son who discovers that his father has been a spy in the war, but a split second later I thought, no, it would be far more interesting if a daughter discovers that her mother has been a spy. Why did I think that? Two reasons, I think. One was because I was entering a genre – I suppose I would think the same if I was trying to write a detective novel or a techno thriller – and I wanted to somehow freshen it for myself, or to come at it from an oblique angle. It is such a masculine world, the world of spies, that it seemed to me that to have a young woman as a spy was going to be far more interesting, and to investigate the particular mindset that spying required, than to do perhaps the slightly over-familiar one of the man who was a spy.

Once you get these ideas there is no going back. So I had two women characters, the daughter, who is called Ruth, and her mother, who she thinks is called Sally, but in fact turns out to be Eva, a Russian émigré recruited in 1939 in Paris. And the other reason I felt happy about doing this is because I realise I have written from the point of view of women for almost my entire writing career. There is a very early short story of mine called *Bat Girl* where I write from the point of view of a young girl working a fair ground in Oxford. My second novel, *An Ice-cream War*, has six points of view and two of those are women, one a German nurse, one the young wife of a British officer. Then I wrote a novel in 1990 called *Brazzaville Beach*, where I took the plunge and took on the first person singular and wrote the novel in the persona of a young woman scientist, a primatologist studying wild chimpanzees in Central Africa. So I felt comfortable and also challenged in writing about a woman spy and writing about her daughter. I evolved this method – which I think would work perfectly the other way around, if you were a woman wanting to write from the point of view of a man – when I was writing *Brazzaville Beach*. I thought what I would do was ask my wife lots of probing questions, and ask my women friends questions. Then I realised I would just get a mass of contradictory answers and so I knew I should find another way of doing it. So what I decided to do was not ask anybody anything, and to ignore absolutely all questions of gender, sexual politics, received wisdom about the difference between men and women and concentrate exclusively on personality, character and the nature of this particular woman, Hope Clearwater, because I knew exactly what she was like. I knew the colour of her eyes, how tall she was, what food she liked to eat or didn't, everything about her. So, whenever I found myself writing and confronting situations that seemed to be slightly gender-driven dilemmas, I wouldn't say, 'What would a woman do in this situation?' I would say, 'What would Hope do in this situation?' and because she is quite tough and smart but also has been emotionally very bruised, everything she does, even if it seems out of character, is entirely plausible because it is based on her personality. It really did work. It was widely reviewed by women critics and I think that is the way to do it, ignore sexuality, ignore gender, concentrate exclusively on personality, and then the character and her actions will have a built-in plausibility and authenticity that has nothing to do with men are from Mars and women are from Venus.

Bigsby: People will think that because you are setting *Restless* in the Second World War Europe is going to be the centre of attention, but there is a rather more surprising aspect to it which not only involves another country, but a surprising and true story.

Boyd: Well, it is surprising to everybody I think because there is a brief moment in Eva's spying career when she is involved in an incident on the Dutch/German border which is true, authentic, though I have changed a few names. One of the questions I asked myself when the novel was in the long process of invention was, if Eva is a spy, where will she spy? I had been asked by the BBC to write a drama about the relationship between Churchill and Roosevelt in World War II and in the course of researching this I stumbled across this extraordinary story, this enormous covert operation that the British Secret Service had run in the USA in 1940 and 41, before Pearl Harbour. They set up this organisation in the Rockefeller Centre in Manhattan called British Security Coordination which was meant to be a kind of liaison office, but in fact became the centre of a huge news manipulation operation. The British Secret Service was able to plant any story it wanted, almost at will, in any American newspaper or radio station. Quite extraordinary. Spin doctoring doesn't even begin to do it justice. Some commentators have said it was the biggest, most successful covert operation of its kind. But it has been completely forgotten. So it is wonderful as a novelist to come across this corner of World War II history which nobody has explored. You punch the air and think, great, terra incognita.

Bigsby: This was because the primary objective of the British was to get America in the war?

Boyd: Yes, because we forget in this era of the so-called special relationship that in 1941, in Britain's darkest hour, eighty percent of the American population did not want to go to war in Europe. American was very isolationist. Roosevelt, however much he was inclined to help us, and that is another complex issue I think, had his hands firmly tied because Congress was violently anti-interventionist. There were powerful lobby groups saying, 'Don't go to war in Europe. We did it last time and all we got was the Great Depression,' so Churchill had set up BSC to try to change American public opinion, to try to persuade the American population and Congress that it was in their interest to join the battle against Nazi Europe. Whether he would have succeeded or not we will never know because on December 7th 1941 the Japanese bombed Pearl Harbour, but there is no doubt that BSC was phenomenally successful. They had penetrated American news media and were able to place stories which were pro-British, pro-intervention. They could place stories that were anti-isolationist, anti-neutral. It is almost as if Portugal had decided to manipulate the media in Greece. I don't know if it has ever been done before. Our own media is manipulated by our own government, of course, but it is not so common to try and manipulate the media in another country. But they did do it very successfully and it has all been brushed very far under the carpet.

Bigsby: These were, in a way, spies as novel writers. They were creating an alternative reality?

Boyd: Yes, because as one of the characters says, 'An untruth can do as much good for us as a truth.' So the whole operation that Lucas Romer runs – Actuarial Accountancy Services – is, in fact, a form of propaganda, dropping things that look like facts into the world and seeing how they grow. A German General is about to be replaced, a new bridge is going over a river, a new type of depth-charge has been developed. These are all fictions but you present them as fact and, as we all know, they are believed. People are credulous. Maybe they were more credulous in 1941 than we are today, but it worked fantastically well.

Bigsby: It is a spy novel, but, as you say, it is also about a mother and daughter relationship. The daughter discovers things that she didn't know about her mother, very dramatic things, but there is a level on which children never actually know their parents. There is a code that they can never break, and perhaps don't want to break.

Boyd: I think you are absolutely right. Ruth has a line in the novel where she says she realises this bombshell has gone off in her life. She asks, 'What do we know about our parent's lives? They are like saint's lives, all legend and anecdote,' and in a way that is true, absolutely true, which is why I have encouraged my mother to write it all down because you forget and there is nobody to confirm that knowledge once they pass on. I am very interested in the history of my father and mother but I realise that my grasp on it is slender and insecure. I need a witness. But, true, the human relationship in this novel, even though it is dramatic, is probably representative of any daughter/mother relationships, or son/father relationships.

Bigsby: *Restless* is a novel that required research. How far do you feel it necessary to visit the places where you set your work?

Boyd: I hadn't been to Tanganyika, which was the background to my second novel *The Ice-Cream War*. I couldn't afford to go. In fact I have now discovered that in some ways it is better not to go to places you are writing about. Researching a novel is a very curious business. Having researched a Ph. D, or having researched and failed to finish a Ph. D thesis, I know what research is all about, but as a novelist you are looking for different things. I wrote a novel, for example, set in the Philippines in 1902 called *The Blue Afternoon*, and after the book had been published I got a letter from a man who was the head of J. Walter Thompson, the advertising company. He was in Manila and he said, 'I loved your novel and I thought you would like to know that every time we get a new client here in Manila, we give him a copy of *The Blue Afternoon* just to explain something about our strange and extraordinary history. How long did you live in Manila? Were exactly did you live?' I have never set foot in the Philippines, but in a way it was a vindication of my method. I have often written about places that I have never been to.

Even in *Restless* there is a section that takes place in Ottawa in Canada, and there is a section that takes place in a town called Las Cruces in New Mexico, and I have met citizens of both places who have congratulated me on the accuracy with which I portray their respective towns. So I know how to do it now. I know how to make it seem completely convincing that I have walked the streets of Ottawa and Las Cruces. I don't feel the need to travel to research a novel, but I couldn't have written novels set in the tropics, for example, if I hadn't lived in the tropics.

Bigsby: *Restless* is set during the war, and war seems to be a recurring theme in your work.

Boyd: There is a lot of war in the world, so my novels reflect the times we live in. It is true that to live in Nigeria in 1968 to 1970, when the Biafran war was on, even though I was far from the fighting, was shocking. We were constantly stopped and searched. It was scary being in a country that seemed to be tearing itself apart. It had a profound effect on me because I thought I knew from the books I had read, and the films and television programmes I had seen, what human conflict was like, but everything I saw in Nigeria in those years made me realise it was completely wrong, that my received wisdom was utterly false and I had to rethink completely. I had two friends who were conscripted into the Biafran army so I heard their stories at first hand. It was such an awful war. A million people died and it was also a strange and surreal war and I thought all wars are like that, so when I came to write my second novel, *An Ice-Cream War*, I transplanted my Biafran war epiphany and put it down in East Africa, in the war between the British and German colonies. Everything about that war is true of all wars. They are utterly vicious, utterly random, uncontrollable, chance-driven events.

Because I became obsessed about it, it has cropped up in my fiction again, particularly World War I which is another one of my pet obsessions. So I want to get it right on a page and I even want to get it right on screen. One film I directed as a war movie was set in the trenches of World War I but there is no doubt that my teenage experience of seeing a civil war made me rethink everything that literature and film have taught me about the nature of warfare.

Bigsby: You were born in Africa. How important has Africa remained to you?

Boyd: Up until the age of about twenty-one or twenty-two, if somebody asked, 'Where is your home? Where do you live?' I would have said Nigeria. I was born in Ghana, but my parents moved to Nigeria when I was about ten, and even though I was sent to school in Britain I went back to West Africa in the holidays. I was far more at home in Ibadan, the capital of Western Nigeria, than I was in Edinburgh, the capital of Scotland, and I often used to unconsciously, unreflectingly, say I was a West African, because I felt that was where my root was, where my stuff was. I knew how it worked better than I knew how Britain worked. It is inextricably part of me but I don't really want to analyse too much what it has done to me as a writer. I think novelists have to keep a sizeable area of ignorance about themselves, a kind of innocence, because if you know too much you won't take risks, you won't make a fool of yourself, you won't go places you shouldn't go. So I am sure it has had a big effect on my writing, but maybe it is for others to chart that precisely.

I think the obvious thing, and this is perhaps the difference between writers like Doris Lessing and Christopher Hope, is that there are no settlers in West Africa, unlike East and South. Nobody owns the land. No white people, no Europeans, own the land. The most interesting thing about my upbringing as a white boy in West Africa was that I never, ever, experienced the slightest bit of racial tension. If you are a South African, or a Rhodesian, I don't think you could say that because the society as it existed was founded on that kind of inequality. That didn't exist in West Africa so it has given me a set of values and attitudes which I think are different from growing up in, say, South Africa, for someone of my age.

I think that consequently I have always been an outsider, not in any kind of racked or painful way. I was born in Ghana, but I can't say I am a Ghanaian. My parents come from Scotland and I was educated in Scotland but I have only lived there briefly. Wherever I hang my hat is where I feel at home. So in the sense that many people say to themselves, 'Where do I come from?' I can't really give that answer, or I have to give a very convoluted answer. I think that is maybe quite good for a novelist because you are always on the outside looking in. I think it probably explains quite a lot about the type of novels I write. I was always more interested in abroad than I was in Britain, and I see now that this novel is the third in which I have been tackling themes of identity, loss of identity, change of identity. The novel I am going to write next is also about loss of identity, so it is obviously on my mind. Why? Well, somebody might say, 'Look at your own life and your own identity problems.' But I am not going any further than that though I suspect it comes from my upbringing.

Bigsby: Before you went to boarding school in Britain you were educated in Ghana. Was that a white school?

Boyd: No, completely mixed. It was a completely inter-racial society. If you went to the recreation clubs, for example, they were completely racially mixed. My classmates and friends were Ghanaians or children of expatriates. It was completely unlike Rhodesian, Kenyan or South African society. People don't realise this because there has been very little fiction written about West Africa, very few novels of West African life compared to the novels that have come out of East Africa or South Africa. So it was a primary school and it had Ghanaian teachers and European teachers, and the classes were completely mixed. We lived on a university campus but Ghana was beginning to fall apart in the early nineteen sixties so we moved to Nigeria because my parents wanted to be safer. Three military coups and a civil war later they realised that perhaps they should have stayed put. But, as a teenager living in Nigeria in a time of incredible internal strife, I never for one second felt threatened. I would go into town late at night to watch movies, and there were soldiers and road blocks, but even though I was manifestly not a Nigerian, I never felt at risk. I think that is an extraordinary blessing that the expatriate children who lived in West Africa received, and children in the East and South didn't.

Bigsby: So the first time you encountered a strange tribe was when you went to Gordonstoun?

Boyd: Yes, a strange society.

Bigsby: That must have been a bit of a shock.

Boyd: It was a huge shock. I hadn't seen snow. I remember that morning in December, in Scotland, when all this white stuff was outside and a boy from Jamaica and I wandered out and picked it up and tasted it. All the other kids were looking on and laughing at us, but it was a strange, magical, substance that we had read about and seen from aeroplanes but had never actually encountered before. But then of course it is a very weird society, the single sex boarding school, a hot house society. I have written a lot about it and made two films about it, and it is another sin of omission by British novelists. There are very few films and very few novels that paint a true portrait of that world. Most of them are fantasies or fairy stories, including the classics. A strange place to be. In all these schools, and perhaps in all boarding schools, there is the public face of the school, which is in the brochure and which the teachers know, and then there is the private life of the school in which the boys and the girls control the mood of the school. It can be benign and druggy or it can be ferocious.

Bigsby: I am very interested that you use that word because John Fowles went to one and he became head boy, as you became Head of House, and he suddenly had this sense of power. In later life he felt terribly guilty about this. Did you ever have that sense of power?

Boyd: Yes, you do, and you also have a kind of renown in that tiny little hot house society which you can't replicate as an adult in the real world, unless you are some incredibly famous film star or musician or something like that, so it does warp people. You meet people in later life who were idols and you wonder what on earth were we thinking about? So it is very warping, particularly for the young adolescent boy to be given these kind of powers. You could certainly ruin somebody's life if you felt so inclined with that power. When I published the screen plays of my two school films I quoted Auden who said that every English schoolboy, he meant every English public schoolboy, knows what it is like to live in a fascist state because school is that kind of environment. I was rebuked for being over-dramatic, but it all depends. It can be sunny and easy-going but it can become a very terrifying place of fear for thirteen and fourteen year old boys.

Bigsby: You wrote that it took a year to recover from the education you had had at Gordonstoun. You then took yourself off to France.

Boyd: Yes. I wanted the then unheard of thing, a gap year, because I had been nearly ten years at a boarding school in the north of Scotland and I said to my father, 'Before I go to university I would like some time off,' and he said, 'Well, okay, but you have to do something useful.' My mother, as a teacher of French in a Nigerian school, had been on a course that certain French universities offered, so I went off to the university of Nice on the Cote d'Azur to do a diploma course in French studies. As soon as I arrived in Nice, at the age of eighteen, I realised that my education had not fitted me out for life alone, away from friends, family, culture, language, so really that academic year I spent there was a year of re-education in the Mao Tse-tung sense almost. I realised that I had been fitted out for a certain kind of life and it was wholly inappropriate for the kind of life I wanted to live. For a start, it was a life that had two sexes in it. So I see that year I had in Nice, alone and really hard up but learning another language, as incredibly informative and I think instinctively I wanted to be different from the person that I had been as I left that school. I set about becoming European.

Bigsby: France was going to become quite important to you. *An Ice-Cream War* was a best seller in France. Why did the French take to that particular novel?

Boyd: French journalists are constantly asking me that question. There is a very simple initial explanation. In France at that time there was a book programme called *Apostrophe* which was live at ten o'clock on a Friday evening. It ran for an hour and a half, or a bit longer if it was interesting, and it drew audiences of seven million, nine million, unheard of. It ran for fifteen years. It doesn't exist any more, but if you appeared on *Apostrophe* it guaranteed an extra ten thousand copies sold. Maybe it is the Richard and Judy phenomenon, but I duly went on this terrifying TV programme, in French, with four French authors. Luckily, due to my year in Nice, I could speak French but the presenter, Bernard Pivot, who is not an intellectual, went bananas about *An Ice-cream War*, and said I will personally reimburse anyone who doesn't love this book. It was like a news event. My publisher practically fell off her chair but I wasn't aware of this because I was sitting like a rabbit in the headlights thinking how long has this got to go on for? Anyway, he was so enthusiastic about it that he broke all his own rules of serene neutrality. The next day I had to do a signing session at the Grand Palais in Paris, where the Paris book fair was on, and as I was making my way to my publisher's stand I saw this enormous queue, hundreds of metres long and I thought, 'God, who the hell is that for?' It was me, and I signed books for seven hours without stopping, thanks to Bernard Pivot. So *The Ice-Cream War* became an enormous bestseller in France because of his endorsement. The Pivot effect hasn't warn off, so my books, to my delight and continued astonishment, do fantastically well in France.

Bigsby: But there was a down side to this in that you had to sue your French publisher?

Boyd: Yes, I did. It took eleven years as well. My French publisher was a small publisher and to have a bestseller success like this was extraordinary. It was unheard of. We sold one hundred-and-fifty or two-hundred-thousand copies of *The Ice-Cream War* in a few months. For him, it was like a gusher of money coming into his little publishing house. Foreign authors, though, don't get paid for eighteen months after the book is published so of course I had already spent this money because I could calculate two-hundred-thousand copies at ten percent. I knew roughly what I was due to get and for me it was riches beyond the dreams of avarice. The day came when the cheque was due and it never showed up. A couple of weeks went by and I rang my agent and said, 'Where's the French money? I need it badly.' It was my second novel and I had written a third but I was making my way as a writer and a windfall like this doesn't happen very often in your writing career. I remember to this day the call I got from her about an hour later. She said, 'Will, bad news. I'm afraid he has spent it all.' He was a gambler and he owed money and he used to go up to Deauville with my loot and his loot as well, because I only got ten percent, and he just blew it all away. He said, 'The banks half-own my company. I am nearly bankrupt. If you want any money you will have to sue me.' So after days of white rage and seething injustice I hired a lawyer in France, an amazingly competent lawyer. She said, 'We will win because he has obviously stolen your money, but it will take a long time. That will be five thousand pounds please.' French lawyers don't even open a file until you have paid them.

I was owed about eighty-five thousand pounds, which was a lot of money in 1983. It is a lot of money now. He had given me about ten thousand pounds, and so I was suing him for the rest, but as we investigated we found that he had been ripping me off in other departments. He had been stealing my paperback royalties. He had been stealing my book club royalties. Then he went bankrupt and was bought by another company and they proceeded to continue to rip me off as well, so I ended up suing not only the publisher but a Parisian taxi company that had bought my French publishers for some reason. We did win. We kept winning, because we were in the right, but they kept appealing so the case moved through the French courts with incredible slowness. It was Dickensian. Eventually we wound up in the highest court in the land which just pores over details and looks at full stops and subordinate clauses to see if anybody has misspelt something, and there is no appeal once they have given their verdict. They said I was owed the money, but of course there wasn't any money left any more so, after eleven years, I ended up getting about thirty thousand pounds out of the eighty-five I had been owed. But luckily I was able to get my books away from him and I resold them to another publisher who I am still with, so it has a happy ending.

Bigsby: There is an even happier ending in a way in that you now have a place in France. You have a vineyard and make your own wine?

Boyd: I do, yes. I don't make it. I am the proprietor. I just drink lots of it.

Bigsby: Rosé wine.

Boyd: We have a Rosé but we have a very nice red as well.

Bigsby: Let me just quickly take you back. You left school, went to Glasgow university and read English. Then you went to Oxford and you started writing a series of books before the ones we know about. Could they ever have life breathed back into them or are they dead?

Boyd: I cannibalised them. Nothing is wasted. I don't come from a literary background at all. My father, as I say, was a doctor and my mother was a teacher and I didn't know anybody who had anything to do with writing or publishing or agenting, so when I said to myself, around about the age of eighteen or nineteen, 'I really want to be a novelist,' I had no idea how to become one. So it was a process of on-the-job learning in a way.

I wrote three novels before my first novel was published, which in a way taught me how to write novels. My first novel, which was all about me, a fascinating person that the world must know about, got it out of my system. I put that away. Then I wrote a novel about the Biafran war, the Nigerian civil war, but it was far too smart arse for its own good. It was a kind of collage novel. Then I wrote another novel. I was getting desperate by this stage. It was a strange conspiracy thriller about a poet who gets drawn into a kind of drug-running scam. But at the same time I was doing other writing. I was writing short stories and a lot of literary criticism and slowly moving my way up the magazine world of the *Times Literary Supplement* and *The New Statesman* and things like that. So I was writing and seeing my name in print.

I tried to get a collection of short stories published first because I had published about nine, but I had said to the publisher, 'I have written a novel featuring a character in two of these stories.' He said, 'I would much rather publish that novel first before the short story collection'. The only problem was I hadn't written it. I was lying. And so I said, 'The manuscript is in terrible disarray. Give me a month or so to write it.' It was all there, so I borrowed some money from my mother and I got a little grant from the Southern Arts Association. I gave up my teaching – I was teaching at Oxford at the time – for three months and I wrote *A*

Good Man in Africa in a kind of white heat of creative energy and presented it to the publisher as if I had just been tidying the manuscript for the last few weeks. I have subsequently told him the story, but he published that in January 1981, twenty-five years ago, and here I am.

In Conversation With
André Brink

- 13th October 2004 -

André Brink was born in Vrede, South Africa, in 1935. A part of the Die Sestigers (the 60-ers) movement, which used the Afrikaans language as part of an anti-apartheid stand, he found his first novel banned. He writes in both Afrikaans and English and is the author of some twenty books including *States of Emergency* (1988), *The Other Side of Silence* (2002) and *Other Lives* (2008). He is also author of a memoir – *A Fork in the Road* (2009)

Bigsby: You were born in the mid 1930s into an Afrikaans family. As you grew up through the 1940s and the 50s did you have the sense of being part of a separate tribe with its own values, its own standards, its own assumptions and myths?

Brink: I am afraid so. We were always God's own people. Until after seven years at university, when I decided to go to Paris to continue my post-grad studies, I lived in an airtight little enclave. My parents were members of the National Party, great supporters of apartheid, and that was the world in which I grew up, in a whole series of tiny little villages in the deep heart of the country where my father was a magistrate. He got transferred every few years from one of these little places to the next but they all resembled each other in the arid nature of the landscape and the arid nature, I am afraid, of the people.

Bigsby: Was religion a part of that life?

Brink: Oh, yes. Everything was completely determined and defined by religion, a very dour protestant Calvinist religion which was I think one of the main reasons why apartheid was made to succeed because it had the full weight of the Afrikaans Protestant church behind it. Without that support, without the sanction of God, I am pretty sure that as an ideology, as a system, it could not have functioned as smoothly as it did, and be as diabolic. That was the kind of world in which I grew up until, at the age of twenty-three, twenty-four, I went to Paris.

Bigsby: I once interviewed the South African playwright Athol Fugard and he recalled an incident, when he was growing up, when he had spat at a black man. A second later he regretted it. In some way it lived with him. It was the moment he first realised something about himself and his relationship to the black world. Was there ever a moment, as you were growing up, when you had an acute awareness of race and of the relationship with black South Africa?

Brink: They were always around us, around the little white enclave of whites, but of course they lived physically, geographically, topographically, completely apart from us.

Bigsby: Were there servants?

Brink: Yes. They were around in the house and, in fact more and more in the last few years I have started remembering – remembering is too strong a word – recalling vaguely the way in which I was brought up because during my first few years my mother used to be very sickly. She couldn't personally take care of me. There was an old black nanny who carried me on her back and sang stories to me in her language of which I can remember a few snatches. But I find, in the last few years, that these things are beginning to come back to me more and more and I realise how much that has fed into my subconscious.

But on the conscious level I hardly existed until the time I went to Paris. I had never, with one exception, encountered one single black person who was not a servant or a labourer. So it never occurred to me, in this cloistered little world, that black people could be teachers, professors, lawyers, doctors, or whatever. They were made by God – and in fact that was how the Bible was very specifically explained to us – to be our servants. That was the way it had been intended. That was the way the world worked and it was a perfectly comfortable way to grow up.

The one exception was when, towards the end of my university career, a very famous black professor, Professor Z. K. Matthews, visited our small white university and addressed the students. We all went because this was a very curious thing, to hear a black person speak fluent English, which to us was largely a foreign language. There was a hint, a sudden flash of lightning, no more than that, from another world, suggesting there were other things happening around us that we simply didn't know.

Very soon after that I went to Paris and two things happened at the same time. One was the Sharpsville massacre in South Africa, when almost seventy black people who had been peacefully demonstrating against the enforcement of the passbook law on black women were killed by the police and about one hundred and sixty wounded. Seeing that from a distance of six thousand miles it was a ferocity to discover in one terrible moment what my people, the Afrikaners, were responsible for, the way in which they had been totally, morally destroying the whole country, and I had to deal with that. I had to start rethinking my whole world from scratch. And at the same time this was happening, for the first time in my life I had the opportunity of sharing university facilities and amenities with black students from all over the world. Suddenly, after this protected white life of mine, there was the opportunity of sitting down at table with black students and discussing. I must even confess to a terrible thing. The first time I could hardly eat because one didn't do that. Black people didn't eat with whites, but it was just a moment of hesitation and then I started feeling both terribly ashamed and amused at myself. I discovered that this was in fact a fantastic opportunity. People who I had never known as people were suddenly entering the world I was entering.

After having spent seven years studying literature at university I thought if there is one thing in the world that I knew something about, it was literature. Now here were these black students, mainly from West Africa, but also the Caribbean and elsewhere, who, when we started discussing literature, I discovered knew infinitely more about literature than I did. So once again I had to start from scratch. But whereas the first shock was negative, breaking down everything I had taken for granted before, the second one was enormously creative, challenging, stimulating, and from there it just continued and took off.

Bigsby: The idea of being a writer came to you when you were very young. You wrote a novel at the age of twelve and sent it to a publisher at fourteen. They rejected it. So you were a precocious child.

Brink: You should also add that one of the reasons the publisher turned down that novel was that he said it was too erotic.

Bigsby: You haven't changed! I want to come on to sexuality later but not just yet because you were still only twelve and fourteen at the time.

You said something interesting just now when you mentioned going to a lecture in English. When you were growing up you spoke Afrikaans. Were you also speaking English?

Brink: That was one good thing about our education. We were forced to be bilingual so from the age of about seven we started learning a bit of English at school, but it was very strange and it was taught as a foreign language. I think that was in fact where my aspiration to write began. After the first couple of lessons at school I would come home, and our home was situated in, I can't call it a garden, a very dry patch with almost nothing growing there but I would walk about there and speak loudly, not just aloud, but loudly to myself in the few halting broken phrases of English that I had learnt at school. I would just listen with amazement at the wonder of language. I discovered that language consisted of sounds and rhythms and cadences and I could transfer this to my awareness of my own language, Afrikaans, and discover that this also consists of sounds and rhythms. Language was a material thing, a thing that you could almost touch but certainly hear intimately not just through your ears but through every pore of your body. It became something that so enthralled me that I knew that whatever I might become one day – and I might become a house painter or train driver or something – I would also be a writer. I would have to be a writer because this feeling of being totally enamoured, carried away, by language has never left me since then.

Bigsby: And when you came back from that first trip to France you had a new perception of South Africa, but also a new perception of literature. You became part of a movement called, in English, The Sixties, which was a breakaway from what Afrikaans literature had been before. In what particular way? Was it a move away from realism?

Brink: That was probably at the heart of it. Afrikaans poetry had taken off quite some time before that, but I think in any culture poetry tends to flower first. Certainly as far as fiction was concerned we had got stuck in a very dry kind of naturalism, dominated by droughts and poor whites and locusts and things like that. It was just too boring to contemplate. We were all heartily sick of it and we grew up with the idea that literature with a capital L means boring writing. As it happened at the time when I came back from Paris – and I should add I had to come back very much against my own will simply for the banal reason that my money had run out – I wasn't ready emotionally. I came back with a sort of resentment against the country. I had become so totally ashamed of what I had seen of South Africa from abroad that I didn't want to write about it, I didn't want to think about it. My mind was still in Paris, dominated by all the existentialist trends that were so tremendously exciting in the middle of the last century. I admired Sartre intellectually but always at a little distance. I was totally swept off my feet by Camus and I think he is still perhaps the single dominating influence in my life. But when I came back there were a few other writers, about six or seven of us, who had spent shorter or longer periods abroad, specifically in England or Germany, and the one thing that fired us, because we were very, very different temperamentally, ideologically, in every imaginable respect, was that we wanted to write new things, things that would be in tune with what was happening in Europe at the time. So that came as a thunderclap to Afrikaans literature at the time.

We were immediately denounced from on high. Sermons were preached against our work. Our books were burnt in town squares and they were discussed in parliament. It was wonderful to have all this attention. It was totally trashed and denounced by the old generation, but the student population, those in their twenties like us, just came rushing on with an enthusiasm that carried us along on this wave, and that meant that although previously the Afrikaans establishment had been terribly effective in crushing any kind of revolt within the bosom of the family, in our case they couldn't do it because we had this tremendous surge of support among the young that helped us to carry on.

Bigsby: But then you went to Paris in 1967/68, a time of revolt. The French government very nearly fell. There were riots in Germany and the United States. Radical change suddenly seemed an international possibility. Were you still thinking at that time of staying in Europe?

Brink: At that time much more. Previously I had gone over to do some doctoral research and, as I say, my money ran out and I had to come back, but I had one idea fixed in my mind and that was to go back to Paris as soon as I possibly could. By the end of 1967 that was possible. I had a very good friend in Paris with whom I could stay in the Latin Quarter and I went with at least the idea of exploring the possibility of settling there. He had already settled there. Nowadays he comes and goes but he is still based in Paris and I thought that was what I wanted to do. But in the course of 1968, as a result of all the things that were happening around me – the incredible social, political, moral, intellectual turmoil that was happening, so much of which concerned interaction between the individual and his or her society – I was forced to rethink who and what I was, and wanted to be, in terms of my writing because writing was important to me. I wanted to continue writing but I realised that to do it in Paris, six thousand miles away from where my life had been shaped, from where my people were perpetrating the atrocities that were happening there, was just the kind of luxury that would cut me off completely from everything that could be vital for my writing.

This time when I came back it was because I wanted to come back. I wanted to start looking for my roots, to find out what is it about South Africa, about Africa, that had shaped me. Of course I was very aware of the kind of schizophrenia that comes from the fact that I am shaped not only by Africa, but by my roots in Europe. I had taken note of those European roots for a long time. I had grown up with it, but now I wanted to find out more about the world of the old nanny who had literally defined and circumscribed my early infancy.

Bigsby: And now you published a book that was much more of a direct challenge because it was banned. Did you expect that?

Brink: I was totally naïve, thinking that they wouldn't because there had been bannings of English books before that but the general feeling was that the government, being predominantly Afrikaans, could afford very easily to ban English writers, like Nadine Gordimer and others, because they were not members of the family. The government, even though they loathed what we were doing, still regarded us as children in the family, so we could be slapped down. They thought they could keep us in check but it had become obvious by then that that just wasn't possible. We were getting out of hand and they seemed to have decided to make an example of my novel *Looking on Darkness*.

There were days when one was simply driven to such extremes of rage and despair that you wanted to rush in and do something. I knew from the beginning that I would make a very, very bad revolutionary. I am simply too impulsive and too emotional, but by channelling it into writing I think I felt able to exert some kind of control over the seething anger inside myself and in my generation.

I lost a number of friends who I had thought of as being very close friends before, but who now totally rejected me and said that I was a traitor and a back stabber. But the wonderful thing was that – especially since the ban on *Looking On Darkness* – I found that I had more and more access to black people and coloured people who would approach me simply to say, 'We haven't read this book' – at that stage it was only in Afrikaans – 'because we can't read Afrikaans, but thank you for having written it.' Sometimes that would be the beginning of a real friendship that still continues many years later. Sometimes it took much longer than that but on the whole I think that for every white friend I lost at the time there were at least five new black or coloured friends entering my life. Some of them were musicians, some painters, some dancers. We could devise ways of directing the anger and in that way there was something not ultimately controlling about the violence because it has always been an incredibly violent society and still is. We could direct it, give a sense of purpose, give a sense of meaning to the chaos in the country, what Robert Frost meant when he spoke about poetry as a momentary stay against confusion.

Bigsby: You write in Afrikaans and then you translate into English. Can you say something about how you use those languages? Why does a novel in one language sometimes radically differ from the original, and then feed back into the original?

Brink: Basically what happened was that when *Looking on Darkness* was banned, because I had been operating exclusively in a small restricted language like Afrikaans suddenly I was a non person, a non writer. I had no reading public and purely in order to survive as a writer, to ensure that I could at least still be published even if it had to be abroad, I then started writing in English alongside of the Afrikaans. I translated that one into Afrikaans. I also translated the next one, *An Instant in the Wind*. But from then on every book has been written in both languages and it is not a matter of writing it in one language and then translating it. They usually grow alongside each other all the time. I may sometimes write the descriptive passages of a book, say, in English but the dialogue in Afrikaans, or one chapter in English, one chapter in Afrikaans, or if there are two narrative timetables, I might use English for one and Afrikaans for the other. When I wrote *A Chain of Voices*, in which there are thirty different narrative voices, I used English for some and Afrikaans for others. Two of the characters grew up together as friends and playmates and then became enemies. In my first version of the book they literally couldn't understand each other because one spoke one language and the other replied in the other. Of course it couldn't go on like that. I had to get a literary tweezers and disentangle the two different versions. Since then, that is how I have been writing, even though now that it is no longer necessary. There is no more censorship in the country, but it has become part of my creative process in thinking my way through a book.

I may take years before I actually start working on a book, but when I start writing it goes very fast. I must get it out of me, and this dual process reins me in all the time. I have to force myself to think at least twice, but that is really only the beginning of every episode, every line. What happens then is that when I have written a chapter in English I then rewrite the same chapter, sometimes without looking at the original, sometimes looking at it, in Afrikaans. But while working in the second language I discover certain things which, as a result of the idiosyncrasies of language itself, I had missed the first time round so I go back to the first version and I make those changes to make it compatible with the second. But in doing that I discover things that I had overlooked in the process of the first transposition. It can go on interminably. At some stage you just have to decide, no, this has got to stop.

Bigsby: Afrikaans is a relatively young language. Does it have absences? Is there a different tonal quality? Are there things you can't say in Afrikaans?

Brink: That is not so much the case now as it was in the sixties when this little group of us started writing because then we were very, very conscious of the fact that, for instance, there was just no vocabulary in Afrikaans for the whole philosophical realm of existentialism, or the whole experience of love, especially physical love, sexual love. You had your choice between words taken from toilet walls or from manuals for surgeons, but there was nothing in between so we had to make up a vocabulary, and boy did we enjoy that.

Bigsby: When your book was banned you turned to a form of self-publishing to get word around. In some way there seems to have been a covert power that came precisely from the banning. When I was talking to Athol Fugard, just after the end of apartheid, I got the feeling that I was talking to somebody who had just lost a subject. He had been pushing against a door and as it swung open he really didn't know quite what to do because part of the power of his work came from resistance. Did you reach such a point when suddenly it disappeared?

Brink: No, I can honestly say I didn't have that experience. I know Athol battled with that, and a number of writers very understandably had that sort of experience. To a certain extent perhaps we must all have had that because one does become conditioned to write in a certain way. I have been thinking ever since that thank God it ended then, not just in terms of the politics, but in terms of the writing because it is dangerous when an entire literature starts defining itself purely in terms of what it is against. If there was a sense of bewilderment for a moment it was the bewilderment a person who has been in jail for a long time experiences when suddenly he is released. He is bewildered by freedom. He can go anywhere. He can go and have a drink. He can go and eat something. I know from some of my friends that in jail they would get their supper at 3 o'clock in the afternoon and then nothing until the next morning, but now if you get hungry you can go and eat. If you write you can write what you want. Any writer worth his or her salt in South Africa wrote about apartheid during those dark years because we felt obliged to do that.

Apartheid wasn't an ideology, a system, it was something that we lived every single moment of our lives so when we wrote about that we wrote about the most intimate things we could possibly imagine. But it also meant that if I had a choice between two stories, let's say a story simply concerning a man and a woman who are in love and another story in which you may also have a passionate involvement of two people but with certain social, political repercussions, then I would have gone for the second one because there was an urgency inside me which impelled me to write about certain things in a certain way. Theoretically apartheid is over. The system has been abolished. There is a new South Africa operating, but the mentalities, the mind-sets, those will persist I am afraid for a very long time, but that is something else. That is something we have to continue to battle against. I should add that if one has the habit of fighting against something, then it wasn't so much apartheid as such that provided us with the temptation and the challenge to write, it was something behind, something even bigger than that, and that was the abuse of power. In any society there is abuse of power so there will always be something to write against and that at least can provide a certain satisfaction. But there are so many more things.

Bigsby: You are not just a novelist. You are a playwright and theatre director. How important has that side of your life been, because very often in oppressive circumstances theatre has been a recourse for writers?

Brink: Unfortunately it no longer features to the same extent now as it used to, especially in the sixties and even more especially in the seventies. The theatre was enormously important for me as a means of discovering things about the country, about myself, but, unlike people like Athol Fugard – who had access to his own theatre company and who could bypass the state subsidised theatre where there was a stranglehold by the authorities – if one single member of an audience complained about a play put on by a state subsidised company the play was taken off and that was the reason why I opted out of theatre. At the university I could from time to time work with students to produce a play, and that was wonderful. I couldn't do it professionally. I couldn't do it all the time and I had the recourse of novel writing so I thought that with the danger threatening my existence as a playwright being so inhibiting I would rather turn to the novel where I felt I could do more. I could go further in my contestation. I could go further in my challenging of the authorities, and that meant that unfortunately I then practically stopped writing theatre, but I am still firmly persuaded that I will return to the theatre. It is just a matter of time. There are only ninety hours in a day.

Bigsby: How long was *The Other Side of Silence* in the making?

Brink: I tried to shy away from writing *The Other Side of Silence* for about fifteen years. A friend of mine gave me the essence of the story and when I told him that I was fascinated by it he kept on feeding me with hundreds upon hundreds of pages photocopied from the archives dealing with this importation into Namibia at the turn of the twentieth century of young German girls and young women to provide the needs, the blatantly sexual needs of the German army stationed in Namibia. There was then this terrible dimension to the story that the men who wanted women, and most of them did, entered their names into a register and a number of girls would be imported, most of them only in their teens. The German authorities had deliberately decided that they had to be fertile otherwise they couldn't be exported. When they arrived they were assigned to the men who had handed in their names. There was a four or five day train journey during which there was a wild process of mixing and matching going on. At the end more or less everybody had found somebody, but there was always a small handful of women who at the end of this train journey had been rejected by all the men and it is difficult to imagine what a woman in those circumstances could possibly have felt being rejected by men, who by dint of circumstances, had started consorting with animals because that was all that had been available to them. Suddenly the women came and this handful was rejected even by them. They were loaded on wagons and transported into the desert to this strange, weird lugubrious building which was part nunnery, part lunatic asylum, part brothel, and left there to die.

Then there is this woman who decides that this is enough and she starts a revolt against the whole of the German Reich, marching through the desert, mounting a little rag-tag army of women and indigenous black people who had all suffered at the hands of the German authorities in order to reclaim their life, their freedom, reclaim the country. Of course it was doomed from the beginning. This story so gripped me, but at the same time was so terrible that I wanted to write it, but I couldn't and, as I say, it took fifteen years. I tried to do anything but that, but then I realised that this would haunt me, would not let go of me, until I had written it out of my system. Once again it was the old thing of trying to contain a certain violence and that is why I had to write it.

Bigsby: It is not only in this novel that sex and sexuality prove crucial. Why is it central to your work?

Brink: I wish I could give you a comprehensible answer or an easy answer. Partly I suppose the incredibly repressed, religious, rightest, little world in which I grew up, added a kind of fascination to sex which I felt was an almost diabolical attraction. But I shied away from it until I was well into my twenties. Then of course I had the opportunity of going to Paris. I think all writers are basically solitary people. That is one reason why the theatre is so attractive to me because there you work with others, you produce something new, interact, but in writing you are terribly isolated and I think by nature I am a loner. I always find it a little bit difficult to engage in interaction with people. As a result of teaching at a university for a decade, I have got used to speaking in public but that doesn't mean that I can easily interact with people. To me the most acute form of interaction between two people, the most acute form in which one can reach out of one's loneliness and touch somebody else, grasp a hand and find that there is a hand waiting that you can grasp and that can grasp yours, is a sexual relationship. I think that is why it occupies an absolutely prime spot in my thinking about human relations and the interaction between individuals, and within a social context too. And I should think that that is really the driving force behind this, call it preoccupation, because I suppose it is.

In Conversation With
Geraldine Brooks

- 16th October 2008 -

Geraldine Brooks was raised in a suburb of Sydney and went on to work as a journalist for *The Wall Street Journal*. Her first book, *Nine Parts of Desire* (1994) emerged from her experiences in the Middle East. She followed this with *Foreign Correspondence* (1997). Her first novel, *Year of Wonders*, was published in 2001 and was followed, in 2005, by a second, *March*, for which she won a Pulitzer Prize. *People of the Book* appeared in 2008 and *Caleb's Crossing* in 2011.

Bigsby: Your latest novel is *People of the Book*. Can you tell me something of the journey you have taken that has brought you to it?

Brooks: I would like to take you back with me for a moment to an experience I suspect everybody has had which is the experience of the very first book that absolutely transported and carried you away. I was nine years old when I had that experience and the book was Enid Blyton's *The Valley of Adventure*. It was the book that turned me from the goody, goody student who never put a foot wrong in class to the naughty girl who is reading in geography lesson under the desk. It was the book that turned me from the obedient daughter to the one who was reading after lights out under the blanket. When I got to the end I was delighted to see that this was part of a series of seven books Enid Blyton had written and I couldn't wait for Saturday because Saturday was library day in our family. We all went and we all came home with a big armful of books. When I got back to the library I found that *The Valley of Adventure* was the only one in the series that the library had and I was devastated but fate was kind to me because a few weeks later, in the children's pages of the Sunday paper, in the classified ads section where kids exchanged things, somebody had listed the entire series for sale. We didn't have a lot of money when I was growing up and the very modest asking price for these books seemed exorbitant to me so I was a bit reluctant to raise it with my family, but I did finally get up the nerve to mention it to my mum. I learned something about my parents that day which was that in our family books were in a special class, like food and school uniform, that you somehow found money for. So they bought me the books and the day they arrived I was so excited. They were beautifully-kept hardbacks with wonderfully illustrated jackets and they had been carefully covered in plastic. I lined them up from one to seven on the dining room table and I started to feel most peculiar. My heart was beating faster, there was a tightness in my throat and I was a little flushed around the neck. I had never had this feeling before. It wasn't unpleasant exactly but it was definitely new to me and I didn't have a word for it.

I was nine then and it would be six years before I had that feeling again, under very different circumstances, and by then I had a word for it and that word was 'lust.' I think the fact that I felt my first stirrings of physical desire for a bunch of used books was possibly predictive that I would wind up writing novels and possibly even predictive that I would write *People of the Book*, which is a book about a book, and about the people who love books, people who make books and who protect them and sometimes even give their lives for them.

Bigsby: And that particular book had a remarkable history, though your particular introduction to it was not without danger.

Brooks: There is a picture of the National Library of Bosnia seen in flames after the deliberate targeting, with phosphorous bombs, by the Serb ultra-nationalists who waged war on that city. By the time I got to Sarajevo as a newspaper reporter covering the siege of the city the smell of the burnt pages still lingered in the air. In those days there was only one functioning hotel and that, in the circumstances, was the rather inaptly named Holiday Inn and you didn't want to be asking for a room with a view when you checked in because if you could see the beautiful mountains that rise all around Sarajevo then the snipers and the artillery men on those mountains could see you. There was one night of particularly heavy shelling and my esteemed colleague Kate Adie was staying at the Holiday Inn. She didn't get a good night's sleep and you don't want to see Kate Adie when she hasn't had a good night's sleep. She woke very truculent and insisted on crossing the front lines and having it out with the artillery commander.

She confronted him and said, 'Why are you shelling the Holiday Inn? You know that only civilian foreign journalists are staying there.' He said,

'Yes, madam, we do know that and we are very sorry. We weren't aiming for the Holiday Inn. We were aiming for the Bosnian National Museum.' So this was a brutal war even in the harsh catalogue of wars because it was a war against civilians, but it was also a war against an idea, the idea of Sarajevo as a multi-ethnic city that had thrived for hundreds of years, where Muslins and Christians and Jews had lived and created together. So when you make war on a idea like that you target things like the Bosnian National Museum and the Bosnian National Museum was home of the Sarajevo Haggadah, which is the book that inspired my novel, *People of the Book*.

So how do you get an idea for a novel? It is probably the most frequently asked question that any novelists gets from readers and I always loved Ernest Hemingway's answer to that question. He said an idea for a novel can be something that you are lucky enough to overhear, or it can be the wreck of your whole damn life. I think Hemingway would approve of the fact that the idea for *People of the Book* was something that I overheard and that I overheard in a bar in a war zone at that. It was in the lightless bar of the Holiday Inn, because there was no electricity and reporters would gather at the end of the day by candlelight for a few drinks to share the fairly horrific details of their day's work.

One evening the talk turned to this priceless rarity of the Bosnian Museum Library, the Sarajevo Haggadah, which was a medieval Jewish manuscript created in Spain around 1450. It was missing and nobody knew its fate. Journalists love rumours and there were all kinds of rumours swirling in the bar that night about what had happened to this manuscript, that it had gone up in flames, as so many wonderful priceless works had in that conflict, that it had been sold on the black market to buy arms, that it had been spirited out of the city through the tunnel under the airport by a team of Mossad agents and taken to Israel. I filed all this away and thought I must investigate, but I didn't get around to it.

Then, towards the end of the war, the true story was revealed and the true story was more interesting than any of the rumours. The true story was that in the very first days of the war, when Sarajevans couldn't quite believe that this madness had come to their city and so no preparation had been made and the Museum stood on the front lines of the war with nothing secured, a Muslim librarian named Enver Imamovic realised that the Sarajevo Haggadah was at risk, and that he was probably the only museum employee who could get there through the shelling. So he went first to the Sarajevo police and said, 'Can you send a party with me because I need to save the treasures of our museum collection?' And the police said, 'Are you nuts, risk our lives to save some dusty old stuff?' He said, 'Okay, don't come, but I am going anyway and after the war I will just tell everybody that a librarian had more guts than the Sarajevo police.' So five of them went with him and they managed to get there just in time because a shell had hit the water main and the basement of the museum was flooding. The basement was where the safe containing the Sarajevo Haggadah was. They managed to crack the safe and he brought the book out to a safe hiding place for the duration of the war. So I heard that story and I became really fascinated by what was so special about this book?

Bigsby: So what was special about it?

Brooks: This book was already old in 1609 and I think that the beauty of it initially is part of the reason that people were drawn to protect it. I think aesthetically it is a very moving piece of art. When I first saw it, it was in a room of a bank in Bosnia with a lot of security. When they brought this book in for the conservator to work on it there was a flying wedge of bodyguards and there were UN security and police and everybody you could think of. The museum official breaks the seal on the box and they open it and you look at it and you go, 'All this for that?' because it is just this horrible looking thing that you could see in a used book store and not look twice at because it was really bound very clumsily in the 1890s, with just awful cardboard. Then the conservator opens the book to the illumination, the first one, and you go, 'Oh,' and if it is doing that to me with the twenty-first century bombardments and all kinds of visual inputs that we have, what must it have meant to people who lived in a much more visually sparse world?

So the first thing about the book is that it is illustrated, at a time when medieval Jewish teaching was very much against illustration of any kind because of the commandment which says: Thou shalt not make graven images or likenesses of anything. Yet here is a Jewish prayer book lavishly illuminated with images of all kinds of things. What I love about these images is that they are a wonderful amalgamation of medieval Spanish life and very familiar biblical stories. In one you have Moses being found by Pharaoh's daughter in the river Nile, but interestingly the river Nile appears to be flowing by a medieval Spanish city that looks rather like Seville or Barcelona. Then you have Moses grown up coming to Pharaoh demanding that his people be let go from slavery but Pharaoh looks for all the world like a Spanish medieval prince. At the bottom of the illustration the plagues have started. The plague of frogs shows them hopping out of a Spanish medieval bread oven. This is what is so intriguing about the book and makes it such a wonderful document.

There is a series of illuminations that I particularly love. It is the Genesis story. It starts with the division of the light and the dark, and the water and the land, the making of the plants and the animals, and ends with God resting. It is an image of God which was a total no-no among both Muslims and Jews at that time. And the other striking thing about this series is that the world is shown as round, and in the fourteen hundreds that was still a pretty radical idea. So who was this illuminator who already knew that? We will never know. That is where the line of fact runs out and the fiction begins because as a novelist I have to invent that person, and that is the great pleasure to me of making fiction from fact. You follow the line of fact as far as you can and then you have to take the swan dive off the cliff into the worlds of imagination and empathy with the past.

Bigsby: How much is known about the history of the book?

Brooks: The facts that we know about the Haggadah are plentiful in recent history. We know that it was not only saved by a Muslim librarian in the recent war but also saved by Muslim hands during World War II, when a librarian risked his neck and tucked the book in the waistband of his trousers and then went to confront the Nazi general who had come seeking it and told him that the book had already been given to another German officer. He was terribly sorry that there must have been a mix up. When the General demanded the name of the man the librarian quickly replied, 'I didn't think it was my place to require a name.' Then he carried the Haggadah out of the museum, still tucked in his trousers, and took it up into the mountains where a friend of his was the imam of the local mosque. It spent World War II safely hidden among Korans.

We know it was in Venice in 1609, because a Catholic priest at that point saved the book from burning by the Pope's Inquisition, which took away countless Hebrew codices at that time. He saved it by writing on the front page of the manuscript that it contained nothing against the church, and he signed his name and dated it. So we can place it in Venice in 1609. Before that there is very little, so you have to make it up. We know it was in Spain, and my job was to tie together the six hundred years of history and half a dozen different cultures. I was scratching my head about how to do that when I had a stroke of luck, which was that I learned that the UN was funding conservation on the actual Sarajevo

Haggadah. So I nagged and cajoled my way into the room to watch a real book conservator taking the book apart and re-stitching the quires.

I had no idea what a book conservator did until that day. I found that it is a marvellous job because you have to be a scientist, a chemist, who understands the structure of parchment and the lethal toxins of the old pigments, and you have to be an artist who can get the intention of the illuminator. You have to be a detective, a sleuth, because if you can find any little artefact in the binding that can be an invaluable clue as to where the book was at the time of its creation. If it is a quill paring, for example, a kind of flight feather, it could tell you a geographical range of where the book might have come from. If it is a bread crumb it might tell you whose hands it was in during its long life. So I decided that my connective tissue would be a character of the near present and she would be a book conservator.

Bigsby: And she would be the narrator.

Brooks: I like to write with a first person narrator so voice is very important to me and I got a very good lesson about voice from the British novelist, Jim Crace. He told me a wonderful story about his research for his biblical-era book *Quarantine*. To research that book he went on a camping trip in the Judean desert with a Bedouin guide and the first morning of that trip he woke up and the guide said, 'Mr. Jim how did you sleep?' And Jim said, 'I slept like a log.' Then he said he raised his eyes to the bare rock-ribbed hillsides of the Judean desert. There were no logs, so he turned to his guide and said, 'How did you sleep? And he said, 'Mr. Jim, I slept like a dead donkey.' So Jim Crace told me that the business of historical fiction is the business of turning logs into dead donkeys, and I have been trying to do that ever since. So I saw the book taken apart and put back together and there it sits today in the Bosnian National Museum as an emblem of the survival of the multi-ethnic ideal of that very beautiful city which is painstakingly putting itself back together.

One of the illuminations that intrigued me, perhaps more than all the others, is a picture of a medieval Spanish Jewish family celebrating the Passover Feast. You see what you would see in any Jewish home at Passover. The unleavened bread is there, the cups of wine. The patriarch reclines on a cushion, and that is symbolic of the fact that Jews are now free men and free men who can recline at meals. But who is the African woman seated with the Jewish family? She is taking part in the meal. She is holding a piece of matzo. She is not serving. She is a participant. She is wearing saffron, which is a pretty fancy kind of robe. She is obviously somebody quite important, but who she is and what she had to do with this Spanish Jewish family is lost to us. So I was free to make it up and doing that was one of the great pleasures of the novel.

It is a bit presumptuous trying to think yourself into the head of somebody as different from you as this medieval African woman at a Spanish Jewish table and I guess I took the courage to do it from something I read once that the African American novelist James Baldwin wrote. He was coming to the defence of the white southern novelist William Styron, who had written a book called *The Confessions of Nat Turner* in which he thought his way into the head of the leader of a slave rebellion in the Tidewater region of Virginia before the Civil War. Styron had been taken to the wood shed for this by a number of prominent black writers who said a white man had no business doing this. But James Baldwin came to his defence most eloquently, I thought. He wrote, 'Each of us helplessly and for ever contains the other, male and female, white and black, black and white. We are part of each other.' I believe that, and it is where I get the courage to be as presumptuous as I am.

I love the digital world but there is nothing like the serendipitous encounter that you can have in the stacks of a great library. For me, this was when I was researching the Venice chapter of the book. I wanted to find out who these Catholic priests were who were the Hebraists, who could read Jewish books in order to determine if there was anything against the church, and quite by chance I stumbled upon the autobiography of a Venetian rabbi. It was as if this character flew in gift wrapped because in the pages of that autobiography I saw how I was going to tell the story of the wine stain that appears on the pages of the Haggadah and which my conservator tries to extract information about the book from. I decided that I would tell that story as a story of a friendship between two men, a Christian Hebraist Catholic priest and a rabbi, and what the limits of such a friendship would be at such a time.

Bigsby: What struck me when I was reading *People of the Book* is that it is not just one novel. Every time you go into a new period you have to set yourself the task of writing a completely different novel. Was it more difficult the more remote you got from the present or were there particular periods you found most difficult to inhabit?

Brooks: Actually I wrote the earliest historical periods first because I am more comfortable there.

Bigsby: Why?

Brooks: I think because you are more free. When I got to World War II, I had to put the book in the drawer and leave it there for a couple of years. The Nazi thing just totally threw me. I thought this has been done by writers so much more skilful than I am. What new is there to say about Nazis and how am I going to tell this story? Then I got the idea for my novel *March*, and it was so much more clear-cut to me how to write that book.

Bigsby: So you were writing this book and then you interrupted it and wrote another novel.

Brooks: Yes, and I wasn't sure if it would ever come out of the drawer. But while I was working on *March* it just occurred to me that I should stick as close to the known facts as possible and that the way to tell the story of what happened in World War II was to go back and research what had really happened with the librarian who saved the book. I had another really wonderful stroke of luck. It is the old journalist in me that loves to get the facts straight. The story of what he had and hadn't done had been told numerous different ways in different scholarly publications, and I really wanted to nail it down. So I went looking and found that his niece worked for the U.S. State Department teaching the Bosnian language. I went to Washington to meet with her and she very kindly brought along a lot of family documents. As she was translating them for me she looked up and said, 'If you really want to know what happened during World War II, why don't you ask his wife?' My jaw dropped to the floor because it hadn't occurred to me that a man in his sixties at the time of these events would have a living widow. She said, 'Auntie was twenty-seven years younger than uncle' and so my ticket to Sarajevo was bought and paid for before I left the State Department. I was able to sit with her and learn not just about the rescue of the *Haggadah* but those other brave acts of resistance that this woman and her husband performed during World War II.

Bigsby: Of course Islam, Judaism, Christianity are all religions of the book. *People of the Book* is a novel about a community, cutting across time and cutting across religions. People save the *Haggadah* not out of religious convictions, but out of a historical respect, an aesthetic respect.

Brooks: Yes. This book has lived through the same catastrophe perhaps four times, maybe more. We seem to be capable as human beings of building these wonderful societies where we appreciate difference and at the times when we do that we move the ball forward intellectually and artistically. The *Haggadah* was very much a product of that intercommunication between the three faiths. Yet we also have within us the seeds of hatred of the other and that rises up to smash these societies, as it did in the Inquisition, as it did with fascism, as it did with the ultra-nationalist movement in the former Yugoslavia. Yet even at the time when these beautiful societies were being torn apart there were always a few people who could stand up and say, 'No, what unites us is greater than what divides us.' And at this point this tiny little book is the very loud witness to that.

Bigsby: You were born in Sydney, but not the Sydney of Sydney Harbour?

Brooks: No, it was the western suburbs, which is a red brick expanse of little suburban bungalows with hot afternoons and bleached buffalo grass.

Bigsby: Presumably history, as taught in school, wasn't your history?

Brooks: I definitely had a colonised imagination when I was a child. I like to say that my bookshelves were garrisoned by foreign troops, predominantly British troops. I read these books about things that I had never experienced, like frost and reddening rowan trees. The idea that trees lost their leaves was an oddity because in Sydney, of course, trees lose their bark and keep their leaves. Imagine the magnificent irrelevance of phrases like 'cold as the grave' to an Australian kid who has just buried her aunt in a cemetery so hot that she can't keep two feet on the ground at the same time. But in a way I am grateful for that cultural noise in my head because it helps me hear these other voices when I need to call them up.

Bigsby: Did that mean that you felt in some way that reality existed somewhere else?

Brooks: I thought that history and culture happened elsewhere. Australia exported concrete things, like wool and iron ore, and brought back abstract nouns, like art and culture. That was very much a product of my times because it is not that way any more, thank God. It was wonderful as a young person to see that a place could change so enormously. It partly had to do with immigration and the end of the stifling white

Australia policy and the opening of the door to others. So we didn't have to look abroad as it was bubbling up all around us.

Bigsby: But you also had pen pals. Was that your way of projecting yourself into this other world, this other place where reality did exist?

Brooks: Exactly. I always thought that these kids in the Middle East or in America or in France were having much more exciting times than I was. So I would write away to these pen pals and then I would project my fantasy life on them. There was a poor girl from France that I wrote to for a year or two. I thought she was going to be one of the cobblestone flinging radicals but she was a rural girl from south-western France who had never been to Paris. I kept pressing her about what she thought of Camus and she wanted to talk about much more mundane subjects and so when my dad died and I was looking through his papers I found that he had kept all my pen pal's letters and suddenly I had these old addresses. I decided to go and look these people up and see how their real lives had squared with the fantasies I had projected on them. So I wrote *Foreign Correspondence*, which is part memoir and part travel adventure.

Bigsby: You eventually left Australia by means of journalism. You became a journalist in Australia and then won a scholarship to Columbia and ended up working on *The Wall Street Journal*. Then, somewhat bizarrely it seems to me, you got a job as a foreign correspondent reporting from Australia. So you went home and there you were looking at your own culture as though it were in some way foreign. But then came a crucial moment because you became a real foreign correspondent, going to the Middle East. Was that the beginning of war reporting?

Brooks: Yes. I had never had that dream of reporting with a flak jacket on. It really was one of these oddities of journalism where you are doing one thing that is completely unrelated and then they decide, well, you might as well do something else. It was so clear-cut in this case because I had just been in New Zealand writing a story about global warming research. New Zealand had a unique opportunity to study the greenhouse gas methane because it had so many sheep per square acre, and I had been following climate scientists as they chased sheep up verdant hillsides to get methane samples. I had come home and written this story about global warming and flatulent sheep and I got a call from the foreign editor. It was the first time she had called me since I had taken the Australasian bureau job and I thought, 'My god, I am going to get the sack for putting too many tasteless farting sheep jokes on the front page of *The Wall Street Journal*,' but she was actually calling to offer me the Middle East correspondent's job. For somebody who had always craved adventures in foreign places, I didn't hesitate. I said 'yes' immediately.

Then I had a month before I had to go and do it and to think how extraordinarily unqualified I was. The first year was a frequent flyer programme from hell. I would be on my way to some uprising in Yemen in the middle of the night with this stack of briefing books on my lap. I really don't think this is any way for newspapers to go about sending people out there but out of necessity I had to find a way to do my job and the way I found was through the women of the region.

You had to be completely oblivious not to notice this incredible ground swell, happening in every country I was in, of young women choosing to re-adopt the veil that their mothers had in many cases cast off and returning to this much more orthodox form of the faith. It seemed to me, as a secular feminist, not to offer them very much. So my journey to try and understand that led me into some extraordinary reporting opportunities, such as being invited home to Ayatollah Khomeini's place for tea with his wife, and spending the first Gulf War visiting Queen Noor in the royal palace in Jordan while King Hussein scrambled to avert open conflict with Iraq. So it turned out that by turning to the women of the region I got wonderful access to the stories that really mattered at that time.

Bigsby: And that led to *Nine Parts of Desire*. You were raised a Catholic but you then converted to your husband's religion, Judaism.

Brooks: There was a period in between those two when I was cruising as a happy atheist, having come to some difficulties with Catholicism on feminists grounds. The conversion was really more about history, I think, than faith. It wasn't that I found God in the ancient Hebrew prayers. It was that I couldn't really stand to see the end of the line of a heritage that had made it through the Babylonian exile and the Spanish Inquisition. I didn't want to further the project of getting rid of Jews in the world.

Bigsby: Did this coincide with your Middle Eastern posting?

Brooks: No, it was before.

Bigsby: So you were going there as a Jewish person in the Middle East and then interviewing Khomeini's wife. Did your conversion put you in an awkward position in writing a book of that kind?

Brooks: Not so much writing the book. I don't think what I am getting at in the book has anything to do with Judaism, or Islam for that matter. It has to do with how patriarchal customs insinuate their way into all religions, though actually when Islam arrives in seventh century Arabia a lot of what it brings to women is good news initially. It gives them property rights, which is something that it would be several hundred more years before women in the west had. When Mohammed sanctions four wives he is not giving licence, he is actually setting limits because before that you could have any number. It brings an end to female infanticide. But as it moves on, in the great march that would take it all the way to the gates of Vienna, and all the way up into Andalusia, every time the faith came in contact with an anti-woman custom it absorbed it and then that custom was carried on as if it were part of the teachings of Islam. So you get genital mutilation, you get veiling and seclusion, which are not part of the original message of the faith. Yet the faith is a warm medium.

Bigsby: What was your attitude towards the translators with whom you had to work?

Brooks: It was a very fraught business having to work with translators but I had no choice. I didn't speak Arabic or Hebrew. I learned some just to get by but not nearly enough to do a job of work. You didn't want to bring a translator who might be working for the secret police so I usually would get to the place where I wanted to report and then find somebody from there who had the trust of the people that I wanted to speak to. I was very lucky in some of my translators. I had some marvellous experiences, particularly with women in Iran who translated for me brilliantly and also gave me a lot of insight into their own lives and how they navigated within the Islamic regime. The only time I had an absolute disaster was in eastern Turkey. I was trying to research an incident that had happened where the local Kurdish population had been caught between the hammer and the anvil of the Turkish army and the very violent Kurdish separatist groups there. Something horrible had happened in this village and people were totally traumatised. I was trying to get it down and they brought the English teacher from the local high school to translate. Well, I had no idea what this man taught but it wasn't English and we were working desperately. Then I had the wit to get him to write it all down in Turkish, because he was telling me that they had taken all the young men of the village, made them kneel down in the town square and then made them eat their pussy cats. I thought, 'oh, horrible. That is nasty. What will the animal rights people say about that?' But there was something that didn't sound right. Anyway it turned out that the word he was looking for was 'excrement' but I only got that when I got back to Ankara. Luckily I didn't tell the readers of *The Wall Street Journal* that the Turkish army had made people eat pussy cats.

Bigsby: You mentioned Kate Adie. You look at her and think that she is probably as tough as nails. I look at you and I don't. Are you?

Brooks: I don't know if I am or not but I think being physically unassuming is a great asset in that job. I look very, very silly in a flak jacket and people feel sorry for me a lot. That gives you a lot more access, so I think there is something to be said for it. Nobody ever feels threatened by me.

Bigsby: How dangerous were the circumstances in which you found yourself?

Brooks: Not as dangerous as they are now. At the time I was doing this job there was a different set of assumptions. You might find yourself in a dangerous situation but nobody would be looking to kill you because you were a journalist. That has changed now. I think the murder of *Wall Street Journal* journalist Danny Pearl was a turning point. Occasionally I would think, gee, I miss that life, but not now. I think, who are you kidding? He was doing what we had all done a million times, which was go off to see somebody who had a different set of opinions. If they had agreed to see you, you were in their care. They would in many cases risk their lives to protect you. I had actually gone into the Bekaa Valley to meet with Hezbollah women in the middle of the Lebanon conflict, and I never thought twice about that. The dangerous situations I found myself in were situations where everybody there was in danger, like when the Kurdish uprising was crushed and everybody made a run for the border. I lost colleagues in that attempt to escape from Saddam's army and it was really generally harrowing, but it wasn't personal.

Bigsby: I gather that in case you got a call you had a kit waiting. What does the kit consist of?

Brooks: The call would come in the middle of the night, more often than not, and you would have to be ready to get on the first possible flight. So it had everything in it, from the bullet proof vest, if applicable, to mundane items like handy wipes because there might not be any running water. You must have your short wave radio, so that you could hear the BBC World Service, and little notes to yourself like a purge contact book. You take out a loose leaf binder and remove the pages with any contacts who you didn't want to alert that repressive regime to. I had this list in my bedside drawer for about eight years.

Bigsby: I remember talking to Don McCullen, the famous war photographer.

Brooks: He was with me on that flight out of Kurdistan, and when he got nervous I really started shitting bricks.

Bigsby: I remember him telling me that there came a moment when he thought he had taken enough photographs of war and that he couldn't take any more. He came back and started taking photographs of nature. Was there a point when you felt you'd had enough of this?

Brooks: There were probably a couple of things that happened. One was covering the conflict in Somalia, which was the most pointless conflict I had ever covered, and realising that if I get popped here I will be really pissed because this is not worth it, whereas most of the time I felt a real identification with the people, at least with one side or another of the people I was reporting on. You felt that bearing witness to their struggles and their suffering was really worth it. There was another time when I thought that maybe it is time to let somebody else experience the wonder of otherness because I was getting too blasé about it. I was sitting in a cave in the Atlas Mountains in Morocco interviewing a woman about her life and her weaving and her goats and I was thinking, 'Oh, another woman in a cave.' I guess the very last straw was the Nigerian secret police. I was reporting on Shell oil's ignominious relationship with the military dictatorship where they called in the military to fire on unarmed protestors in the oil-producing region of Nigeria. I got thrown in the slammer and accused of being a French spy. I was sleeping on this concrete floor and I had no idea how long they were going to keep me and I started thinking of Terry Anderson and his seven years in captivity. In seven years I would be too old to get pregnant. So when they deported me after only three days I went home and greeted Tony with more than usual enthusiasm and our son was born the following year. At that point I didn't want to go off on long open-ended assignments.

Bigsby: He was also a reporter?

Brooks: He was, yes. We were foreign correspondents together for a number of years and then he became a national reporter cruising all around America. I couldn't give up the foreign correspondence at that point so I would hop on a plane and come home, first to Hampstead and later to our place in Virginia, a very bucolic rural village that was very different to my work place.

Bigsby: Having been a reporter you then turned to the dark side, becoming a novelist and so inventing things. Having reported on the present you turned to the past and you have largely stayed in the past with your novels. The first one – *Year of Wonder* – wasn't even an Australian past or an American past. It was an English past. Where did that come from?

Brooks: It came from a beautiful June day when we were based in London and I was still covering the Middle East. Whenever Tony and I had a weekend at home together we loved to go rambling, because this is something that you can't generally speaking do in Australia. It is too hard to get into the country from Sydney. It just takes too long. In America you can't do it because the farmer will likely shoot you for trespassing.

We found out about these ancient rights of way, and that you could just walk all over the place. That was a revelation to us so we did a lot of it. One day we were in the Pennines, in the Peak District, and saw a sign saying rat plague village. I have reflected on that since then. Very few towns try to attract tourists by putting up signs saying plague village, so I went there and bought this souvenir, which was a rubber replica plague rat. Somebody needs to work with them on tourism. In the parish church was the account of what had happened there in 1665 when bubonic plague struck the village and the villagers came together and took this unique decision to quarantine themselves rather than flee in different directions and spread the infection. It was effectively an act of altruism because no outbreak of bubonic plague was ever traced back to the main outbreak, and yet it cost a great deal to the people of that village because many of them would have saved themselves had they fled. As it turned out, two-thirds of the villagers were dead in a year. So I was thinking about what that must have been like to come to such a momentous consensus and then to live with the consequences of it.

I guess it banged around in my imagination for about ten years before I came back from Nigeria and had my infant son and needed a new gig. Suddenly I started hearing the voice of Anna Frith in my head. She was a woman of this village. So I thought, okay, let's see what we have got here.

I sat down and wrote a couple of chapters and sent them off to my non-fiction literary agent and said, 'Be brutal, because I can always get another non-fiction idea and work on that.' I didn't hear anything from her and I thought she hated it and was just too polite to tell me. Unbeknown to me she was peddling these chapters all over the place and she sold them. Then I had to write it.

Bigsby: There is a connection between that and *People of the Book* in this sense of altruism, of people doing things they don't have to do, that is not necessarily in their own interest.

Brooks: I think it comes out of the foreign correspondent years, seeing people under great stress, seeing them in times of catastrophe, and realising that nobody knows who they are going to be until it actually comes upon you. Some people become their best self, and you see acts of incredible bravery and generosity and kindness, and some people become their worst self and turn into monsters and brutalisers. I guess that fascinates and draws me: how will people be changed by catastrophe?

Bigsby: You were explaining earlier that you broke off working on *People of the Book* and wrote another novel, *March*, which won the Pulitzer Prize. That was a book that had its starting point in another book.

Brooks: It had its starting point in self-preservation from my husband's obsession with the American Civil War. I knew he was interested in the Civil War but I didn't know that he was an absolute bore on the subject until we moved to Virginia after we had been married ten years. It was almost too late to do anything about it because we had been engaged in all these more contemporary conflicts. There is a saying in America that the Civil War was fought in ten thousand places, and it soon became depressingly clear to me that he intended to take me to every single one of them. Our weekends were just eaten up with these battlefield visits and these re-enacters would be sleeping in the garden. You would only find out because the dogs couldn't stand them. They are very smelly. They don't wash, to get more authenticity into their re-enacting, and it was just driving me completely spare. I though I am either going to have to find something that interests me about this or I am going to have to leave him. So I found it in thinking about what happens to idealists at war, and the idea of war for a good cause.

The abolitionists went off to fight that war because they thought slavery was a greater evil than violence. That was very vivid in the village where we were living because it had been settled by Quakers and Quakers were ardent abolitionists but also pacifists. So for the young men of that village it was a big crisis of conscience and a few of the villagers formed a unit to fight on the Union side from the heart of the old dominion. So I was thinking about that, and those traces, and what happens if you are an idealist and you go to war for moral ends while the means by which wars are waged are never moral and you find yourself doing unspeakably immoral things. As I was thinking about the idea of the idealist at war I thought of the absent father in Louisa May Alcott's *Little Women*. That was a beloved book of my childhood, though I couldn't have told you, as a ten-year-old when I read it, that it was an American book. I thought it was English, like everything else I read. As an adult it occurred to me that when Louisa May tells us on the first page that the father is away down south, where the fighting was, being a minister to the Union troops, he seemed the perfect vehicle to explore this idea of what happens to a good man in a bad war.

Bigsby: Have you thought about writing a book based on Australian history?

Brooks: I think about it quite a lot actually and I did start one but there was a problem. There was too much information, because the woman at the centre of the story had kept a journal every day of her life in which she wrote down in minute detail what she thought about everything. So there wasn't that void for my imagination to work. The only void was one that I couldn't quite get my novelist head around because she commits an inexplicable act in her life and I just couldn't imaginatively come to grips as to why she had done it. And if I couldn't, then I couldn't possibly write it. So I set that one aside. But I am very fascinated now with the story of a very early woman anthropologist who went to live among the aboriginal communities. She is not well known, but I want to spend more time discovering what happened to her.

In Conversation With
A. S. Byatt

- 2nd December 2009 -

A. S. Byatt was born in Sheffield in 1936 and was educated at Cambridge, Bryn Mawr and Oxford. Her first novel, *The Shadow of the Sun*, appeared in 1964. Other novels include *The Virgin in the Garden* (1978), *Still Life* (1985), *Possession: A Romance* (1990), *Babel Tower* (1996) and *The Children's Book* (2009). She is a winner of the Booker Prize, the Irish Times/Aer Lingus International Fiction Prize and the Shakespeare Prize, among others. She was made a Dame of the British Empire in 1999.

Bigsby: Your latest work is *The Children's Book* but I wonder if I could start not by talking about the book itself, but by taking you back to your own childhood and asking which children's books you grew up with?

Byatt: I was like Angela Carter, I found myths much more real than stories about children doing things in schools or kitchens. My very favourite book was called *Asgard and the Gods*, which was not a children's book but a book my mother had used at Cambridge as a crib for studying ancient Norse and ancient Icelandic. I then went to Iceland and the Icelanders told me indignantly that there was no such language as ancient Norse. It was simply Icelandic and Cambridge should have known better. But at the time I thought that was what it was and I lived in that book, and I lived in various fairy stories. I did read Arthur Ransome but, looking back, I think it was Kipling I most loved of the children's writers of the period. I loved *Puck of Pook's Hill* and I loved *The Jungle Book*. I didn't read *Kim* until I was grown up. I read the *Just So* stories.

Bigsby: You once said that you weren't very happy being a child, that childhood wasn't something you would look back on necessarily warmly?

Byatt: No, I disliked being a child intensely. I wanted to be an adult. I had no idea what being an adult would entail but I knew it must be better

131

than having to be a child. I didn't like the structures I found myself in, schools and gangs and playground groups, and then when I was sent to boarding school I didn't like other girls sleeping in the same room as me. I think partly I didn't like being a child because I am a natural solitary. I have no capacity for group life, almost at all. I like coming out and talking to somebody for a few hours and retreating back into the attic with my books. Also I think I felt that childhood was a series of people telling you how happy you were to be a child, how wonderful childhood was, and it didn't fit. I am writing a myth now, for the Canongate myth series. I am writing the myth of Ragnarok, which is the end of the world. But it has to be remembered that my early childhood was passed in a war. My father was fighting in the air force in North Africa and, looking back, I now see I never really expected him to come back. So I was a child overarched by something that nobody spoke about that was terrible.

Bigsby: Does that mean that in some way story was where you went?

Byatt: Yes, I just went into stories. I told myself an endless myth. Some of it was out of *Asgard* but a lot of it was just me. There was a female character and there were an enormous number of articulate animals. There weren't any more people in this story. I wrote things down and never showed them to anybody. You start making up myths about yourself when you reach the age I have reached and I have now convinced myself that the moment I could read I knew I had to write.

I remember being on about page four of a reading book and hitting the word 'machine.' I read it 'ma'–'chine' and I looked at it and thought, 'This isn't a word.' Then I think my mother explained and I thought, 'Alright, this can all be mastered,' this idea of all these words, in this order, making a place that I wasn't in. I loved doing it. I loved writing as much as I hated sewing.

Bigsby: You mentioned your mother and she went to Cambridge but at that time women couldn't get a degree at Cambridge?

Byatt: No, I think it was 1948 before women could get a degree at Cambridge. Oxford women, I think, were allowed to have degrees in the thirties. Cambridge women hung on. I was absolutely horrified when I was doing my research for this novel because several of the female characters go to Newnham College, Cambridge, before the First World War. I didn't realise that the male students hated the females so much that they actually invaded the college and broke down the wonderful bronze gates. I didn't realise that there was a riot in Cambridge against the women. I just thought there were a lot of rather irritated old men who didn't want them getting into their common rooms, which can be understood. It wasn't that. There was a gut feeling against the women that is quite frightening. They were not allowed to go anywhere without a chaperone. There was one I read about – and I put the fact in the novel – who was doing some kind of rather arcane economic history. She was the only woman doing it. But the Principal of the college had to chaperone her, and walk to the lectures she was allowed to go to. You were allowed to go into lectures in men's colleges if the men's college would let you in, but some of them wouldn't. It was very precarious. When I went to Newnham, I didn't know any of this. I just thought women went to Cambridge. My mother had gone to Cambridge. I didn't know how much they fought, or how stressful it all was, and how meaningful it therefore all was. I was deeply moved by the amount of work they did and how hard they studied.

Bigsby: But for your mother Cambridge didn't lead out into the world but into a domestic, enclosed world?

Byatt: The story is rather strange really. My mother and father were in the same class at Mexborough Grammar School, at the age of eleven, and my mother said to me, 'If he didn't come top then I did, and if I didn't come top, he did.' She went to Cambridge, although she was a working class girl from a poor household, because the English teacher there believed in educating all these people in a South Yorkshire coalfield. My father's parents were rich. They said there was no point in him going to university. He could be a commercial traveller in his father's firm and he therefore, unbeknown to his father, worked secretly at night and got himself into Cambridge. Then he went to his father and said, 'Papa, I am going to cease to work for you now. I have got a scholarship to Downing College, Cambridge'. My father said his father was an inconsequential person and flung his arms around his neck and gave him two thousand pounds. When my parents married the thing my mother didn't tell me, until she was really quite old, was that teaching was all she could do because of the Depression. This country forbad women who were married to teach in the Depression so that there would be jobs for the men.

She went back to teaching in the war in Pontefract. She was senior English master at a boy's grammar school, and I am probably the only one of her children who remembers that she was happy. I wasn't happy. I thought she shouldn't leave the house, but she came home and she talked to me about Shakespeare. When I was five or six she taught me English grammar. She said, 'This is the subject and that is the verb and this is a sentence. Brightly waved our banner. What is the subject? So I said, 'Our banner,' so she said, 'Yes.' But all the boys got it wrong and said it was 'brightly.' I remember that because we were happy and she was not very good at being happy.

Bigsby: You said once that your father always told you the truth and your mother always lied?

Byatt: That was his version, come to think of it. My mother was a fantasist. Any story she told she embroidered, and this drove my father mad because he was a lawyer and a judge eventually. He was a religious man, a Quaker, and he felt that everything you said should be the truth, the whole truth and nothing but the truth, so help you God. My mother thought that simply wasn't interesting. Any story she embarked on became the shape my mother was choosing to tell stories in. Some of them were awful; some of them were terrible. Why on earth she didn't tell me she hadn't been allowed to teach before the war, given all the things she did tell me about, I don't know. She seemed to assume one would have known it. I wrote a story called *Sugar* about the two of them, and there is a poem by Goethe in which he says that from his father he got his rigorous nature and his truth telling and from his mother he got his capacity for fantasy. So I used that as an epigraph. It is called *Sugar* because sugar is what my grandfather dealt in. He made boiled sweets which he sent all over Yorkshire in horse-drawn vehicles.

Bigsby: You mentioned Quakers and you had a Quaker education. Is there any sense in which that has fed into your subsequent life?

Byatt: The older I get the more deeply I see it did affect me. Quakers believed they were the primitive Christians. They tried to do those things which Jesus told people to do – love their neighbours as themselves. They had no ceremonies. They had no creed. What I loved about them was that their religious meetings were conducted in silence. You just sat there and if anybody felt, as they put it, moved by the spirit to communicate something to the group, then they stood up and said something, and if they didn't you all just sat there. They had this rigorous sense of truthfulness and accuracy and the school was said to have no punishments, which meant of course that it produced quite dangerous mental punishments. It made you feel very, very bad if you did anything it thought was a bit bad and so it wasn't exactly as comfortable as you might think. But it was deeply serious. My father became a Quaker after sending his children to Quaker schools, not before. None of his children became Quakers.

Bigsby: Your books are not lacking in humour and wit, but you are a serious novelist. Do you think that traces back in some sense to that education?

Byatt: It traces back through the Quakers to both my parents who were serious people. My mother, God help her, was supervised by Dr. Leavis and he taught her to take literature seriously, so it is very deep in me. It never occurred to me there was any other way to live, unless you were Becky Sharpe or somebody like that, all the bad people in novels. I was quite surprised to find people who were not serious in the world. I found them fairly early. They were in the gangs in the playground.

Bigsby: When did you first think of yourself as a potential writer?

Byatt: I was writing stories and plays when I was six. The Quakers taught me to doubt myself and they didn't set much store on art or writing or anything, but I felt from the age of about ten that I might be a writer as long as I never told anybody and as long as I made a provision for my life when I failed to be a writer. I wrote, probably, three novels while I was at boarding school.

Bigsby: How old were you then?

Byatt: I went there when I was thirteen and left there, gleefully, when I was seventeen-and-a-half, and I sat there writing all these novels.

Bigsby: What did you do with them?

Byatt: I put them in the furnace in the basement. They were no good.

Bigsby: By the time you left school, then, you had developed a critical faculty that enabled you to judge yourself as not coming up to the required standard?

Byatt: Yes, I think that was all I had really got. I couldn't run. I can swim now, but I was no good at it then. I wasn't very good at making friends. I was very good at languages, but I was no good at any other subject. I always came bottom in domestic science practical, and top in domestic science theoretical. I was a narrow-minded, narrow creature with one thing in its head and I did get into university and went to study literature. In those days if you studied A level English literature you were given a sense of what was good writing and what was bad writing. You were told to discriminate and we read an awful lot of books compared to children nowadays. I learnt the rhythms, and you know if you have written a bad rhythm, if in what you have written the rhythm is dead. You don't necessarily know how to make it any better, which is very sad, but you do know it is not any good. Reading and writing were the same thing to me really. When I read I wanted to write. I remember writing little things that were rather like Dickens because I had just been reading Dickens.

Bigsby: When you eventually began to write more seriously than the ones you threw away, what kind of writer did you think you were going to be? What kind of novel did you think you wanted to write?

Byatt: This is a question I need to work my way around rather carefully. I didn't want to be a woman writer. I always say I call myself A. S. Byatt because of T. S. Elliot and L. P. Hartley and D H Lawrence and H G Wells. It was normal. When I finally did publish I wasn't trying to avoid being thought of as a woman. I just wanted it not to come into it. Every week, both at boarding school and at home, we went to the Boots library and we got out a heap of books like that and I didn't want to write most of those, although I read them avidly. I read Georgette Heyer like crazy, and bits of *Possession* are indeed directly derived from Georgette Heyer. I didn't want to write about people's emotions, and I didn't know anything else. I wanted to make something that was also an object. One way of putting it is that when I was a student I wrote about poems in exams. I never wrote about novels, partly because I didn't know the novels by heart and I did know most of the poems by heart, so if I needed a quote I could drag it up and put it in. It was easier. But it was partly because I was afraid of the shape of the novel. I hadn't mastered it, whereas I could write an elegant thing on a John Donne religious sonnet that would say most of what needed to be said, and I could talk about the rhythm. I didn't want to write about people in houses and women in kitchens and people falling in love and people falling out of love. Because of the Quakers I thought there were more important things in the world.

Bigsby: Did you want to write about now, the time you were living in?

Byatt: I believed I ought to write about now, what you read in newspapers, and to a certain extent what you were taught at university.

We weren't taught novels very much. I did poems and plays but there was a general theory that what you should do is write about now and my now was again extremely narrow. I wasn't even young in the nineteen sixties. I was young in the fifties, and although I agree entirely with Doris Lessing that the fifties weren't nearly as boring and arid as everybody now says they were, you actually had to be a better novelist to find something interesting in the fifties than you do to find something interesting in the sixties or the seventies. You need to be very, very subtle indeed to make that interesting. I gave a talk at the ICA once, with David Lodge. David was complaining that my novels were not about the big things and I had just been talking to Doris Lessing who said that there were no novels about the machinations of international companies. Then this lady stood up and said, 'All political struggles can be found in the kitchen.' I said, 'No, they can't. It isn't enough. You have got to be able to do the kitchen if you are stuck in it but probably you should go and work in a hospital, if you are stuck in it as a housewife, or if you are stuck in it as a writer.' That was the Quakers, you see. The hospital came in sideways through the Quakers.

Bigsby: How important has it been to your writing that you can work in French and German as well?

Byatt: Enormously. It never occurred to that young woman trying to write novels in the nineteen fifties that if I got to be a novelist I could then become a European novelist. It just would never have occurred to me. I always knew it is good for writing English to be able to read another language and hear the rhythms and the thought structures of another language, because that makes you know what English is, if you can read French or German. Also it has been enormously good for me as a writer to have read Balzac and Thomas Mann as well as Racine. I am intensely English. I am not British. I am English. It is narrow again, but I know all these other things are there and I get terribly excited when the Europeans notice that I know a bit.

Bigsby: You studied literature at university, and you then went on to teach English and American literature at a university. On the other hand literary criticism has at times been very restrictive. You mentioned Leavis, who had a very defined canon. If a writer fell outside that he or she wasn't really worth looking at. When you were teaching at University College, London, it was a period in which literary criticism, more especially in America perhaps, was going through a phase which made

137

writers feel uncomfortable. Critics often deployed a language which did not seem to address the essence of what they were doing, and that is reflected in some way in *Possession*, isn't it?

Byatt: Yes, it is very strongly reflected in *Possession*. I got into university teaching because I met Frank Kermode at a party and he invited me, just as a woman in a house, to come to his graduate seminar on literary theory before there was any literary theory. He had read my novel and I was reviewing for him. So I was a particular woman in a particular house. Anyway, he invited me and I left my house, with my bag of books, and went to this seminar, and that was in fact how I got the job at UCL. I didn't apply for a job. I got shovelled into one. Then, as you say, theory took over, and when theory became this extraordinary linguistic and institutional power structure in the teaching of English literature and professors swept across America with a huge train of people behind them as though they were Good King Wenceslas I felt that something had gone wrong with the language. I believe in writing criticism in what I call common speech, which I know I got out of Tolkien. I do believe most things you can say about books, though not all, can be said in the same language as the one in which you write novels, and I felt rather lost. Sometimes I thought this extra language was obfuscating and sometimes I thought it was saying really interesting things. The study of linguistics said really interesting things, but they weren't my things, and so I left.

What I noticed in this country was that the Martin Amis, Julian Barnes generation, younger than me, had rather gleefully given up on academe and that there was a freedom to their writing. My generation was afraid of Dr. Leavis saying we were not serious enough. That generation said, be gone to all your schools and theories and ideas. I am going to write a good story. It was wonderful. We won't talk about it here but an interesting case is Anthony Burgess because he could do the theory and I think it inhibited him that it was around.

Bigsby: David Lodge could as well.

Byatt: Yes, and David always claimed, which is clearly not true, that his critical side never speaks to his writing side which any reader of either can see is not true, but he needs to say it.

Bigsby: You have been drawn to the past as a setting for your novels. Is the attraction particularly, say, of the nineteenth century, that there is a different language waiting for you back there, a richer, more allusive, more metaphoric language.

Byatt: I once did a broadcast with a wonderful broadcaster who had been interviewing a series of British writers about why they chose to write in the past. I think he expected to get a lot of answers about history, and how the present is made up of course of history. But he said every single one of them – William Golding, Anthony Burgess – said they needed to write something in complex sentences, to write dependent clauses. That was a great deal of why I wrote *Possession*. I wanted to write the sort of sentence that I took great delight in and that there was no place for in a good straightforward modern novel about now. So I wrote *Possession* as a kind of romp, just to play with the language, because, after all, language is why you start writing. I never started writing in order to set the world to rights, or even to describe my feelings. I started writing because I was fascinated by words and it is surprising how many of these historical novelists were doing it for the same reason.

Bigsby: Is there another reason? There is a different conception of character waiting for you there as well, not the ironic, attenuated version that you often find in contemporary writing.

Byatt: When I wrote *Possession* I went to interview Nathalie Sarraute, who had said that you can't have characters any more, you just can't have them. It is far too vulgar. There mustn't be any people with buttons on their clothes, because buttons have been described to death. I could write that if I wanted to but I don't think that characters and buttons and plots have been exhausted. I think it was when I wrote *Possession* that I came to see just how important plot was, and that was going against the tendency of the kind of writing that was being admired. I subsequently met John Hawkes who said, 'The chief enemies of the novel are plot, character, theme, and setting,' and I looked at that and I thought that that was a terribly clever thing to say but is simply not true. He was a very interesting man, and his books were amazing, but it seemed to me that it was almost revolutionary to make a really good plot at that point in writing history.

Bigsby: The other thing nineteenth century novels had was elbow room, that is to say they were large. You have a tendency to write large. Is that space valuable in itself or is there a risk that you will be tempted to put everything in?

Byatt: There is a an intellectual need to grab everything. If you think you are writing about the Victoria and Albert museum you find you need to know the whole of theory of how to make museums in nineteenth century Europe, and very interesting it is too. Publishers won't publish the book if it gets that long. I think there is a moral reason, too. My natural need is to write books with more than one person in. I like there to be a lot of characters to show that the world is full of different people, with different needs and different desires and different histories.

Bigsby: That is very nineteenth century.

Byatt: It is totally nineteenth century. I am invigorated more by Balzac and George Eliot than I am by E. M. Forster or by Jean Paul Sartre, who I haven't read for ages. Iris Murdoch once said that when she had finished a novel she felt she had done down the marginal characters at the edges, and that they hadn't had their story told properly. She wanted to start the novel again and tell it from the point of view of the minor characters. Of course you can always do that, then you can do it again, and then you can do it again.

Bigsby: She also said that she wanted her novels to be a house fit for free characters to live in. Are you drawn to that conception of character and the relationship between the characters and the person who creates them?

Byatt: Yes, I am. They should be free. They aren't, of course. I think the difference between me and Iris is that she was a moral philosopher who thought the persons in the novel were the most important thing, even though she knew that the form of the novel was crucially important and that the balance and the structure and the metaphors mattered. For better, for worse, and in some ways for worse, I am a linguistic being and see all my characters as part of the run of the language in the book. They have their own voices which come to the surface.

Bigsby: But if they are free they can surprise you. Are you surprised by your characters?

Byatt: Yes. I am not going to give the plot away but I was quite surprised by what happened to Florence in *The Children's Book*. It was inevitable, but I was quite surprised by it, and I was surprised by one or two of the others as well. You can be surprised in a little way even if the scene you are writing is something you had intended to write. You get to this point in the plot you had intended to get to and people say some things you didn't know they were going to say. They do surprise you. I spend a lot of my time just watching them as though I was in the room with them. I watch them and think, 'What's he going to say next?' Or I think, 'What would he look like if I was looking out of that one's eyes at this one?' They surprise you. People write letters to writers saying your characters simply take over. Mine have never done that. It has never turned into a completely different story because one of the characters wouldn't do as they were told, but then I don't ever tell. I listen to them.

Bigsby: Can you tell me why you were drawn to the period when *The Children's Book* is set?

Byatt: I wasn't, in a way. It is not a period I like. It is full of people who are very conceited about themselves and very sure they can improve the world and generally less tragic than the high Victorians, the Edwardians. It started with the idea of children's writers. I noticed that a very large number of great writers for children have children whose own fate is tragic and I thought this is a phenomenon. So I did a bit more research. I did know that Kenneth Grahame's son had killed himself. I didn't know that Alison Uttley's son had driven himself off Beachy Head. There was something very powerful about the effect of people who wrote compelling books for children and what happened to their own children. So I started with that idea, and obviously this was the right period to set this in as it was the period of Kenneth Grahame and Peter Pan and E. Nesbitt and Kipling.

Bigsby: But it was also the period, as you point out, of the establishment of the great museums in London, of the arts and crafts movement, Fabianism. Everything was going on. You once said that you didn't like the phrase 'creative writer' because you like to think of yourself as a maker and there are makers in this book. There is a potter, who creates beauty from clay, which is I suppose what writers do in their own way. But we also discover that there is a price to be paid for that in that his mother had been involved in that industry and had been slowly poisoning herself in the process. And that is not the only instance in the novel in which there is a price to be paid for creativity.

Byatt: I think there is. Sooner or later I always get a question about what sort of a mother do you think a writer can be, and some of the real and imaginary writers round about then were pretty bad mothers, though they lived in a period when they had so much domestic help that nobody

141

really expected them to be mothers that much. Then the next cliché that comes along is Grahame Greene talking about every writer having a splinter of ice in the soul.

Bigsby: A central figure in the novel is a spinner of stories, a writer of children's stories. And she writes the stories of other people's lives in the sense that Dick Diver, in *Tender is the Night*, gives people a story to inhabit. But there is danger in this process.

Byatt: There is a lot of danger in this process. The children's writer, Olive, writes a fairy story for each of her many children and that is meant to be their fairy story in which their imagination shall live. This is the sort of thing that could well have happened in that period and it was an immensely generous act you would think to give your child a whole story to himself or herself, yet it is also an invasion. Nobody gave the child I was trotting along to school with, my satchel on my back, my story. I did it. So she is both immensely generous and immensely invasive. I think the word 'creative' sounds as though you are a God making a world whereas if you are somebody making a pot you have half a chance to go away and be a human being when you are not actually making the pot, half a chance.

Bigsby: You are looking at the last decades of the nineteenth century and the first decade of the twentieth century, a period alive with a ferment of ideas, but ahead lay an event that was going to resonate down the century, much of it anyway. When you started the book did you think of the fate that was inevitably awaiting that generation and of which they knew nothing themselves: the First World War?

Byatt: I didn't think about it. I said I am narrow. I was actually never very good at history and I started thinking intensely about the eighteen nineties and nineteen hundred and it was only really when I started chronologies for all these characters that I suddenly saw where they were all heading. I think this was very good for the novel because I tried very hard, and succeeded in this country, in keeping the word 'looming' out of descriptions of the First World War on the book jacket because in my novel it doesn't loom. One of the historical things I think I discovered was that the Second World War probably did loom. I think everybody knew Europe couldn't go on the way it was. But as far as I could see, reading an enormous amount of history, the First World War could just as easily not have happened. The people who weren't expecting it weren't expecting it for a good reason. In fact the more I read the more I came to think that an enormous amount of it depended on the fact that the Kaiser was mad. If you look at all the Kaiser's letters he sometimes thought it should happen and sometimes thought it shouldn't and wanted to be loved by all his relations who were on the thrones of all the countries. Indeed right at the last minute he thought that, although he was going to war with Russia, war with England could be stopped. In a way I think my novel, owing to my lack of historical knowledge, makes a falling of the axe feel like a falling of an axe. People right up to the last minute were completely obsessed with whether the poor were going to rise up and slaughter the middle classes. The Suffragettes were completely obsessed with smashing windows and getting the vote. Nobody said, 'Is there going to be a war?'

Bigsby: Were you ever tempted to stop the novel just short of that?

Byatt: I thought of that, but partly because, as you rightly say, all my novels are too long I thought to myself if you stop in nineteen fourteen you don't have to do it. And then I thought if I was a reader of that novel and it stopped in nineteen fourteen I would simply be enraged and throw it down the stairs. I would say this is a cheat, this is terrible. I never in my life wanted to write a war novel. I didn't think I would write a First World War novel. I thought I would write a novel about the Fabian society and pottery and arts and crafts, and so then I had to get the war into a reasonably short space because of the length of the already existing novel. My husband has had a huge library about the First World War all the time I have been married to him. His father was buried alive on the Somme at the age of seventeen. But I had been brought up by the Quakers to believe that war was wrong, and so I had never read any of all this. Then I read it all and got terribly distressed.

In Conversation With Jung Chang

- 24th November 2008 -

Jung Chang was born in 1952, in Yibin, China. She grew up during the Cultural Revolution in which she was a Red Guard. She was allowed to leave China in 1978 to study in Britain, receiving a PhD four years later. In 1991, she published *Wild Swans*, an account of three generations of her own family. It has sold over ten million copies and was British Book of the Year in 1993. In 2005, together with her husband, the academic Jon Halliday, she published *Mao: The Untold Story*.

Bigsby: Though you have lived in this country for many years, you were born in China. What was it like to grow up under Mao Tse-tung?

Chang: I was born in China in 1952, three years after Mao took power. As I was growing up there was the intense personality cult of Mao. He was like our God. When we were children if we wanted to say that something was absolutely true we would say, 'I swear to Chairman Mao.' There was a song every child in China learned to sing. It went 'Father is close, mother is close, but neither is as close as Chairman Mao.' Mao was able to do this partly because he had sealed China off and isolated it completely from the outside world. I didn't see a foreigner until I was twenty-three, so when we were children the West was this horrible, terrifying place and westerners were terrifying people. Because my parents were communist officials I was sent to an elite nursery and if the teachers wanted us to eat up our food they would say, 'Think of all the starving children in the capitalist world.' When the boys played guerrilla warfare the baddies would always have something glued onto their noses to show they were foreigners because the Chinese think foreigners have longer and sharper noses than the Chinese. The baddies would say 'Hello' all the time because in propaganda films evil foreigners were always

147

drinking Coca-Cola and saying 'Hello' so we all thought 'Hello' was a swear word.

In this world Mao indoctrinated us with his personality cult and the reason he was able to do that was that no parents in China dared to tell their children anything different from the Party line. Parents who loved their children and didn't want them to grow up to become non-conformists and ruin their lives always said to their children, 'Do as Chairman Mao says.' Our teachers would say to us, 'If you work hard you will be able to go to Beijing and see Chairman Mao.' The goal of my life was couched in Mao's name. When I was fourteen I went to Beijing on this pilgrimage to see Mao. I didn't see him clearly. I only caught a glimpse of his back. I was so heartbroken that for a fleeting moment I thought perhaps I should commit suicide. But it was in that year, 1966, when I was fourteen, that my faith in Mao began to wane. This was because that year Mao launched his violent Cultural Revolution and there were a lot of atrocities around me. In virtually every school and university in China teachers were designated targets and children set them up as prisoners to torment and torture. Many teachers were tortured to death. I was so terrified and appalled and disgusted by what was happening all around me it just went against my nature.

Bigsby: Your own family suffered at this time.

Chang: My parents became victims of the Cultural Revolution. My father was one of the few who stood up to Mao and protested. When he was about to write to Mao to make his protest my mother said to him, 'do you want to ruin the lives of our children?' But my father was somebody who always put his principles before the interests of his family and he said, 'what about the children of the victims?' So he went ahead and, as a result, was arrested, tortured, driven insane, and exiled to a camp. He later died prematurely. My mother was under tremendous pressure to denounce my father. She refused, although she had felt a lot of bitterness towards him because he was a very difficult man to live with. My mother refused to denounce my father and as a result she was put through over a hundred of those ghastly denunciation meetings that were an everyday feature in China. Basically, the victims would be stood on the stage and their arms would be violently pushed back and their heads pushed down. They would be kicked and beaten. My mother was made to kneel on broken glass. She was paraded in the street where children spat at her and threw stones at her. She was exiled to a camp but survived and today still lives in China.

While all this was happening I started to doubt the society I was living in, a society we were always told was paradise on earth. On my sixteenth birthday, in 1968, I wrote my first poem. I was lying in bed polishing my poem in my head and I heard the door banging. My parents' tormentors had come to raid our flat so I had to quickly rush to the toilet to tear up my poem and flush it down the toilet. Afterwards I was lying in bed thinking, if this is paradise, then what is hell? This was the first time I openly questioned the society I was living in, but I didn't question Mao. In the following years I blamed people around him. I blamed his wife, but I just couldn't bring myself to say Mao's name. Mao's personality cult had produced that kind of impact and effect.

Bigsby: When did you begin to realise that Mao himself was the moving force?

Chang: In 1974, eight years after my first questioning of Mao, a friend secretly gave me a copy of *Newsweek*, and by then I had learnt a little English. In the magazine there was an article about the Cultural Revolution and a little picture of Mao and Madame Mao. The caption said, 'Madame Mao is Mao's eyes, ears and mouth.' Suddenly, it was as if a window had been thrown open in my head and I thought, 'Of course, Mao is responsible and how come that I am fairly intelligent and didn't even realise that?' It was Mao, not the Gang of Four, so called. It was not his wife. It was Mao, and that is the first time I openly challenged Mao in my head.

Then, in 1976, Mao died and China began to change. In 1978, for the first time, scholarships for going abroad were awarded on an academic basis. I sat for a national exam. I did reasonably well so I became one of a group of fourteen people to come to Britain for studies. As far as I know I was the first person from Communist China to come to the west. So when I got my doctorate from the University of York, in 1982, I was so lucky to have become the first person from Communist China to get a doctorate from a British university.

When I first arrived, of course, Britain was like Mars. Everything was so different. I remember that when I arrived at Heathrow airport I nearly walked into the men's toilet because I had no idea that the figure wearing trousers on the door was supposed to be a man. In China, in the Cultural Revolution, for many years women were not allowed to wear skirts. Also the man walking in front of me had long hair. When we first came we were all wearing these Mao suits and were not allowed to go out on our own. We had to move in a group, so we were quite a sight in a London street. Also, before I came the only foreigners I had met were some sailors in a port in South China. I managed to get into a university when universities re-opened in China in 1973. I was one of the lucky ones to get into a university to learn English. We were sent to this port in South China to practice our English with these sailors. We would be sitting in this bar or restaurant eagerly awaiting our sailors and we would grab them as soon as they came on shore. Of course we had no idea what must have been on their minds.

Also, when I learnt English my textbooks were written by teachers who had never seen foreigners themselves, so textbooks were direct translations from Chinese. I remember this lesson on greetings. In China, when we bumped into each other we would say, 'Where are you going? Have you eaten?' So those were the English greetings I learnt. When I first arrived in England I would go around asking people where they were going and whether they had eaten. Ten years after I came to Britain, in 1988, my mother came from China to stay with me. This was her first trip abroad and for the first time she was in an environment free of social and political constraints and was able to open her mind and heart. She told me stories of my grandfather and stories of herself and my father. Once she started she couldn't stop. She stayed with me for six months and talked every day. By the time she left London she had left me sixty hours of tape recordings so while I was listening to her I said to myself, 'I have got to write all this down.' That is how I wrote *Wild Swans*.

Bigsby: What led you to write about Mao?

Chang: After *Wild Swans* was published, in early 1990, I was thinking about my next project and Mao seemed to be the obvious subject because he dominated my early life and I saw him turning the lives of a quarter of the world's population upside down. Yet I felt the world knew little about him. The Chinese knew astonishingly little about him and I myself knew very little so I wanted to find out. Writing this book was also a journey of discovery for me and my husband, Jon Halliday. He is a historian and was also interested in Mao so we embarked on this project together.

We divided our research by language. Because I am Chinese I dealt with the Chinese language sources. Jon unfortunately speaks many languages so he was landed with the rest of the world. In particular, he speaks Russian and spent years working in Russian archives, which turned out to be a treasure trove. We travelled all around the world together and interviewed virtually anyone who had interesting dealings with Mao outside China. In China we interviewed Mao's family members, friends, colleagues, colleague's widows and Mao's staff. Outside China we interviewed everyone from Edward Heath to George Bush Sr, from Henry Kissinger to the Dalai Lama, and we worked in all the archives which had Chinese documents. We were the first to go into the Albanian archives because tiny Albania was China's only ally in the Cultural Revolution.

We had great fun. One encounter was with Sese Seko Mobutu, the tyrant of Zaire, now Congo. He was a man who was supposed to have strangled his opponent with his bare hands, and was supported by Mao. One day we were in a Hong Kong hotel. Jon was reading his morning paper in the bathroom and he suddenly yelled, 'Guess who is in this hotel? It's Mobutu.' He said, 'Shall we try and find somebody to introduce us?' And I said, 'Oh, Jon, I have done two months of interviews. I am exhausted and I can't be bothered. I am going to the hair salon.' So I went to the hair salon and ten minutes later who but Mobutu strutted in. He was sitting near me and was underneath the hairdryer. He had bits of cotton wool around his hair and towels around his neck and was trapped, so I was able to approach him. I rang Jon to bring the album of us with the world's dictators and statesmen so I was able to approach Mobutu with this album and ask him for an interview. He never gave interviews in those days but he agreed.

We also had a rare interview with Imelda Marcos, the Philippine First Lady who had thousands of pairs of shoes. Mao was a womaniser. When he met her he was nearly blind but his eyes sparkled and he got into a flirtation with Imelda and kissed her on the hands and the cheeks. This so shocked Mao's photographer, because he was in the Cultural Revolution when these gestures were deemed bourgeois and dangerous, that he didn't dare to take photographs. The newsreel camera, though, was running and recorded the moment of Mao flirting with Imelda, so we had a rare photograph in our book. Imelda also tried to flirt with my husband and batted her eyelids furiously. She said, 'Oh, western men simply don't understand us eastern women.' So Jon said, 'Have you come across any western men who understand you? She said, 'Only one person, Richard Nixon.'

Following more than ten years of research, hard work from morning until quite late in the evening, I was shocked by our discoveries. Almost every day there were big and little discoveries and shocks. I was shocked by how Mao treated his people. I was shocked by how he treated his colleagues and I was shocked by how he treated his family. For example, there was a great famine in China between 1958 and 1961. Nearly forty million people died of starvation and overwork. I knew about this famine and wrote about it in *Wild Swans*, but then I thought, like most people, that the famine was the result of economic mismanagement and that Mao was no good at managing the economy. Then, suddenly, as a result of our research, I realised this wasn't the case. It is true that Mao was no good at the economy but this wasn't the reason. Mao knew these tens of millions of people would die because he was exporting the food these people were dependent on for survival to Russia and to Eastern Europe to buy nuclear technology and equipment for the arms industries so he could build China into a military super power, so he could dominate the world. That Mao had these ambitions was completely new to me because we had always thought he was just messing about with the Chinese people and wasn't thinking about the outside world. Not true. From the day he took power in China, even before then, he had set his eyes on dominating the world or imposing his tyranny on the world. Mao was heartless. We discovered what he said when he was told the peasants were starving, having only tree leaves to eat. He would say, 'So what? Educate the peasants to eat less. Then they can fertilise the land.' So, in many places when people died they were not allowed a proper burial. They were buried in the farm land and the crops were planted on top. Mao even said that to achieve all his projects half of China may well have to die.

So I was really shocked. Mao's actions were so heartless that even his number two, President Liu Shaoqi, felt this was too much. Liu was a hard man but even he thought this so unacceptable that at the beginning of 1962 he ambushed Mao and got together with seven thousand party officials at a party congress and together they forced Mao to change his policies and avoided tens of millions of deaths. Mao was furious. He hated being outsmarted and wanted revenge. This was why he launched his Cultural Revolution a few years later, in 1966, in which Liu became his number one target. He suffered appallingly and died an appalling death. Most of the time he was imprisoned in his house, a stone's throw from Mao's own house, and Mao had his agonies filmed and photographed and took pleasure in his former colleague's agony.

Mao's number three was the charismatic Zhou Enlai who charmed statesmen all over the world and Edward Heath sung his praises. Henry Kissinger said he was the most impressive statesman he had ever dealt with. He served Mao like a faithful slave. He collaborated with Mao in the Cultural Revolution and, according to the official statistics, made possible the appalling suffering of one in nine Chinese. When Mao was ill he tasted Mao's medicine and even tried Mao's eye-drops to see whether they stung. But when he was diagnosed as having cancer of the bladder Mao ordered his doctors not to treat him. Mao wanted him to die before him and this is exactly what happened. He died eight months before Mao.

Most tyrants had a soft corner for their family but I was astonished to see how heartless Mao was towards his family and his wives. Mao was married four times. He always said that his number two wife, Luo Yixiu, was the love of his life but, as we discovered, Mao actually abandoned her together with their three young sons, the youngest only four months old. When she was in danger of being arrested and executed by the nationalists, Mao's domestic enemies in 1930, he could easily have saved her, but he didn't lift a finger and she was executed. Mao's third wife, He Zizhen, bore him many children and they were either abandoned or died in infancy. Mao was completely indifferent. On The Long March, in 1935, his third wife gave birth to a baby girl in very difficult circumstances and the baby girl was immediately given away to a family who had no milk. So the baby girl soon died. As she went on The Long March a few weeks later she was hit by a bomb and nearly died. In both cases Mao was in the same town as her but he didn't go and visit her. He was said to be too tired and his third wife suffered a mental breakdown and was in and out of insanity for the rest of her life.

Mao's fourth wife was the notorious Madame Mao, Jiang Qing, who many, including myself in the past, still blame for the horrors of the Cultural Revolution. They say that she was this evil woman who manipulated Mao, but in fact we realised it was Mao who used her. She said, 'I was Chairman Mao's dog. Chairman Mao asked me to bite and I bit,' and that was accurate. She initiated no policies. All orders came from Mao. Mao knew she was a vicious woman and he once said to a family member that she was like a scorpion, full of venom. Mao wriggled his little finger to imitate a scorpion. So Mao then used her venom to do the kind of dirty work other people wouldn't do. Mao knew everybody hated her.

In the last couple of years of Mao's life he was suffering from an incurable disease and felt very vulnerable. He was terrified of a coup. So Mao said to his military commanders, 'You are welcome to do in my wife and her gang as long as you leave me to die in my bed,' and this was exactly what happened. Mao died in his bed. Less than a month later

Madame Mao and the rest of the Gang Of Four were arrested. Madame Mao later committed suicide in prison.

Mao ruled China for twenty-seven years and was responsible for the death of over seventy million Chinese in peace time yet today his portrait is still hanging on Tiananmen Gate. His corpse is still lying in the centre of the Chinese capital for people to worship. His face is still on every bank note in China and the regime is still upholding Mao's image and the myths about Mao. People often talk about the future of China. For me, the day Mao's portrait is taken down from Tiananmen will be the day when a fundamental change will have happened in China and the country will have become a really nice place and a benign force for the world.

Bigsby: I can't find one redeeming moment in Mao's life in your book. Was there one?

Chang: Mao loved some things. For example, he loved books.

Bigsby: But he had them destroyed?

Chang: Yes, but he loved books himself. He became a Communist not because he believed in Communism but because he was given the job of running a leftwing bookshop selling Communist literature. He needed the money but he also loved the books. This is how he got together with the Communists back in 1920/21. In his later life he had a giant bed. Half would be piled a foot high with books so he could wake up, roll over, pick up a book and start reading, but the problem is, as you say, he wouldn't allow one billion Chinese to read. This man's cynicism was really in a league of its own. In his later years, when his eyesight failed, he had two factories built to print books with large print for him, but the print run for each book was five copies, all for Mao. During the time I was growing up in China books were burnt across the country. Until Mao died the books we could read could be counted on the fingers of both hands. I myself read over a thousand books because I had an entrepreneurial brother who had discovered the black market selling books, foreign and Chinese. I was able to read the books that went onto the bonfires of the Red Guards. Most Chinese weren't able to read books and a generation of people grew up not having read them.

Bigsby: You said that for Mao Communism was not at the centre of his concerns. He simply wanted power and the Party was a mechanism for acquiring it. It was not something that he essentially believed in. He came from a peasant family but you already hinted that his attitude towards peasants — despite the fact that he was supposed to have led a peasant revolt — was vicious.

Chang. He didn't care about the peasants. He didn't join the Communist revolution thinking that he was going to give the peasants a better life, which I think some of his colleagues did. They did have a certain degree of idealism when they joined the Party, but that wasn't Mao. Having said that, after he joined the Communist Party he soon realised this suited him. The Stalinist model suited him very well and the promotion of violence and atrocities suited his gut feelings. Mao loved violence and wrote about it in 1927. When he first encountered a Soviet model in the Chinese countryside, he said he felt a kind of ecstasy that he had never felt before. He loved that and he also realised that the Communist Party was the ideal mechanism for him to get absolute power and for him to have an instrument because the Party was a totalitarian organisation. Popular opinions did not make any difference. What did make a difference was about half a dozen people at the very top and Mao was very good at manipulating this half a dozen people. He would blackmail this one, poison that one and intimidate a third. He was able to dominate this less than half a dozen people and through this tiny group was able to dominate the vast Party and, through this Party, control the vast China.

Bigsby. One of the things you do in the book is to look at some of the principal myths that attached themselves to Mao. One such was the famous Long March.

Chang. There are just so many myths about The Long March, which took place between 1934 and 1935. One myth was that this march was six thousand miles long and that Mao walked heroically, according to the American writer Edgar Snow, like a soldier. In fact Mao was carried most of the way. He even designed his own transport, which was a bamboo litter, and he designed a kind of awning so he would be shielded from the sun and the rain. He actually said to his staff during The Long March, while he was lying in the litter, 'I had nothing to do so what did I do? I read. I read a lot.' This was one myth. There were many others.

There was this famous image of the Red Army crossing a river on a suspension bridge under a hail of machine gun bullets. The Red Army was supposed to have crawled on bare chains, set on fire by the nationalist soldiers. It was a myth because not one of the soldiers suffered a single injury, not even burnt skin or a broken ankle or anything, let alone died. It is clearly a myth. Zbigniew Brzezinski, the

American National Security Advisor, went to visit China in the nineteen eighties and after his trip he told Deng Xiaoping that he had had been to all these heroic places including the famous river bridge and Deng smiled and said, 'Oh, it is all propaganda you know. We created the battle to boost our morale.'

I think the worst thing about The Long March was that it was basically the Red Army going from the heartland of China, and from the southeast to the northwest, to receive arms from the Soviet Union. The Soviet Union was the single most important factor in putting Mao into power but he needed Soviet help so they marched to the Soviet border. It could have much more straightforward if they had gone in a straight line. The soldiers would have walked about only two-thirds of the route, but Mao didn't want to go on this particular route because he was afraid of joining up with a Party rival, somebody who could dislodge him as the Party boss. So, for purely personal power reasons he dragged the Red Army on the long route and caused thousands of deaths in order to avoid his rival.

After they met up he slaughtered the Red Army under his rival. Altogether Mao caused tens of thousands of deaths of his own men, his own Red Army soldiers, for personal power. I was very shocked and it took us a very long time to piece together the truth about this Long March and I was very shocked again when our book was published and we were attacked. Some people said, 'I can't imagine Mao would do this to the Red Army.' Nor could I when I first encountered these new documents but I was convinced this was the case. We were attacked but then more Russian archives were opened and in one document we had Mao saying to Stalin's envoy that, 'During The Long March I was in terrible danger,' because his Party rival was going to swallow him up, 'but I kept my cool and eliminated thirty thousand in his army.' Mao could say this to Stalin because they were very alike. In the Stalinist party the brutalists, the most unscrupulous, the guy who would not bat an eyelid at slaughtering old people, would be the man who would get on top.

Bigsby: Another thing that surprised me had to do with the Japanese invasion of China, reverberations of which are still around today. Mao, far from going into battle with the Japanese, was apparently only interested in fighting with his potential rivals in China, in effect working with the Japanese.

Chang: Mao did not want to fight the Japanese but this was because he was very smart and he knew that if he had fought the Japanese the

156

Communist Army would have been wiped out and he would have had no chance of getting to power. His real enemy was Chiang Kai-shek, who was a nationalist. Mao wanted to use the Japanese army to destroy Chiang. He didn't see the Chinese war against the Japanese invasion as China versus Japan. He saw it as triangular warfare, Japan, Chiang Kai-shek and himself. Of course then we ask ourselves the question, if the Japanese destroyed Chiang how could Mao expect fiercely anti-communist Japan to spare him, because the Japanese spared Mao during the war and focused on Chiang. After they had wiped out Chiang presumably they would deal with Mao and he would have been wiped out. Then we discovered what Mao was up to. He placed his hope in Stalin, in the Soviet Union, because Russia was an old rival of Japan when it came to controlling China. He knew that if the Japanese were in a position to occupy the whole of China, Stalin was going to come into China with armed forces and beat the Japanese for him. This was Mao's strategy.

Earlier, we were talking about whether he had any positive characteristics. He was completely amoral but he did have very smart strategic thinking. He had foresight because this is exactly what happened. Mao bided his time. In 1945, the Soviet Union occupied a huge chunk of China, larger than all eastern Europe, and with his occupation Stalin was able to help Mao come to power, beating Chiang Kai-shek. In fact, Mao had this scenario back in 1923. When he joined the Party he didn't think that the Communists had a hope of winning power in China. He said the only hope the Chinese Communist Party had was Soviet military intervention from the north so, for his entire political career, before he took power, his whole purpose was to hang on to Stalin and drag the Soviet Red Army in to create a communist country for him.

Bigsby: On the other hand he wasn't that bright when it came to persuading everyone to have a minor steel works in their back garden.

Chang: As Mao himself said, he was very good at destruction and not very good at construction. He knew his strong points and his weak points but one of his weak points was the economy. The Great Leap Forward was this huge industrialisation project which led to tens of millions of deaths. For all his military industries Mao needed one essential thing, steel, but China didn't have enough for his purpose. So he ordered the whole population to make steel. I was six years old then but my major occupation was to cook steel in the school kitchen because every organisation in China – schools, hospitals and bus companies – had a steel quota. Mountains were stripped bare of trees to provide the fuel and people were exhausted because you had to man these steel backyard furnaces twenty-four hours a day, constantly feeding everything from doors to windows to hairclips into these backyard furnaces. But of course nothing like steel came out of these ventures.

In the same period another fantasy of Mao's was to kill sparrows, because Mao suddenly thought that sparrows eat grain, which he needed for export, so he ordered the whole population to kill sparrows. I remember vividly we all had to sit in the courtyard and hit saucepans to make a gigantic noise. The idea was that sparrows would be so exhausted, since they couldn't land on trees, that they would fall down on the ground and we would all go after them. But of course a lot of other birds perished as well and the result was a disaster for agriculture and for the grain.

Bigsby: What did you make of Nixon's supposed breakthrough in opening up relations with China?

Chang: Nixon didn't really make a breakthrough. He didn't open up China. He came to China in 1972 and China was not opened up. China was a still a prison. People were still imprisoned. No Chinese were let out, except a group of young Chinese who were sent abroad to study English, but from the whole of China only a tiny group got out, along with diplomats. A few tourists did come to China but under very tight control. When I was an English student in 1975 and we were sent to the port in South China to learn English from the sailors, every night we had to report exactly what we said to the sailors. We were all given a false name and were told only to say these rigid things, basic Party propaganda. I was once invited to a ship but of course there was no question of me being allowed to go so I was ordered to make up a lie and say I didn't want to go, or I was ill or something, an excuse. On the way back from this port some friends and myself went sightseeing. We went to this beautiful place and saw a foreign tourist, a man carrying a baby, and, eager to say a sentence of English, we said, 'Good morning.' But after the man went past we were immediately detained by a plain-clothed policeman and questioned. We were released because they learned that we were English language students and we were let off the hook. All this happened after Nixon's visit.

Nixon spent one day in Shanghai and for this one day the regime backed off. At least tens of thousands of people, like myself, and people who had been exiled to the countryside, were back in Shanghai for the

Chinese New Year which coincided with Nixon's visit. In the impossible unlikely case that these people might complain to Nixon, which would be impossible, the regime went to the extent of ordering or packing everybody off to their place of exile. Nixon's visit was for Mao basically to put himself in the limelight on the world stage and indeed after Nixon's visit Mao was in vogue. In fact Mao was in vogue thanks to Nixon. There was Andy Warhol's Mao portrait and because Mao spat constantly Chinese spittoons became a fashion item. I remember when I first came to the West I went to a friend's place for lunch and she made salad in a spittoon.

The other purpose was to get military secrets out of America because America was carrying on this embargo on China and Mao had been getting his nuclear secrets and equipment from Russia. But he broke with Russia basically because he was vying with it for leadership of the world Communist movement. He broke with Khrushchev and thus shot himself in the foot by cutting off his supply of military secrets. This is why he turned to America trying to get secrets out of America and Eastern Europe. In fact Britain's Rolls Royce technology saved Mao's aeroplane industry because Mao's factories produced thousands upon thousands of planes every year but they couldn't fly because their motors were in dire trouble. It was thanks to Rolls Royce technology that they eventually took off.

Mao was fashionable with western lefties. Simone de Beauvoir and Sartre never got to see Mao properly because Mao basically had contempt for Western lefties. He liked people to take him seriously as a threat, a menace, but these people had illusions about him. For example, in the index of Simone de Beauvoir's book there is an entry, 'Violence, absence of, under Mao.' Mao didn't see them nor did he care about them. The person he most wanted to see before he died was Richard Nixon and Mao sent a plane all the way to America to fetch him to China to say farewell. Nixon came in February 1976 and Mao said a melancholy farewell to him and died in September. When China got the technology it was already post-Mao.

This is a long story. Mao realised that western democracy was not like Stalin. There are procedures. There are enquiries. He didn't manage to get it in his lifetime and in fact his nuclear industries, his military industries, were in a shambles before his death. He never made China into a military super-power partly because he was no good at the economy and partly because he shot himself in the foot with the Soviet Union and misjudged the democratic west, which was not going to hand over military and nuclear secrets without a significant change in the nature of the regime.

Bigsby: What would it take to change the current Chinese view of Mao?

Chang: The Chinese government has to make the decision to disown Mao, to reject Mao and Mao's legacies. It is the regime that is propping up the image of Mao as the father of the nation. My books are banned in China, although there is a difference now in China. The Mao book is banned but people are not getting into any trouble for reading it and there have been numerous pirated editions. And now, particularly with the internet, enthusiastic readers have scanned this book in Chinese, which I translated, and which was published in Hong Kong. Thank God Hong Kong is still very much separated from mainland China and so books like mine can still be published there and many copies have gone into China. People have downloaded my book and made photocopies. People have made disks and sent it to people as an attachment. So many, many people have read the book, but of course the internet police are also very vigilant and websites are constantly closed down or blogs deleted.

Bigsby: What politically would it take to get the regime to change? Can you imagine circumstances in which they would have a vested interest in blowing the myth away?

Chang: There has to be a trigger, but I don't know what that is. Events sometimes occur that take people by surprise. It is in the regime's interest to distance themselves from Mao. They will make many friends and very few enemies, because anybody who lived under Mao, people of my generation and people of the older generations, suffered appallingly. If this big lie, Mao's image, is not destroyed then we are never going to be rid of the small lies. Many people want to have Mao denounced completely and there are signs that they are distancing themselves from him. In the Olympics they avoided Mao's portrait. I think the current leaders themselves and their parents suffered appallingly under Mao, as well as the Chinese population.

Bigsby: So the very people who suffered have been sustaining the myth.

Chang: Yes. Deng Xiaoping himself suffered tremendously. Deng's son was tortured so badly in the Cultural Revolution that he threw himself from an upstairs window and was paralysed from the chest down. But after Mao died Deng was the one who decided to uphold Mao's myth because he thought that, given the kind of indoctrination of Mao's personality cult in the population, to expose it would be to create such an upheaval, such a big shock in Chinese society, that the Party might not be able to cope. I think Deng's successors probably also think that way, that this is such a major thing for China and that if it is not managed well it might create instability for themselves. I can see their point. I don't agree. I think if it was handled well you would unite the Chinese people far more than divide them.

One problem is that Mao has been dead for thirty years now and in these thirty years there is still brainwashing going on in Chinese schools. Mao is still called the father of the nation. Books like mine are still banned and films and plays, the arts, are not allowed to portray Mao's era. So the young generation have grown up not as brain-washed as my generation but still with serious brainwashing. They don't know what life under Mao was like. Many young people don't believe in the Great Famine. They find descriptions of the Cultural Revolution incredible and therefore don't believe it can be true. That is a very worrying thing, but in my travels in China I have met some very smart young people and I think there is hope that changes will come when these very smart young people take charge. It is even starting now.

In Conversation With
Louis de Bernières

- 20th October 2003 -

Louis de Bernières was born in London in 1954. He was educated at
Manchester and London universities and published his first novel, *The
War of Don Emmanuel's Nether Parts*, in 1990. It won the Commonwealth
Writers' Prize as did his second, *Senor Vivo and the Coca Lord* (1992). This
was followed by the third in the trilogy, *The Troublesome Offspring of
Cardinal Guzman* (1992). *Captain Corelli's Mandolin* (1994) won him his
third Commonwealth Writers' Prize. It was followed in 2004, by *Birds
Without Wings*. In 2008 he published *A Partisan's Daughter* and the
following year, *Notwithstanding: Stories from an English Village*.

Bigsby: This is one of those significant moments as you conclude a project that has occupied you for some time?

de Bernières : I have just finished a novel which I have been working at on and off for about seven years. It is set in southwest Turkey between about 1900 and 1923. It was a time of terrible disruption for everybody in that whole region, as indeed for all of Europe obviously because that includes the First World War. One of my main characters is called Rustem Bey. He is a landlord. He is rich and powerful and has had a disappointment in marriage. His wife has been unfaithful and he has rejected her. He has got the idea into his head that if he finds a Circassian mistress that will be what makes him happy. The Circassians were driven out of the Caucasus by the Russians in their repeated persecutions of Muslims. They all went to Turkey to get away and be safe, and there were quite large communities of Circassians in Turkey. The women were famous for being beautiful and there is a story in Turkey that the reason why women go veiled is that the presence of Circassian beauties caused so many fights among the local men that they decided that the women should cover their faces to prevent the fights.

Anyway, Circassians still have this reputation for extreme beauty in those parts. So Rustem Bey goes all the way from southwest Turkey, right up to Istanbul, trying to find a Circassian mistress. He does what you always do which is take in a Turkish Bath. It is like going to the barbers really; you get all the gossip and the juicy details. So he and his servants are led across the water to what was then part of Istanbul, which was notorious for the worst kind of low life.

Bigsby: How long has this novel been gestating? Did you allow yourself time off after *Captain Corelli* or was this somewhere in the back of your mind even then?

de Bernières : I had the original idea for it very quickly because I found myself wandering around a ghost town in southwest Turkey. It used to be populated by a community of what you might call Turkish Christians and Turkish Muslims. It has become quite common now to refer to these Turkish Christians as Greeks but many of them didn't speak Greek at all. They were an anomalous people but that was what the community was back then. The Christians had all been deported after 1923 because the Greeks and the Turks exchanged populations. So the Greek Muslims, who we have come to think of as Turks, were deported to Turkey and the Turkish Christians, many of whom were of Greek origin, were deported to Greece. This community disappeared and was finally destroyed altogether by an earthquake in the 1950s, although the earthquake doesn't turn up in the novel because I did that in the last one. It was almost the same time funnily enough. That is where the idea came from.

Bigsby: When was that?

de Bernières : Probably the year after *Corelli* was published. It took me about another three years to write the first page, which I did in Canada for some reason. I have rewritten the first page lots of times and then, as the years went by, I did absolutely masses of research and accumulated bits and pieces of story. In a way the book consists almost of a series of photographs which only make sense when you see all of them together.

Bigsby: It is interesting that you said you rewrote that page because you have also said that at times you write an entire chapter in one go. What is the tension between spending three years working on one very small part of it while being able to run off a whole chapter?

de Bernières : I was messing about mostly. I had just quit teaching for one thing, which was such a relief. I was just enjoying being free and unstressed. I have come back to that page many times in the last few years simply because your first page has to be damn good.

Bigsby: Is that where you get the voice for the rest of the novel?

de Bernières : That particular first chapter is narrated by one person in the story so I had to get his voice established. I have made it hard for myself by having lots of narrators, each of whom has to have his own voice. That particular one happens to be a potter and the irony of it is that a few days ago I thought of a better beginning. So my old beginning is no longer the beginning.

Bigsby: With *Captain Corelli* you walked into a certain amount of political flak and now you are taking on the Armenians and the Turks. Is there a masochist in you somewhere? This is dangerous territory, politically, isn't it?

de Bernières : It is very dangerous territory politically because the book could be offensive to Kurds, Armenians, Greeks and Turks, but the thing is if you come to your own opinion as to what really happened, I think you have to be honest and stick to it. I just hope that nobody will find me in Norfolk.

Bigsby: I take it that that the historical, political world weaves into these private stories.

de Bernières : Yes, very much so because it was a time when Turkey was at war for more than ten years. It started in 1912 with the Balkan wars and it didn't really end until 1923 when the populations were exchanged. It is quite difficult to put so much war into a novel without making it fantastically depressing. What I have done is take snapshots of the life of Mustafa Kemel and intersperse them through the novel to try and give the historical background. I don't yet know whether that trick works. I will see what other people think.

Bigsby: Your first novels were set in South America, or in an invented South America. You have set a novel in Greece and another in Australia. Now you are dealing with Kurds and Turks. What is a nice British, French Huguenot doing writing about all these other places? Is there some advantage in setting the works as far as possible from your daily life?

de Bernières :   I generally find it so. I have now been in Norfolk for three or four years and I still don't think I could write a story set in Norfolk because I haven't quite got the hang of the dialect yet. It takes a while for your ears to get themselves round this sort of thing. The other thing is that I find the various accents and the intricacies of the British class system a bit off-putting. In a sense I find it easier to write about foreigners. Having said that I have set a great many short stories in this country, which get published from time to time and will one day be an anthology, no doubt, and future novels will be at least partly set here [in 2009 he published *Notwithstanding: Stories from an English Village*]. I think the real answer to your question is that because I am mainly interested in narrative I will take a story from wherever I find it and then do the necessary work to get it written. I am not frightened of setting stories in exotic or faraway places because I know that, with sufficient work or enough travel, I can get the hang of the place.

Bigsby: So which way around does it go? Is this an invented country that you subsequently earth in research or is it a researched country that generates fictions?

de Bernières :   Those are not mutually exclusive are they?

Bigsby: Do you go to a place and then imaginatively recreate it before doing detailed research?

de Bernières :   That is more or less what happens. I have found it pointless going to places hoping to find a story. I went to Portugal many years ago thinking there are bound to be lots of lovely stories because of all those years of dictatorship. I came up with nothing. All I noticed was that lots of Portuguese people had gammy legs, which I attribute to moped accidents, and I spotted a very strange woman in Oporto who looked like Miss Haversham. She was dressed in a kind of white wedding dress. She was very old but what was extraordinary about her was that she was just draped in lavatory paper. I have always wanted to write a story about her, but I haven't. I really had no success with going somewhere on purpose.

Bigsby: You went to Australia and came back with a flatulent dog in *Red Dog*.

de Bernières :   The same thing happened with that. I was travelling in Western Australia and I spotted a bronze monument to a dog. I stopped and looked at it. It was in the middle of nowhere, in a mining town, and I looked at the plinth. This monument had been erected by his friends and specially commissioned from a sculptress who had had to go through a large authentication committee. It really did look like their dog and I went back three months later to collect the stories and wrote the stories up in the evenings on my laptop.

There were two local libraries which had masses of press cuttings about him and there were two pamphlets written for tourists, though fairly badly. It was relatively easy to find out all the information I needed for a book that I actually intended to be for children in the first place. I wrote it for twelve-year-olds, but no one ever seems to have realised that that is what it was.

Libraries are fantastic, in the sense that they can get you books or archives from all over the world. You just have to ask and they will set the ball rolling. For *Captain Corelli*, the only copy of one book in English was in Ireland and the Irish sent it to me via inter-library loan, so I don't spurn libraries by any means. It is just that it is not enough. You have to go to places to pick up the atmosphere.

Bigsby: If you are going to set future novels here, are some of those stories already floating in your head somewhere?

de Bernières : They are. I more or less know what my next three books are going to be after this one. The particular story I mentioned I wanted to base on the life of my grandfather who lived into his nineties and led quite a quixotic and irregular life, starting in London. During his lifetime he lived in Nazi Germany and in what was then Tanganyika and what was then Ceylon. He was in the frontier police on the Northwest Frontier trying to control the Afghans. He was in the Royal Flying Corp at the end of the First World War and he ended his life in Canada. So this story, if I write it, will probably go to all those places.

Bigsby: This is the novel you are going to be setting in England?

de Bernières : He was mostly here until he was about twenty-five.

Bigsby: After the film of *Captain Corelli* would you be happy to see your other books made into films?

de Bernières : I thought the film was a mixture of good and bad. I can think of a lot of good things about it. I am not as negative about it as some people think I am. My one wish, I suppose, is that I wanted a European art film and they tried to produce another *Gone With The Wind* and just didn't quite make it. The good things about it were Penelope Cruz, John Hurt and David Morrissey. The soundtrack and the photography were marvellous. I don't understand why they had to mess around with the story and although I think Nick Cage is an extremely good actor, I rather wish they had chosen somebody like Roberto Benigni and done it with an Italian who didn't have to pretend to be an Italian. So my feelings are quite mixed. As for selling other books for film, I remain optimistic.

Somebody is interested in doing *Red Dog* and somebody has been interested for years in doing my second novel. It is just a question of coming up with the funding and the right scriptwriter. I would always be happy to have my books made into films. One thing that does deeply annoy me is that for some reason people think that film is much more glamorous and marvellous than novels. I just don't get this. I think film is a seriously inferior art form compared to the novel. I really can't get excited about film as film. I think what you hope for as a writer is to get a reasonably faithful representation that will actually help you to sell your books.

Bigsby: How long did it take to research and write *Captain Corelli*?

de Bernières : *Captain Corelli* was written in not much more than a year. I really got on quite well with that one. Everything happened with the most marvellous synchronicity. For example, just when I got to the point of needing to write about the earthquake my neighbours in London, who were Greek, had a friend turn up who had been in the earthquake. With that kind of good luck it really went very well indeed.

Bigsby: Do you miss anything about teaching or was it just paying the bills?

de Bernières : I pay the bills a lot better now. There were two good things about teaching, one was that the kids always told you the latest most horrible politically incorrect disgusting jokes the moment they were invented. Since I left teaching almost no one has told me a joke. The other thing that I enjoyed in a grisly way was the serious moaning that the staff do in the staffroom. Other than that if I had to go back to it I would shoot myself.

Bigsby: There is a local figure – the black dog of Bungay. Have you ever been attracted to the idea of writing about him?

de Bernières : Yes, I have. I am really a cat lover to tell the truth, not because I don't like dogs, I love dogs too, but I think cats are even better. The thing is I am vexed about the black dog of Bungay because there used to be a statue of the dog on a plinth on a roundabout and for some reason it hasn't been there for years. There is a small label there which says, 'The black dog of Bungay,' but what is there is a vase of flowers. I want to know why there is no statue of the black dog on that plinth and I do actually want to write about the black dog in some context or other. I just haven't got round to it yet.

In Conversation With Margaret Drabble

- 22nd November 2006 -

Margaret Drabble was born in Sheffield in 1939. She was educated at Cambridge before joining the Royal Shakespeare Company as an actress but published *A Summer Bird-Cage*, in 1963, the first of what became seventeen novels that include *The Radiant Way* (1987), *The Witch of Exmoor* (1996), *The Peppered Moth* (2001) and *The Sea Lady* (2006). She has also written biographies of Arnold Bennett and Angus Wilson. In 2008, she was made a Dame Commander of the Order of the British Empire.

Bigsby: Your latest novel is *The Sea Lady*. How was it born?

Drabble: The idea of writing about friends converging at a degree ceremony came to me when I was watching Ingmar Bergman's *Wild Strawberries*, if any of you remember that very remarkable film. It is built on the story of a doctor going to receive an honorary doctorate. As he journeys through Sweden he goes back to the scenes of his life and remembers them. I was very moved by seeing that: the mingled sense of disappointment and fulfilment, the things achieved and the things that went sour and bitter. I just thought, what a wonderful format it was, so in *The Sea Lady* I borrowed it and used it in this novel which, though I didn't know this when I started writing it, is about reconciliation and forgiveness. It could have been about recrimination and bitterness, but I worked very, very hard on that bit and I think they end up forgiving one another.

The public orator in this novel is an ambiguous figure, but not quite as ambiguous as the public orator at Cambridge this summer of whom I have very un-tender memories. Luckily he was speaking in Latin. The public orator in this novel is slightly based on somebody I used to know well very long ago, but he will never spot this and if he does he won't dare say so. I did think it was a good idea to have somebody arranging a

175

degree ceremony at which people met who didn't know they were going to meet, and who didn't necessarily like one another. After this novel was published I did get one or two letters from friends about having to appear on platforms with people who had been so rude to them in the press recently. They had to be all smiling and smirking and pretending to be honourable.

Bigsby: The book has a subtitle which is *A Late Romance*.

Drabble: That was meant to remind people of Shakespeare and the late play. There is usually a bit of Prospero-like narration going on under the public orator's style. There is a bit of manipulation and there are a number of fantastic meetings, but I also find the mood of Shakespeare's late plays very moving because they are about forgiveness and reconciliation and letting grievance go.

Bigsby: Did you know how the book was going to end when you started it?

Drabble: No. I didn't. I had no idea how they were going to end up. What I knew I wanted to do was to set them off on a journey that could end in reconciliation, but I wasn't sure if they were up to it really. They have been through quite a lot of estrangement, difficulty and bitterness and I wasn't sure if they would meet in a human way, or whether there would be yet more malice involved in the ending, so I really didn't know where the novel was going nor did I know where I was going. I am very dependent on the moods that develop in me while I am writing and if I get very depressed then so do my characters. I have to work towards some affirmative feeling and I did feel very much with this novel that if I didn't find an affirmative feeling I would give it up altogether.

Bigsby: Have you abandoned novels in the past?

Drabble: Not as far in as I was with this. Yes, I suppose I have ended up abandoning bits of novels and I don't know if I will ever write another, so it was very important to write one that ended with a feeling of *The Tempest* rather than *King Lear*, with peace rather than fury.

Bigsby: You don't think you are going to write another novel?

Drabble: No. I don't think so.

Bigsby: Why?

Drabble: I am tired of them. I am tired of my own novels. I enjoy other people's very, very much. What happened was that I wrote a couple of novels that involved me in immense difficulties with various legal and personal things. *The Peppered Moth* and *The Red Queen* both had legal trouble and I thought, what am I doing writing a novel and getting myself into hot water? Why bother? So I wrote this novel in an attempt to get rid of all that feeling of resentment and anger, and so I could say I didn't end on an angry note.

Bigsby: But weren't you asking for it with *The Peppered Moth* in that it was both a novel and not a novel at the same time, being based squarely on your mother?

Drabble: Yes, that is absolutely true. I knew what I was doing in that. I knew that I was entering very dangerous territory. Then I wrote another novel called *The Red Queen* which brought down on me the most appalling trouble which I had in no way anticipated or indeed invited or indeed deserved. *The Red Queen* is set in eighteenth century Korea and is drawn largely from, or inspired by, the memoir of a woman who died in 1815, which is quite a long time ago. I worked from a translation. I met the translator. I found other translations of the same work and I got her permission and everything seemed to be fine but when I sent her the first draft she said I couldn't publish it because of cultural appropriation. She didn't say copyright. She said cultural appropriation. I was completely shattered by this because I had been encouraged to think that all was well. I behaved impeccably, insofar as one can ever behave impeccably in writing a novel, but I began to think that writing a novel was not an impeccable pursuit, that whatever you did was going to involve you in trouble.

Bigsby: You did say of this one that there is someone on whom one figure was based and you have talked in the past about there being people you have known who you turn to as models. I suppose all writers have models but do you think you do to a greater extent than other novelists?

Drabble: No, to a much lesser extent because I am so polite and nervous. I know writers who do the most cruel and wicked things, that I wouldn't dare to begin to do. I have novels within me that were I to dare to write them the world would quail, but I don't. I write about the dead, largely. I actually find it impossible to be candid in the way that some writers are. Saul Bellow was just brutal and we all know many writers – Philip Roth, Doris Lessing – who can be brutal. Doris Lessing I know well and admire greatly but she is really brutal in some of her writing. The great writers are brutal. I am not a great writer and try not to be brutal. But it is very, very hard if you are obsessed with being fair and generous to write truthfully at all. This is the dilemma I find myself in very much in my late novels.

Bigsby: Coming back to this novel, I read an interview that you gave before you wrote this and you said, 'I have got an idea of possibly writing about a marine biologist' and that you like watching fish because fish have meaning and messages. I am not on those kind of terms with fish. What messages and meaning do they offer?

Drabble: They move freely in dimensions. They are not trapped in a flat plane as we human beings are. I have repeated dreams about fish and in some of the dreams the water is running out and the tank is getting dry and the fish are gasping, and that is bad. In some of the dreams I am going into the water and the fish are there and it gets deeper and deeper as you are entering this eternal world. I am absolutely a great fan of the work of Elaine Morgan. The aquatic ape hypothesis is her view of the fact that we all came from the water. I have read nearly all her books. They are wonderful. She is now not as ridiculed as she used to be. She dismisses the Savannah Ape theory, and her dismissal is completely convincing to me. She goes into seals and body hair and sweat glands and all the rest of it. She believes that human beings spent a few millions of years in the water and then resurfaced.

That is why our bodies are so different from other animals and why we have this yearning for the water, which some of us do. I gather not all people do but I think we are basically sea creatures and have evolved into land animals and it has been greatly to our disadvantage. We have not only evolved into land animals, which was a mistake in the first place, but we then evolved into two-legged bipedalists. She is very good on bipedalism. But I have become so neurotic about using people's material, being accused of appropriation, that I didn't dare write to Elaine Morgan and say how much I admired her work in case she said, 'Don't steal it.' I was immensely pleased to get a letter from her saying she had picked up *The Sea Lady* at an airport and had read it and was so astonished and delighted to find her own name in the book. She said that it validated her as a real person, and how much she enjoyed being taken so seriously. But I have become so nervous about using material that I thought she would be displeased.

Bigsby: There are two main timescales in the book. There are childhood scenes and then, later in life, we see the characters moving on their trains towards this degree ceremony. The young Humphrey is a kind of sickly child. He seems quite lonely and has a fear of being left out. I have read an interview with you where you describe yourself in almost exactly those terms.

Drabble: Yes.

Bigsby: So there is a sense in which you are drawing on yourself? You had two sisters, one older, one younger, and I wondered why you felt left out in that sense.

Drabble: I think all children feel left out. I decided it wasn't just me. I think almost all children feel, for quite a lot of their life, that the other people are having more fun next door. I certainly did feel this but so does everybody. If you talk to people they have all been through periods of going to a new school and feeling that no one will play with them and I have a character, a completely incidental character, who is the little girl that they don't play with or ever talk to and people have written to me and said, 'I was that little girl.'

I still feel moments of complete panic when I go into a room and I know that there is no proper seating plan and I am going to have to sit somewhere and they might not want me there. I don't think that is an abnormal feeling. I think it is abnormal to stride in and imagine that you are the most important person in the room and that if you sit down everybody will want to sit next to you. That is abnormal. What you do in a novel is exaggerate characteristics and in fact Humphrey gets over that and becomes a completely normal, attractive, rather handsome sort of swashbuckling guy, but his childhood comes back at him because things begin to go a bit wrong, because he is a bit too ambitious in the wrong direction.

Bigsby: The narrator figure strikes me as a magus, the writer manipulator who takes these characters, puts them together and watches, as a novelist does. Is that how you work as a novelist creating characters and then allowing them to interact almost as a scientist watching the behaviour that develops?

Drabble: Yes, that is exactly what I feel as though I am doing. You may have noticed I am not very good at plot, really. Complicated plot is not my forte. I am more interested in how people change and what the meaning of their lives is. So what I try to do is to create characters who have a history and reality to them and then I like to see how they evolve in contact with each other. This novel had quite a long time span so I was able to put them in touch with the movements, the historic social movements, with which they interacted as well as with their family movements. That was quite satisfying because I realised that I was a product of a certain kind of feminism, or a certain kind of feminism was a product of me. It is the same thing, really.

I find exploring the marine biologist more interesting because it is not my life at all. When I am doing research for a book I go and talk to real human beings, a real marine biologist, and something that that person says suddenly reveals the whole dimension of plot possibility. Then you are back in the territory of appropriation. So there is a whole process of taking things out of the real historical background and putting them into a character and seeing where it leads them in conjunction with the other characters.

Bigsby: You mentioned Doris Lessing and she said something very interesting about *The Golden Notebook* once. She complained about being appropriated by a certain kind of feminist who wanted to make it her property and interpret it in a particular way. Is the writer the person who actually understands what a book is about necessarily?

Drabble: No, not necessarily, no. I used to believe more in authorial control than I do now. I think Doris is a particularly interesting example of somebody who works with extreme imaginative daring and is not always quite sure where that is taking her. Her imagination has got increasingly dark as well, as history has impinged on her. I maintain that what she has written means something to me in my life which she may not have intended it to mean. She doesn't want it to mean that, therefore she will be in denial that it did mean that to me. I am quite prepared to agree that my books have meant something quite different to other people. This is limiting in a way but it is very exciting when you meet somebody who has read your book in exactly the way you meant it to be. Then you feel, yes, that's good, you and I understand that bit and that is very, very satisfying.

Bigsby: You said once that you read books to find out about the world. Is that why you write as well?

Drabble: Yes, exactly. That is the only reason I write them, not to make money or to make patterns, but to find out what I believe, what I think, and what is happening.

Bigsby: So why are you going to stop? Don't you want to find out about the world any more?

Drabble: I know.

Bigsby: Aren't you tempted to write a book that might appear posthumously in which you would be protected from the assaults you have suffered?

Drabble: That is what my husband is always saying, and I have actually started that novel. I have written about a paragraph and at the moment it is called *The Solid Gold Baby*. It could be brilliant if ever I were to write it but some inhibition overwhelms me when I try and write this story.

I obviously can't write my memoirs as other people write their memoirs. I could deposit them but then in what tone would I be writing them? So that is another whole problem. The writer who amazes me most, the writer who perhaps I admire most next to Shakespeare, is Wordsworth who wrote *The Prelude* and didn't publish it in his lifetime in the form in which we know it. I find that such an extraordinary act of restraint and pure creation, but most of us aren't up to that. Most of us want to see what happens after our death.

I think all that I know is in this book and there comes a stage in your life when you wonder if you are going to find out anything else. I am not sure that I am. I think if I can stand fast and hold to what I know I am in a good place and if I learn more I may not wish to know it and I may be diminished by the knowing of it.

Bigsby: It is an oddity about writers. Everybody else retires. The assumption is that writers never retire. Actors never retire.

Drabble: They die on stage, like Henry Irving. I am actually writing another book. I only said I wasn't going to write another novel. I am writing another book and I am deeply engrossed in it at the moment [*The Pattern in the Carpet*, 2009]. I had a very, very happy time this afternoon in Norwich pursuing my research in Stranger's Hall with boxes of tricks, so I am writing a book which has been very good therapy for me and which does not require the answer to the universe. On the other hand I may discover little bits more as I write this book. It is a book about jigsaw puzzles and my aunt. It started off as a very short article about jigsaw puzzles and then it grew into an essay on jigsaw puzzles. Then it grew into a memoir of my aunt, and now it is about jigsaw puzzles, memory, childhood in the nineteen-fifties, my aunt's childhood, and all that area, so it is completely engrossing. But what is good about it is that it enables me to go and look at things that have absolutely nothing to do with me, like eighteenth century, nineteenth century jigsaws. With jigsaws you fit the pieces together. You have a purpose in assembling the bits and pieces and of course I will eventually go into some profound last chapter about shape and the meaning of it.

Bigsby: In *The Sea Lady* you say we are brought up to believe that stories have meanings and that meanings have stories and that journeys have ends. We are brought up to believe that there will be an ending, that there will be completion for each and every life, for each and every organism. But now, surely, we know that that is not true. It was true once but it is true no longer. We have passed the point in time and in history where that truth applies. You start a jigsaw knowing it will be complete, that there will be an end to it. It will have a shape. What looks like anarchy and chaos in front of you resolves itself and that is what the novelist offers the world, a sense that between two covers you will find a completed story.

Drabble: I think that that is quite true although the fashion now is very much for open-ended books, but nevertheless there is still a sense of a journey having been completed within the compass of the book and, yes, that is one of its appeals but, unlike the jigsaw, the pieces are not already necessarily invented. You may never ever resolve it. You may never finish the pattern. In a jigsaw you know that patience will resolve it, and I have had very touching emails from people saying that this gives them faith in life, that they know that they can finish their jigsaw, whereas they don't know that they can finish writing their novel or whatever. They know that they can stick to the jigsaw. In writing a novel there is always this feeling of horror and despair that the pieces aren't going to fit, that there is no ending, so you are caught between the feeling of there being no shape and a shape that if you waited long enough would evolve, as creatures evolve.

Bigsby: I remember you saying that you believe that there is an immanent order and that it would eventually be revealed to you. Is there a sense that you have reached that point, that there is a kind of coherence and that looking back it has now become apparent or is that always going to be arbitrary?

Drabble: I feel I have discovered things that mean I don't need to look for them endlessly. I actually do feel that I have reached a plateau when I am not looking for further solutions. I have discovered the immanent shape and I am happy with it.

Bigsby: You have been writing novels for over forty years now but at one stage you were going to be an actress. Why did you abandon that?

Drabble: It was because of children, really. Children are very difficult to combine with a life in the theatre, whereas writing, although not wholly easy, is a lot easier and I wasn't single minded enough for the theatre. I once said that I became a novelist because I was bored, and there is an element of truth in that. I do get bored quite quickly but I can then start writing a book. If you are an actor or an actress, and those of you who know the theatrical profession well will know, there is not much you can do if you are out of work. You just get more and more bored and more and more restless and more and more angry, whereas if you are a writer you can turn those feelings to good use. So although it is a reflective and inward-looking and at times a very isolated life, it is also a life over which one has much, much more control.

Last week I went to a reunion of the Marlowe Society, which was the hundredth birthday of the Cambridge Marlowe Society. People say it was founded by Rupert Brooke, but it wasn't. There were various other characters involved, but that was really very, very interesting seeing a group of theatricals, some of whom had stayed in the theatre, like Trevor Nunn and Griff Rhys Jones and Ian McKellen, and others who had gone into totally different walks of life but still remembered their theatrical days with great affection. But those who stay in it are so single-minded about staying in it that they would stay there through anything. I couldn't stay there through children and baby-sitting and anxieties and I probably wasn't good enough either.

Bigsby: So you turned away from the stage. Looking back at the books you then went on to write, which of them has meant the most to you?

Drabble: Every time I look at any of them I am completely appalled by them. I think, how did I get away with that? I'll tell you my least favourite, that was a novel called *The Middle Ground*. It was of such slightness of plot and journalistic tone. It is perfectly good-humoured but it really isn't a novel at all. I am amazed that I got away with that. I think my most serious novel is *The Needle's Eye* which I worked extremely hard on. I can look at that without shame, but I look at it with tears of regret in that the world has become darker than I thought it was going to. It is a book with a kind of optimism in it which hasn't quite been fulfilled. I look at it and think, 'Well, that was the statement I made then and it hasn't worked out like that but the book in its own terms is well worked through.' So I think that is the one I am most proud of. It is out of print here but there is a very nice edition in the United States with a very nice new introduction. Books come, books go.

In Conversation With
Richard Eyre

- 7th October 2009 -

Richard Eyre was born in 1943 and educated at Cambridge and Oxford universities. Beginning as an actor, he quickly turned to directing, working as Artistic Director of the Nottingham Playhouse from 1973-8 before working as Director of the National Theatre for ten years from 1987. As well as plays he has directed operas (including *La Traviata* for the Royal Opera House and *Carmen* for the Metropolitan Opera) and films (*Iris*, *Notes on a Scandal*). His honours include five Olivier Awards. In 1997 he was knighted for services to drama. His book *Talking Theatre* was published in 2009.

Bigsby: One of the themes of your autobiography, *Utopia and Other Places*, is the question of your identity, of who you are, but the theatre would seem an odd place to go to answer that because people spend their time there not being who they are.

Eyre: I suppose so but one of the reasons we have such a rich theatre in this country is because we have a love of dressing up, of play acting in our public life. But I also think class is so important. We are marinated in ideas of class, and a lot of class is to do with pretending to be something that we aren't. Like it or not, and I don't particularly like it, I can't help myself instinctively gauging class when I meet someone. This may seem a very, very archaic idea because of course class changes, but in this country it seems to change rather slower than elsewhere. So I would say it is not a particularly strange thing going into the theatre to be something that you aren't.

The theatre represented, and was, everything that my upbringing wasn't. What it was also was family, and I have always felt an absence of family. Both my parents were only children and there was just my sister and myself. Three of my grandparents had died before I was born and the only surviving grandparent was a figure I would love to have written about except that fiction could never quite do justice to him. You would

187

never really believe him. He was a man who lived in a ramshackle house in North Devon, a very remote part of North Devon, and he dressed like an old Edwardian. He had Edwardian tweeds and Edwardian jackets, which I think dated from before the First War, and he looked like a Prussian officer. He had stopped the clock in about 1914 so his house never had electric light and never had running water, not because he couldn't afford them, but simply because he thought they were all new-fangled devices and the devil's work. So that is the house where I grew up, taking a candle to bed and watching the titanic rows between him and my father. So I suppose getting into the theatre gave me a chance to create a life that was as theatrical as that but without the terror.

Bigsby: You have said that what actors are implicitly saying is, 'Love me, love me, love me,' and that in some senses they are looking for something that isn't necessarily there. Is that the absence that you were hinting at in your own family background because your father was in the navy and so was away?

Eyre: My father was in the navy and then retired early and became a farmer. He was away three years in South East Asia when I was ten so from the age of ten to thirteen I didn't see him at all. He was away because he was serving in South East Asia, but he never got my mother to join him so I think they were on the edge of breaking up at that time. I was aware of her many liaisons with nice men who used to take me out to lunch and were always referred to as mummy's friends. I didn't see him and I remember going to Stansted when he came back and not being quite sure, when seeing people come out into the reception area, which one was my father.

Bigsby: There was some theatre around in your family because your grandmother was an actress?

Eyre: My grandmother was an actress. She was quite racy. I would really like to have met her. She was rather tall, quite eccentric and looked a bit like Sybil Thorndike. She always wore purple and a load of bead necklaces. She had three brothers, all of whom died in the First World War. She eloped with a racing driver, but that didn't work out. Then she married my grandfather, who was an Antarctic explorer and was with Captain Scott on his first expedition. I wish I could have met him, but he died. For some reason he was in the navy and went to the Antarctic but didn't get on with Scott so didn't go on the second expedition. He became an admiral and then, as they did in those days, he was appointed

Deputy Commissioner of the Metropolitan Police because of his total lack of experience in criminal activity. He died dancing the waltz for the police ball at the Savoy. He was quite young, in his fifties. He died when my mother was eleven and then her mother died a few years later, when she was eighteen, so I was very aware of the absence of family and the fact that my father absolutely hated his father who was very, very brutal, with a terrifying temper.

Bigsby: Then you went off to boarding school?

Eyre: I was seven when I went, and that was something that I found very difficult to forgive. I can so vividly remember seeing my mother – my father wasn't there – dropping me off and fighting back tears and then seeing the car disappear. I was simply unable to imagine why this was happening to me. I remember when my daughter was seven thinking I simply couldn't. I would rather go to prison than see my daughter taken off at the age of seven. It is so much at the core of a middle class background that you just have to cauterise your feelings at a very early age. You have to teach yourself not to expect to be loved. So when you ask about actors needing approbation I think it is true of anyone who puts themselves in front of the public, whether they are a writer, a painter, or musician. But it is particularly true of an actor because the audience isn't distinguishing between the character and the person because they are indistinguishable. The person is the vessel for the character, so part of the audience, or part of each person, is thinking, 'Well, they are a bit odd looking aren't they? They look old. I thought they were younger.' There is a judgement of the body as well as a judgement of the talent. It is a dangerous thing because if they are not loved then they are rejected.

Bigsby: And while you were going through this experience in the school you did start doing some acting.

Eyre: I did, yes. I played Julius Caesar and Benedict to a male Beatrice. He was very pretty. That was the beginning of a rather disturbed school career. Eventually I got expelled.

Bigsby: Why?

Eyre: I was very confused and quite unhappy. I had done maths and physics and I had actually got into university to read natural sciences. As soon as I got accepted, though, I realised it was a complete disaster because you can fake it up to a certain point with science, and I was good at maths, but only up to the level that you can blag it because with conceptual maths, pure maths, you can either understand it or you can't and I had to admit that I couldn't. So at school I didn't know what I was doing so I said I will do English, because I thought English just involved reading books and saying what you thought about them. I thought, well, this is a soft option. But I was bunking off school telling the science people I was still doing science and the English people that I was doing science.

Anyway the college that I had got into at Cambridge were thrilled when I owned up and said that I didn't want to do natural sciences, I wanted to do English, because they had taken on their first English don, who was Kingsley Amis, and they said to me, 'At the moment we have got no students for him so we would be very pleased if you read English.' Anyway, back at school I was disaffected with everything and eventually was very rude to the School Chaplain. So I went off to London. He tried to stop me because I had been very rude to him. When I got back I discovered that everybody in the school knew I had been thrown out except me.

Bigsby: Your father didn't want you to go to university. Why?

Eyre: He just hated higher education. He joined the navy when he was thirteen and was a bright guy but he resented what he didn't know. He thought that most of higher education was in some way a conspiracy to prove to him that he didn't know enough. He also resented the arts. He resented Shakespeare. We lived in the heart of Hardy country and because he knew how much it annoyed and upset me he used to say he couldn't stand Thomas Hardy. 'Whenever they get down to it', he said, 'you can't tell what they are doing,' meaning sex of course, which was one of his major obsessions or major hobbies I would say. He wanted me to screw my way around the world, though he said it slightly more graphically, and thought it was a waste of time for me to go to university. So I was very defiant.

Bigsby: While you were at Cambridge you weren't directing but you were acting. At what stage did you decide that you wanted to be a professional actor?

Eyre: I think about half way through my time at university. I was very flattered. It is such a hothouse, an hermetic little world. You can have a star career as a university actor and be fooled into thinking that the outside world operates exactly like a university drama department.

Bigsby: You refer to something you call 'university acting,' which is meant as a pejorative term.

Eyre: It is a pejorative term. It is a kind of knowing acting. It is acting when you see actors offer a commentary on the part they are playing as if in some way they are more intelligent than the character. I find it very, very, very, irritating. There are other genres of acting. There is dog acting which you see a lot of in the classics. It is when you see actors cocking their legs on furniture. In real life you never see anyone put their foot on a table, do you? The other thing is what I call telephone acting. You see a lot of it on television. It is when somebody finishes a phone call and looks meaningfully. It is just that we have life around us as our model and it is astonishing that it is so frequently ignored in acting.

Bigsby: So you left university and went into acting. At what moment did you decide that it was not for you?

Eyre: Proper actors have a third eye, which is their way of monitoring what they are doing. In a good actor, let's say Judy Dench, who is a brilliant actor, if you are doing a play with her she will do a bit of business, pick up on a certain line and pour a drink and do it in a different place. Then you say to her the next day, 'Oh, you did that in a different place,' and she says, 'Yes, I thought I would do it on this word rather than that word.' Then you might be talking about the audience and she would say, 'Did you see that extraordinary woman who was sitting over there?' You realise that there is this monitoring device which is saying, 'How well am I doing this?' And then she also has that ability, like a musician to whom you say, 'We will go from bar 36 and give a downbeat,' to go straight into a performance without winding up to it. So that third eye, that monitoring thing, is a paradox in acting, the paradox of needing to be conscious of yourself but not being self-conscious. For me, self consciousness started to take over until I became paralysed by self-consciousness. Then I started to feel ashamed because I knew that I wasn't able to do what was in my head and I would forget words.

I was in a very, very bad production of a very bad musical when I had this epiphany, which was partly occasioned by bursting into laughter during the opening number because the girl I was partnering told me she had forgotten to put her knickers on. Any professional, proper actor would have gone through the whole thing but I just collapsed into laugher. It was shameful. What made it memorable for me was that it coincided with the death of Churchill and Churchill's funeral and I was acting in this show and we had Churchill's funeral on the radio that day. Anyway, around that time I encouraged some actors who were in that production to let me direct them in a play by Ann Jellicoe called *The Knack*. Then, by extraordinarily good fortune, John Neville, who ran the Nottingham Playhouse at the time, and Judy Dench, came to see that production, in Leicester, and the man who was running Leicester made me choose between being a director and an actor.

Bigsby: A musician recently said, 'We don't really need conductors. I seldom watch them.' What is the function of a director?

Eyre: Anybody who has had anything to do with the production of a Shakespeare play and gets to the last scene and has not had a director will know that there has to be somebody who at very least controls the traffic. There has always been somebody in charge who has said, 'You are going to come up there.' There has always been a traffic controller, certainly in the twentieth century, which is really when the idea of a director with, if you like, a concept or a guiding idea for a production grew up. I was at a Q and A thing with Peter Brook once and somebody asked Peter what a director did. He said, 'A director gets people on and off the stage,' which, like most of Peter's rather gnomic statements, is really rather profound because if you come on stage you have got to decide what is on the stage. You have got to decide where you come from onto the stage and, most importantly, you have got to decide when you come on. So it is a question of timing.

The really mysterious thing is why some conductors get extraordinary sounds out of a group of musicians and others get commonplace sounds. There is always that sort of mutinous feeling, sometimes in the string section. If you are the second violinist you can get very disaffected. To me, it is about timing, in the sense of getting the right thing happening at the right moment in the right way. What illustrates this for me is actually conducting. I saw a master class in conducting once. There were six postgraduate conducting students and they had to bring in the English chamber orchestra at the end of a Mozart piano concerto, at the end of the cadenza, and then bring in the orchestra, and I thought this is incredibly easy. I could do this. But only two of those students did it successfully. The others appeared to be making the right movements, and it appeared the timing was slightly different, but only two of them could actually bring the soloist and the orchestra together, and they were all equally expert as musicians. So it is very hard to quantify but there is some element of leadership in it. There is an element of making a proper society so you can gather your actors, your group, together so that you have a potential model society where each person contributes, some more than others. You have to balance them out and make the whole greater than the sum of the parts.

Bigsby: I am interested in that remark about a society. I remember, when Margaret Thatcher was saying there was no such thing as society, going to the National Theatre past the homeless, who used to camp underneath those pillars, into a theatre which couldn't exist if there was no such thing as society. There is a society on stage. There is a society in the audience. It seems to me one of the amazing things about theatre, that you don't get in television.

Eyre: Yes, that is one of the things that really attracts me about the theatre because it is a poetic medium. It all depends on the imagination of the audience because the audience know that they are looking at a stage, that there is nothing real about it. It is a poetic journey to embrace it and imaginatively fill in the non-real bits. But also the theatre is uniquely good at presenting a community on stage. In all of Shakespeare's plays there is a sense of a world even though it is just supplied by sixteen actors. In Arthur Miller's *The Crucible* he creates a world on a stage. Film, contrary to that, is very literal. It is very hard for film to create a community. For instance, in the film of *The Crucible* I don't think that there is a sense of a community because it is too literal. It doesn't resonate in a poetic, in a metaphoric way. So I love the fact that the stage is social, that you can create worlds on a stage and play them to a community. One of the things that excites me about the theatre is that with audiences you go in as an individual and, with a successful piece of theatre, you end up part of a group in spite of yourself if you are entering into that sense of engagement.

Bigsby: And there is a dynamic to it because the next night it is going to be a different community and the play may run ten or fifteen minutes longer as the actors respond to what is going on out there even as the audience think they are responding to what is going on on the stage. You said that a director has a concept. If we were having this conversation in Germany the director's name would probably come before the writer's.

Eyre: It would, and that is one of the many reasons why most of German theatre is incredibly moribund. It is the director's concept and there is a glass wall between the stage and the audience. I remember taking a production of *Richard III* to Germany. To British eyes it was a rather concept-driven production, although the idea simply came from a systematic reading of the play with the leading actor, who was Ian McKellen. Not a single word of the play was changed, and there wasn't anything that smacked of the twentieth century, but the costumes were nineteen thirties. It was positing a fascist Britain of the nineteen thirties impacting on the medieval world of Richard III, a play that is an archetype of the rise of the tyrant. I took that production to Hamburg, as part of a world tour, and all the reviews said, 'How exciting it is to see a production which puts the actors at the centre of the event.' That is one of the reasons I like the theatre because it seems to me it is irreducibly about the actors, about the human dimension, about the human voice, and the human proportions, in a way that film isn't and that the human being at the centre of it is what resists conceptualising. In fact there is no such thing as modernist theatre or abstract theatre because you are always stuck with representational form. There will always suddenly be a human being there, fallible, vulnerable, all the things that we are.

Bigsby: I think the production that even today was the most exciting that I ever went to was a concept production – Peter Brook's *A Midsummer Night's Dream* – and that raises the problem of talking about theatre, because it is like trying to describe a party that the other person missed. It is impossible. You can say this happened or that happened but where is the party? The theatre is a party. That is the greatness of it. You were there or you weren't there, and if you were there you all shared that moment and will always share that moment. So it is difficult to talk about theatre because it is always this event that most people weren't there for.

Eyre: Yes, absolutely. That is another reason why I like it because you have a unique experience. I made a TV series about the history of twentieth century theatre for the millennium and when I was researching I happened to be reading Georgio Vasari's *Lives of the Artist* and I discovered this wonderful story that for me is a great metaphor for the theatre. There was a snowfall in Florence, a very rare snowfall, and the current Medici commissioned Michelangelo to make a snowman. Vasari said it was the most beautiful thing that Michelangelo ever made and, of course, it lasted as long as the snow. Then it was gone, and only those who had actually been in the snow witnessed it, had had that experience.

Theatre is like that. It melts away and you can't really describe it. You can make claims for it, but it only lives on in your memory, and I loved that because we are so drowned in people urging us to digitise everything, to rely on digital memory which is endlessly inexhaustible and immortal, but I think we should value more and more the things that are unique in our individual memories, and the experience of going to the theatre, when it is really good, is one of those.

Bigsby: Opera is sometimes not like that. They will put the scenery and everything away and then ten years later they will take it out of store and recreate that production. The Moscow Art Theatre tries to preserve Chekhov as it supposedly should be, and as it once was.

Eyre: It's true, but I've had this strange experience recently. I did a production of *La Traviata* fifteen years ago at the Royal Opera House with Georg Solti, who was conducting shortly before he died. They revive it almost every year because it is one of their staples. Recently Renée Fleming, who in my opinion is one of the greatest if not the greatest soprano in the world and who I knew from New York, said to me, 'I would love to sing in your production.' She had seen it and she said, 'Will you rehearse it if I perform in it?' And I said, 'There is nothing I would like to do more.' This was in May of this year and this production, which as you say was like a Moscow Art Theatre war horse, had a new cast. I rehearsed with them for four weeks. They were absolutely fantastic and the whole thing just came alive. It didn't seem in any way dated. The production had become embalmed, because it was rehearsed by Chinese whispers, not by my original assistant, but by my original assistant handing on to someone else, who handed on to someone else. So when I came to re rehearse it I was taking off layers of varnish. But it was so thrilling doing that and the climax of that was that it was broadcast in one hundred and fifty cinemas all over Europe, and live in Trafalgar Square. I went along to Trafalgar Square and there were fourteen thousand people who had bought tickets and were there on this warm summer evening to watch this fifteen-year-old production with these great, great singers. So I am less critical of that. Theatre has to live in the present tense.

Bigsby: And that is the joy of theatre, that it is in the present tense, the same tense as the audience exist in, whatever games you are playing with time on the stage. Can I ask a related question? You have directed the same play more than once. You directed Jonathan Price in *Hamlet* and

Daniel Day Lewis in the same play. Is it like taking an exam? Do you wipe your mind and then go into the next one? Have you got that other production in your mind as you start the rehearsal or can you completely wipe away what you did before, because they were very distinctive versions?

Eyre: In 1980 I did *Hamlet* with Jonathan Price at the Royal Court Theatre, and it was in many ways quite anarchic. In some ways it was not at all reverential to the text. I had made a lot of cuts and cut the ghost altogether, so Hamlet was actually the ghost that possessed Hamlet. The ghost was speaking, like demoniacal possession, through Hamlet. Then I decided it was a mistake, really. When I took over the National I decided that because Peter Hall, my predecessor, had done *Hamlet* with Albert Finney I would do *Hamlet* with the leading actor of my generation, who was Daniel. I decided I would do the whole play and I would do a classical production. I think with hindsight it was because my experience of the theatre was a lot more to do with modern drama and new plays and it was like putting a stamp or mark on the wall saying, 'You have got to take me seriously as a director of classical plays,' whereas actually what I had done at the Royal Court was treat *Hamlet* like a new play. So although there were some things that I thought were terrific about it, it had to me a slight feeling of a lesson not well learned. So it was like the exam, and wiping the previous production. But I now feel that I wiped in the wrong direction.

Bigsby: In 1956, Arthur Miller came to England with Marilyn Monroe, who was going to be in *The Prince and the Show Girl* with Laurence Olivier, and an event was held at the Royal Court Theatre which was based on the idea that the English theatre was going nowhere. As it turned out, 1956 has acquired a magical connotation, and you can understand that in the British context. In a world context, though, *Look Back In Anger* would not have seemed in any way revolutionary. In fact *The Entertainer* was more radical. Nonetheless, something happened in British theatre. You came into the theatre at a very exciting time. Even on television you were a producer of *Play for Today* in the seventies and *Play for Today* addressed people's lives. If you wanted to be a writer then you wanted to be a playwright. If you wanted to be a writer today would you want to write for the theatre?

Eyre: I think you would want to write for the theatre possibly not because it is in the forefront of fashion, or because it is a conspicuous opinion-forming medium, but partly because of the process of television and film. It is very difficult to get the voice of a writer on television. Very few individual pieces of drama are commissioned and if they are commissioned they are so fed through a filter of people commenting on them and what is called input that it gets more and more like doing a film for Hollywood. So a lot of screen writers are coming back to the theatre as do actors who do a lot of movies because they feel in charge in the theatre.

Last night I saw David Hare's new play which is called *The Power of Yes*. It is a journalistic play. It is a very, very cunningly constructed account of the credit crunch and its origins. Its mysteries are to some extent revealed and I don't know how this information can be better conveyed than in the theatre. I remember Arthur Miller telling me about the Federal Theatre's Living Newspaper project, which was the theatre bearing witness to events that were actually happening in society in the 1930s. I happen to think that theatre is a very good forum for that. At the same time young writers wouldn't be writing for the theatre, at least initially, for the same reasons as they were in the Sixties because in the Sixties it was absolutely the dominant medium and it coincided with the age of the modern director if you like.

Bigsby: As a director you direct actors who come out of different acting traditions. How difficult is that?

Eyre: It is one of the problems, but I would say that it is a problem you almost don't think of consciously because, to some extent, that is what you are doing with every production. You are extracting from one individual something altogether different from another individual, and you are probably using a different language to talk to them. You could say it is manipulative but it is instinctive. You just think, 'Well how do I speak to this person?' Some people can take very, very brusque criticism, and other people you have to cajole and caress and support. You have to bring them all together so you have a common language, but that takes a long time and sometimes, very, very rarely, you get to the end point and find somebody is still outside the chorus and won't come in. I would say almost invariably they are not the good actors.

Bigsby: On the other hand dangerous actors are really attractive, like John Malkovich or Marlon Brando.

Eyre: Oh, sure. I talked to Kim Stanley, who was Stella in *Streetcar* with Brando in the theatre and on the screen, and I asked her about him. She said he wasn't at all difficult at rehearsals. He was meticulous about the text, and he was very caring about other people in the company, but when you see an actor who is unpredictable it is absolutely thrilling and it is quite rare.

Bigsby: How do you structure the early days of rehearsals and how nerve racking are they?

Eyre: They can be nerve racking but what I do is try and create a world in which everybody feels that they can contribute and to some extent that is contrived. For instance when I did a production of *The Crucible* in New York, Arthur Miller was around and I spent the first two or three days sitting around a large table and talked about the play with Arthur. We would read the play and keep stopping to say, 'What does this mean? Why did you write this?' It is quite hard to control because there is always someone who is incredibly garrulous. Some directors organise games but I feel it is contrived, so I prefer to do it as you would with a social group. I gradually loosen people up and get to know them and get people to talk about their own lives. Sometimes we talk about my life to encourage somebody to talk about theirs because what you want is for people to draw on their own lives, their own experience. In something like *The Crucible*, you compare the moral choices involved in the witch hunt with the moral choices we have ever made ourselves.

Bigsby: You drifted into directing, with no training. How would you advise someone who wanted to be a director?

Eyre: I would advise them to see a lot of theatre and watch a lot of good movies and to develop a critical faculty. There are two things I think operate in directing, one is a sort of management of a group of people and how you achieve ideas, put ideas into action. The other thing is taste, discrimination, how you discriminate between something that is true and something that is bogus and that can be learned, I think, in a way that you can teach somebody cooking or teach somebody gardening. There is a wonderful quote from a Douglas Dunn poem that only gardens can teach gardening and I think it is the same. You have got to watch and learn and develop taste and discrimination.

Bigsby: We haven't talked about your films, of which there are now a number. Do you find directing films enjoyable or a challenge?

Eyre: I guess the most successful film has been *Notes on a Scandal*. It wasn't the most fun to make. The most fun to make was *Iris* which is about somebody dying of Alzheimer's. My mother died of Alzheimer's and when we made it Judy Dench's husband had died only three months before, so it was very intense. But actually it was a fantastically joyful film to make and quite often that is the case. I made a film about the Falklands war called *Tumbledown*, and I had an absolutely wonderful time with that, so it is generally not so much the subject.

Bigsby: You mentioned Judy Dench. You explain in your book that she once had an interesting encounter with John Gielgud.

Eyre: John Gielgud insisted in his will that there shouldn't be any sort of memorial do for him. There shouldn't be a solemn ceremonial where everybody got up and read pieces of Shakespeare and poems, but I was fantasising that what there should be would be a load of actors telling anecdotes about him, of which there is an infinity. One of my favourites is one Judy Dench told me. They were rehearsing at what used to be called The Acton Hilton, which was the BBC's rehearsal block in West London. Gielgud was rehearsing something else which only had a few actors in it and Judy had a group of very young people at her table. This was in the canteen. She beckoned to John Gielgud and said, 'Come over and join us,' and he came over and sat at the table and all these young actors who had never met him, and thought he was living God, were just in total awe and silence and the silence was broken by John Gielgud saying, 'Has anybody had any obscene phone calls recently?'

In Conversation With Richard Flanagan

- 23rd September 2009 -

Richard Flanagan was born in Tasmania in 1961. He left school at sixteen but later returned to education graduating from the University of Tasmania before gaining his Masters degree at Oxford on a Rhodes Scholarship. His first novel, *Death of a River Guide*, appeared in 1997. It was followed by *The Sound of One Hand Clapping*, in 1998, and *Gould's Book of Fish* in 2001, which won the Commonwealth Writers' Prize. His fourth novel was *The Unknown Terrorist* (2007) and *Wanting* (2009) his fifth.

Bigsby: You come from Van Diemen's Land, Tasmania, and were born and raised in quite a small town.

Flanagan: Yes. My people were all convict people. We all went out during the famine and most people in Tasmania are the issue either of convicts or the original Tasmanian aborigines. For a quarter of its modern history it was really the gulag of the British Empire, and when that period ended the island went into economic decline. A great silence settled on the island and lasted for the best part of a century, and in that time the Irish convict people all intermarried. No one moved out of this strange nether world. They tended to live in the country, in the bush. They were all labourers. My generation was the first one to get an education, to leave that and marry outside of this strange caste, but within it was a world where story was very strong. Ideology, opinion, aesthetics, those sort of things, didn't matter. We didn't have art and literature. We had Australian-rule football, at which we excelled in a certain sort of operatic fashion. That was really about it. So that is the world I come from.

Bigsby: You were born in Longford.

Flanagan: I was born in Longford, a village of a couple of thousand. There is no middle class there. There is a sort of bastard gentry that were the idiot issue of the English that they didn't want. They were given these very large land grants and then everyone else was compelled to work for them. Up until the nineteen forties people worked on these huge sheep farms and would still be given the convict ration of several pounds of flour, several pounds of mutton and so many ounces of tea and sugar, plus a few shillings to go with it. Longford was where my great, great grandfather, Tom Flanagan, had been sent for stealing eight pounds of corn at the heart of the famine. So we had a long connection with the place.

When I was three my father, who was a state primary school teacher, was sent to Rosebury, which is a mining town on the west coast of Tasmania and that is even smaller, about eight hundred people, and completely isolated. They had only got a road through to it a year before we got there, and that was a one-lane gravel road through the rain-forested mountains and rivers. I loved that strange world. It was full of migrants from post-war Europe. It was very hard and brutal but I found it utterly beautiful and compelling. I think that was a very big event for me, and particularly this extraordinary natural world, the measure of which was not man-made. It was a natural world that was ancient, far more ancient than the natural worlds of Europe, for example. The rain-forest contains, in a mountain about five miles from where I lived, the oldest living thing on earth, a ten thousand year old pine, and I think I had an enormous sense of the antiquity of the natural world, and its immense power. I realised none of this until I came to live here in Britain as a young man and realised that it wasn't so normal to live in such a strange place.

Everybody was sent to this island whether they were slave revolt leaders from the Caribbean, or Canadian patriots, whether they were trade unionists, Chartists or Irish rebels. They all ended up there and John Mitchell, who was sent there as a convict, described it as a strange, misshapen, bastard England. He said, 'I am not so enamoured with the former to feel any like for the latter.' But in truth it wasn't bad. It was some other world coming into being. What was happening was that because of this combination of an old European culture, pre-industrial culture, and the black world a new culture arose. It was ostensibly western but had an unusual relationship with the land and an unusual sense of story being embedded in land, a strong sense of family and the connection of people to one another. Originally, when I tried to write I tried to write in the manner of the great Europeans. I tried to write crowd scenes, city scenes, which were completely disastrous because I had never seen a crowd until I stood in one in London when I was about twenty-three and was utterly terrified because I realised no one knew me and I would know no one. I had never experienced that in my life.

Bigsby: I got the impression from reading your work that there is a difference between Tasmania and Van Demon's land. It is as though Van Diemen's land incorporates the aborigines. It incorporates those who are on the margins, in some way, or the ordinary as opposed to the extraordinary. Is there a distinction between Tasmania and Van Diemen's land?

Flanagan: Van Diemen's land was the name given by the Dutch explorers, and the name remained until the ending of convictism, until the moment it ceased to be the gulag. There is a great shame on the part of the pre-settlers, for a minority, that their island, which is known throughout the empire, had to live with the stigma of being Van Diemen's land. This was compounded by an odd historical moment because the pre-settlers made enormous wealth out of wool. They were sending the wool back to England, but they had land that was stolen from the aborigines through a pitiless war of extermination. And they had the slave labour of the convicts, so they were rolling in it. The one thing they didn't have was political power, because it was still being run as a penal colony from Whitehall. They petitioned and lobbied to be given political power and Whitehall was completely uninterested in it. Then they advanced a moral argument, and the moral argument was that the system was breeding vice, particularly sodomy, in pestilential proportions. So Whitehall sent out a man called La Trobe, and he discovered people buggering themselves everywhere he went. The La Trobe report, in every paragraph, is punctuated by four asterisks. Tasmania became known as the island of Sodom and so they used this moral argument, which also created a sort of international aura of shame about it.

Van Diemen's land was seen to be wild. It invented bush ranging. It had had this terrible black war. It was seen to encompass the spirit of revolt. Tasmania was to be bourgeois. It was to have no memory of what had passed, and proposed a denial of history. Thus was Tasmania born, and really they are the two strands that have persisted ever since. There is a certain underground Van Diemenian world, that is black and convict.

Bigsby: When you were growing up in this small town world what was your ambition?

Flanagan: Rather appallingly I always wanted to be a writer, which made no sense. That was like coming out of the closet and saying you were gay in Tasmania. I didn't tell my parents until I was twenty-six. They did a television programme on me last year in Australia and my sister dug out something which I didn't even know about. It was a letter I had sent to her when I was six saying I would become a writer, and that was the only thing I ever wished to be.

I know it is a curious and strange thing that I would want to be that. If you wanted to be a writer in Tasmania you had to leave. That was the journey, because art and literature were what people did elsewhere. They did it in Europe, they did it in America. We were marginal to Australia, which was marginal to the world. There was no sense that our lives were other than diminished and not worthy of what art is, so why on earth I wanted to be a writer I can't say. My grandfather was illiterate and I guess from my father I got a strong sense about the strange magic of words and the way they can be liberating and the absence of them oppressive. Books and words were the only things that were taken seriously in the family. Everything else was the subject of humour.

Bigsby: So why did you leave school at the age of sixteen?

Flanagan: Well, Mum wanted me to be a plumber and I thought I would be a carpenter. I wasn't quite sure how I was going to be a writer and a recession had set in. I couldn't get an apprenticeship so I became a chainman for a surveyor, and I did that for two years. Then I got laid off and went to university. A chainman just cuts tracks through the bush with a slash hook and axe. One day – it was a very wet day so we couldn't go out – we were sharpening the axes and slash hooks at the back of the surveyor's offices and they threw a lot of old furniture out. We were to burn it but there was one chair which was broken and I fixed it and did it up and I thought, one day I will sit on that chair and I will write all my books on it. And that is the chair I have written all my books on.

Bigsby: There is something missing here. You left school at sixteen and then decided to go to university. Did you have the qualifications that were necessary or didn't you need them?

Flanagan: You didn't need them, thank God.

Bigsby: So you got a first class degree and then you had a Rhodes scholarship which took you to Oxford. Was England what you thought it would be?

Flanagan: No, not at all. I had spent time in the highlands in New Guinea living with native people up there before I came to England. They were stone-age people. We were in a very remote area, so remote that older people had seen white people but younger people hadn't and wanted to touch your skin. But the cultural trauma of that was as nothing compared to coming to Oxford. I only realised much later that it was a very unusual experience even for English people. I realised we shared a language but not much else. I got to read a lot, which I liked. It was also such a strange period in your history. It is said that individuals are rarely mad but societies frequently are, and that was a period of madness for your country.

Bigsby: Which date are we talking about?

Flanagan: I was here in 1984, so it was the height of the new Cold War. Cruise missiles were being deployed. Everyone was wearing black. There was this terrible sense of violence, race riots everywhere, and for me it was deeply shocking. I met an English writer the other day who wants to write a novel about the eighties because it seems far more distant than twenty years ago now. They had stationed these miners from Mardy in Oxford, and they were trying to redo that flying picket thing that was used in the winter of discontent. I went out on one of those pickets. It was about two o'clock in the morning and they rang up and I went out to Didcot power station. It was a grimy, grey, flat sort of place and we stood around. There were about sixty miners and shop stewards from Cowley who had lost their jobs in '84, and three or four students. Then, at about dawn, these buses started turning up, coach after coach, and the riot police got out. In the end there were a couple of hundred of these riot police. We were ordered to disperse and the riot police started putting on their shields. They came up and just started beating people with their batons. People began falling and the police were kicking them and laying into them and it was horrific. To my shame I turned and ran. I ran across the fields and finally found some village and got back to Oxford, and I thought, well, this is unbelievable. You can't do this in a civilised country. This will be national news tonight. I turned on the television that night and there was nothing. Then I thought, well, it will be in the papers, because now I was hearing that people were being hospitalised, but there was nothing. So it was a deeply shocking place. Nothing was as I expected and I longed for home.

Bigsby: But you found yourself in print for the first time. You were a historian and your first published books were history books.

Flanagan: My first book was based on an honours thesis I did in Tasmania. That was published while I was in England, but it had already been lined up for publication.

Bigsby: You were twenty-one?

Flanagan: Yes.

Bigsby: But it wasn't the book you had wanted to write when you were growing up, when you wanted to be a writer. Was it fiction you wanted to write or did you just want to see your name on a cover of a book?

Flanagan: No, I wanted to be a novelist but I wrote histories because you could get them published. It was an apprenticeship, and they were a terrific way of learning the architecture of books. It is understood that the apprenticeship should be poems and short stories and on to novels. There are many fine writers that do this but I think poetry and short stories are fundamentally different forms and they obey completely different rules. Writing non-fiction books allowed me to understand the larger architecture of the novel, the necessity for structure and movement. I think it is very hard, if you come from the short story or poem, to learn that initially because they obey different aesthetic rules. There is a different spiritual element in them.

Bigsby: You returned to Tasmania after the Oxford experience. How did you survive, because you weren't going to get enough money out of those books to keep you going? What did you do?

Flanagan: Misadventure, I guess. I was a labourer through winter and a river guide through summer. We had very young children so I had a family to support. I would write of an evening and slowly things came up. I got odd jobs. One of my best friends ended up as a minder for Australia's most wanted corporate criminal who had defrauded the banks of about seven hundred million dollars and set up this secret army. It was a very strange story. He was a Bavarian con man who had come to Australia and became celebrated. This bloke had been the subject of the biggest manhunt in Australian history. Being caught, he got what those sort of people always got, a very large book contract and, of course, he was criminally indisposed to write anything. They got editors in to work with him and they couldn't stand him and so then they said, 'Well, you find a writer,' because he was about to go to court and go down for a very long time, because the banks weren't pleased with him. So my friend said, 'I have this friend back in Tasmania who wants to be a writer.' They rang me up and gave me ten thousand dollars to write this story. I had six weeks, because in six weeks time he was going to court. The dilemma with it was that he killed himself in the middle of it. He shot himself, and this was front-page news. The publisher said to the newspaper that they had this tell-all memoir but they refused to divulge any details, as well they wouldn't because I was making them up in Hobart in a café. The normal criticism of a writer's first novel is that it is autobiographical but my first was in fact a novel.

Bigsby: There is a lyrical quality to many of your novels. Where does that come from? What was the state of Australian fiction when you began writing?

Flanagan: In Australia, when I started writing, there was a pared-back modernism. A sort of suburban naturalism was the dominant mode and I found it very dull. I also thought it was untrue to how people speak. I grew up in this large crowded house. I was one of six. We used to have all sorts of cousins turn up and stay and the house would often swell up to twenty or so people. I don't know how my poor mother survived it but I just remember these people spoke in a very poetic way – people do – and the best poetry tends to capture and simply recognise the beauty of the way people talk. The worst poetry pretends that literature should be different from the way we talk, so I wanted to write books that captured that beautiful baroque poetry of the language I had heard growing up.

I also grew up with a sense of stories in which time was endlessly circular and not linear as it is here in Europe. When I came to Oxford stories were linear, history was linear, everything progressed down this railway line of thought and development, but in my world everything fell back on itself. There is a beautiful poem by Borges where he writes that time is the river that sweeps me along, but I am the river. Time is the tiger that eats me, but I am the tiger. Time is the fire that consumes me, but I am the fire. That is the sense of time I grew up with.

I had a cousin who was about eighty. She just turned up one day and stayed for six months and she had all these stories about our family that reached way back into the convict days, but she loved watching American soaps and, after a time, we realised that a lot of the family tales seemed to have American Christian names in them and that she was actually confusing our lives with the stories from the soaps, but they were no less marvellous for that.

Bigsby: That edges us towards your first novel. You said that you were a river guide. In fact you kayaked up a lot of the rivers, as well as being a river guide.

Flanagan: It is very hard to convey to people here. I am forty-eight. Tasmania is the size of Ireland. A quarter of it to this day is uninhabited. A quarter of it is still this great immense wild land. Fibre-glass kayaks had just turned up in the island in the early seventies and I got in with a group of people who had started kayaking all these remote rivers. You would go down places and you would know you would be the first white person ever to go through these gorges and these areas of rain-forest. They were difficult and remote but that gives you a strange and beautiful sense of the world, and that affected me a lot. But then I nearly drowned leading a group down the river in 1983 and out of that I wrote the first book, which isn't autobiographical but, just as James Baldwin said of *Go Tell It On The Mountain* that it was the book he had to write if ever he was to write a book, I guess *Death of a River Guide* was that for me.

Bigsby: You set yourself difficult technical problems in that book because it is narrated by a person who is dying. In fact he is underwater for much of the book. How confident were you, as you were writing, that you were cracking this, because it moves around in time, it moves around in space, and yet is narrated by this figure.

Flanagan: I was never confident, but I think you cannot act without the horizon of failure constantly in view. Browning said a man's reach must exceed his grasp. I think when novels have an ambition and fail they are still better for it than seeking to work within the limits of what a writer knows. When a writer knows what he is writing, Faulkner said, he is writing nothing worth reading. So I guess with that rather ludicrous sense of what the novel was I set out to write this.

Incidentally, I did a reading in Germany once. They have actors to read for you and they are very German. What can I say? I was in Hanover, famous for the Volkswagen factory, and they seem to have a similar notion of art as never ending. When I arrived at the reading there was a man just oozing over the top of the table. He looked like Jabba the

Hutt. He was the German voice of Brad Pitt. There were about a hundred earnest Germans and a moderator who was like a Lutheran pastor. He spoke for a very long time and then he turned to the actor who read, I kid you not, for an hour and eighteen minutes. That was his reading, and the Germans just took it all in. No one tried to throw anything at him, and for an Australian this was quite an extraordinary idea of art. I thought, 'Well, that's ended. That's good.' I still hadn't said anything, although it was my reading. Then the moderator, the Lutheran pastor, took over and he spoke for an inordinately long time, again in German. I thought, 'Well, that must be the end of it,' but then, inexplicably and amazingly, he threw it back to the actor once again and he was now on fire and he spoke this time, and I know because I had nothing else to do but look at my watch with an ever growing sense of awe, for one hour and forty-three minutes, at the end of which there was a standing ovation because even the noble literati of Hanover had had enough and just wanted this idiot to go home.

Bigsby: It wasn't a book that sparked immediate positive reviews.

Flanagan: One thing I have learnt is that you must be true to your readers. I became a writer because of readers. When my first novel, *River Guide*, was published, because I was from Tasmania *The Sydney Herald*, which is the leading broadsheet in Australia, refused to review it saying it didn't fit into any recognisable school of Australian writing, which was perhaps the greatest compliment I have ever had. That book took off because readers loved it and they kept on forcing reprints. In the end reviews started appearing and prizes started turning up, but it was because of readers, and for readers you must have story. But story doesn't have to be linear.

When I was working on the script of *The Sound of One Hand Clapping* I worked with one of the leading soap opera writers in Australia and I learned so much from her, but I also learned the limitations of linear plotting which is what soap operas are. Linear plotting isn't story. Story is so many things but it is essentially musical in composition. It is often about strange juxtapositions. What do I mean by that? If you take, for example, the extraordinary moment in *Anna Karenina*, where Anna dies, everyone remembers those pages, with the flickering candle, and everyone is moved, but what Tolstoy does then on the next page is have a character who has written a book about agrarian reform in Russia and has just published it and thinks the Walls of Jericho are going to fall because this is a profound work he has devoted his life to and this is the defining issue for this great country. But nothing happens and, after about two months, a desultory notice appears in some journal and he grows angry and disillusioned. Then there is one other review. And what Tolstoy has done there, to my mind, through that strange juxtaposition, is to take you back to this tragedy of a woman whose life in that society is viewed as nothing, which is the great tragedy at the centre of the novel. To me that juxtaposition is story, but story doesn't have to be linear. It is about so many other things. At heart it is about the music of the novel. Story is the motley the novelist throws over the fundamental emotions he or she wishes to communicate, but one must be utterly true to it and respect its power.

Bigsby: *The Sound of One Hand Clapping*, is altogether bleaker than your first novel. You are married to someone from Slovenia, and there is a Slovenian in the book. A new Australia emerges in this book from the country which announced to the world its whiteness – White Australia. Things have begun to change and there are tensions to do with that change. In a sense the Slovenian woman in your book already came from a marginal world, in European terms, and now finds herself physically on the margin in a small town rather like the one you were describing, a small mining town, lacking love, lacking something that can sustain her and yet looking for something that could sustain her. Was there a sense in which, though it is set in Tasmania, you were looking at some version of Australia?

Flanagan: That is a far more interesting question than any answer I will be able to make. The rather dreary truth of all these things is that a writer understands what they are doing but I think there is something autistic to their work, otherwise they wouldn't need a thousand pages and three years to write these things. Nothing is more secondary to a writer's achievements, if they have any, than their original intentions because if the book has any worth it somewhere escapes them and becomes something else. I don't have much perspective looking back on my novels, but I will endeavour to come up with some satisfactory fictions that explain it as best I can.

Australia had a white Australian policy for fifty years, the first half of the twentieth century. Then it threw itself open to immigration and in consequence is now one of the most cosmopolitan countries on earth. As I said, I grew up in this mining town surrounded by people who had come out of post-war Europe. The sort of migrants we got tended to be rural European migrants from peasant Greece, peasant Poland, peasant

Yugoslavia, peasant southern Italy, and it struck me how extraordinary it was that in the heart of one forlorn labourer you might have derived the great historical movements of the age and, in a place beyond history and even hope, you might in that one person's life read nationalism, bolshevism, fascism, total war. All that could exist in that one person if you could find your way into their story.

I guess I was interested in the way we think we must look into ourselves for meaning. What I have learned from those people is that whatever meaning there is doesn't lie in the madness of analysis, step aerobics, colonic irrigation, all these terrible things we do to ourselves in the hope we will be a better person: it lies in others. I guess that is what I learned growing up with these people. It is in the love you find in others and the love they show you that whatever meaning there is in this life is to be found.

I gave it a Slovenian background because that was the migrant world I was obviously most familiar with. It wasn't a conventional Australian story because Australia loves the successful migrant story. It loves the migrant who has become a millionaire. Some people were unhappy with the novel. It also came out at a time of rising racism. When this book came out in the late nineties, there had been a big movement against Asian migration and the neo-fascists were on the rise. A neo-fascist party was polling fifteen per cent nationally.

There were other things that intrigued me at the time. One was the cult of violence that was growing in art, and the obsession with the moment of violence, whether it was in a Tarantino movie or *American Psycho*. Everything was about the moment of violence but, as Clint Eastwood himself said, violence has consequences and it seemed to me that what really mattered, what art should do, was to look at both the causes and consequences of violence. At the heart of this novel is a rape that you never witness but which passes through not just one life but many, and not just through a year or two but through decades and generations.

At the time there were a lot of Bosnian refugees turning up in Australia and it just struck me that the use of rape as a weapon of war had been severely misunderstood in the west because it is a profound crime that destroys not just the individual but the individual's sense of themselves in the community. It ruptures all those relationships. So there were various things feeding into it and I guess all those strange beautiful people I grew up with – and it never cease to amaze me – had come from this ravaged Europe and their job in Tasmania was to remake Europe.

213

This most beautiful place was to be remade as the Ruhr valley of Australia with great power stations and heavy industry, and that always seemed a funny irony.

Bigsby: You nearly won a prize for this one but were probably deprived of it in rather strange circumstances because it went up against a fraudulent novel, by Helen Demidenko, whose real name was Helen Dale, also known as Helen Darville.

Flanagan: If Australia has one noble literary tradition it is literary fraud. We are very good at that. This woman had written a novel that purported to be the story of a Ukrainian mass murderer. It was an anti-Semitic work with fascistic overtones and it was a poor piece of writing. It read like a pornographic comic book, really, but the literary establishment loved it. I think they loved it because it gave them wogs as they thought wogs should be, violent and irrational and nasty. A 'wog' was always the derogatory term used for non-Anglos. It is the old English term. So she was feted as a great writer. She was a tall woman with blonde hair and used to wear peasant shirts. She turned out to be the daughter of an English nurseryman and not the daughter of Ukrainians. Her uncle was not, as she had said, the subject of a war crimes tribunal. It was all a complete lie.

Bigsby: She was a student at the time and took a law degree after this. That must have really pissed you off?

Flanagan: On the awards night it was a great introduction to the idiocies of literary life. She came up to me and said, 'The best book had to win,' and I thought never a truer word was spoken about literary status because these things are never about best books. Prizes become celebrated to the extent that they can succeed in giving it to the wrong book because at that point they become contentious and fixed and talked about. The book has made a global reputation on this basis.

Bigsby: In 2001, you published an intriguing book, *Gould's Book of Fish*, which is rooted in history and has more than a tincture of truth at the bottom of it. There was such a man as Gould, but you had to reinvent the character and invent a language that would go with him. I find it hard to describe this book in terms of any other books. How did the idea of the book first come to you?

Flanagan: Books begin for me in very simple ways. I was in the archives and the old archivist asked me if I had ever seen *Gould's Book of Fish*. I had never heard of it. He kept it hidden in a cupboard and got it out and showed me. There were twenty-eight watercolour paintings of fish, made by a convict called William Buelow Gould, and I found them utterly compelling because there was something intensely human about them. He said they were painted on Sarah Island, which was the Devil's Island of the British Empire. I knew there were no pictures of any convicts who had ever been on that island and at that moment I loved the idea that he had smuggled something out in the eyes of those fish and that it had lived in this cupboard, locked away and lost, for nearly two centuries. Here it was speaking directly to me and I knew what the book was at that moment. I didn't know how to write it or the voice, but I saw it and I wanted each chapter to begin with one of these pictures of a fish and to be about who the person was he was smuggling out in the fish. Each chapter would be written in different coloured inks, but I knew I had to be in a strong position to go to a publisher with such a ludicrous proposal because it was utterly non-commercial. So it wasn't until after *The Sound of One Hand Clapping*, which was a very large success in Australia, that I was in a strong enough position to go to my publisher and say, 'will you back me on this book' because no one knew how to print a book in different colours, with plates, at that time. They knew how to do it as an expensive book but I wanted it done as a book anyone could buy at the normal cost of a novel, and I needed designers and printers to work with.

So I wrote the book according to the technical requirements. All the early drafts were written in multiples of sixteen pages. I had such fun writing that book. It was a way of understanding the world. I just used to sit at my desk laughing but unfortunately it had to end at some point and I had to abandon it and let the publishers have it.

Bigsby: Your next book was a completely different, extraordinarily bleak, book. *The Unknown Terrorist* seems to me partly about the kind of paranoid world that we now inhabit, after 9/11, after the bombs in London. But the portrait of ordinary life is quite bleak. What was the response to the book in Australia?

Flanagan: Firstly, I should say it arose out of two things. *Gould's Book of Fish* was a really big book around the world. It just took off and was a monster and I realised I could become imprisoned in it and that I would never escape it. That is a not uncommon story with writers who write a strange book like this, and I realised I would have to break the mould if I was to be free as a writer again. I wanted to go beyond it as a writer. I always want to do something that I don't know how to do because I think that is how you improve as a writer. So I wanted to write something very pared back and minimal, something that just had a very straightforward story.

Gould's Book of Fish was about the story of language. I wanted to write a book this time around where language didn't get between the reader and the story, where you could look straight through the sentences and phrases to the story and character and aren't aware of the language. As to the subject matter, it was that very strange time which all the west passed through, and I was trying to write a parable for the time. And I guess what I realised at the end of the book is that it is not really about politics. I felt there was a crisis of love in the west. There was a failure of empathy. We had somehow lost that sense of shared humanity that is so fundamental. Somewhere in the book there is a line that says politics is the enemy of love, and that is what I came to believe. In Australia the book was very popular. It was a big best seller. It divided critics. I got some very hostile reviews, but then I think that is inevitable unless you wish to write something that the public wants, work that reflects the stupidities of the age. I think if you really wish to write something worth reading you must try and question those stupidities and look underneath them. That is your role as a writer.

Bigsby: *Wanting*, your new book, which has already been short-listed for an award, assembles an amazing cast of characters. How did you come to put all the component elements of *Wanting* together?

Flanagan: I wanted to write a meditation about the terrible hunger we have for love, and the constant way we say no to that hunger, the way we deny ourselves love. I think if any of us look in our own hearts we would see that there have been moments in our lives when we have turned away from love. We do it because we are trapped in a world that demands we conform to certain idiocies that we call society and community and family. We need those, that is how we get food on the table and shelter, but we pay a great price with our soul. We are only liberated from that in rare moments of transcendence and it seems to me that one of the terrible cruel fictions we live with is that love must be eternal, whereas love is always ephemeral. But we are granted a few moments in life and we should celebrate those. It was all that that I wished to write about.

Many years ago I had seen a painting of an aboriginal girl, painted in the eighteen thirties. She is a very beautiful child and is wearing a regency red dress. It is framed in an oval wooden frame and this painting was at the back of a museum. It had never been exhibited. And when you lift the oval frame off you see two bare feet and realise that she has kicked off her shoes during the sitting and whoever commissioned the painting was so ashamed of it that they used the frame to cut her off at the ankles. It seemed to me to be an image that summed up this dreadful conflict, the rubble of which we walk through all our lives and to which there is no resolution. So I tried to find out who this aboriginal child was. She was one of the few survivors of the war of extermination I spoke about earlier. She came from this very beautiful part of what is still a great wild area in Tasmania and was adopted by Sir John Franklin, who was briefly governor of Tasmania. She was set up as a sort of black princess and then, when Franklin was recalled to London, was promptly abandoned by the Franklins and descended to a sorry and ultimately tragic life. She was despised by white society and she, in turn, despised the despairing black society, what was left of it at that point.

I thought that was a quite extraordinary story but I didn't know how to write it for a long time. Then I came across the story of how, after Sir John Franklin disappeared looking for the Northwest Passage and many years later reports came back that the expedition having succumbed to cannibalism, Lady Jane Franklin recruited no less than Charles Dickens to rescue Sir John's honour, because eating people was what savages did and not civilised great explorers like Sir John Franklin. And Dickens became obsessed with this story seeing in it an image of his own frozen inner life, I think. He staged a play in which he played a Sir John Franklin type figure. He was a sensation in Victorian London but he used the play as a metamorphosis in which he transformed his own life. He fell in love with an actress who he ran off with and thereafter his life was utterly changed and I realised that these two stories, one of an unknown child at the edge of the world, and one of the most famous men of the age at the centre of the world, were connected by wanting. At that moment I roughly knew what the book was, although it took me some time to actually get it down on paper in a coherent fashion.

In Conversation With Richard Ford

- 27th September 2006 -

Richard Ford, the novelist and short story writer, was born in Jackson, Mississippi, in 1944, the son of a travelling salesman. A graduate of Michigan State University, he later completed his MA in creative writing at the University of California, Irvine. He published his first novel – *A Piece of My Heart* – in 1976. It was with *The Sportswriter* (1986), though, that he broke through. It introduced the character of Frank Bascombe to whom he would return in the Pulitzer Prize-winning *Independence Day* (1995) and *The Lay of the Land (2006)*.

Bigsby: You were raised in Mississippi, with family connections in Arkansas. Your father was a salesman. You once said that you were left alone a lot when you were growing up.

Ford: I was an only child and my father was a travelling salesman. He left on Monday mornings and came back home on Friday afternoons, so I was in the house with my mother all of the week. By saying I was left alone I didn't mean to voice a complaint. She was often one place in the house and I was some place else, or she was in the house and I was in the yard, because that was a more innocent time than now. You weren't constantly worried that somebody was going to haul your kid off. I was usually just on my own from the time I was five-and-a-half or six. When I went to kindergarten I went down the street, turned right, went a block, caught the bus and went to the street where the kindergarten was, which was about a ten minute bus ride away. I got off the bus, crossed a quite busy street, went down about three blocks and went to kindergarten. That's just how life was. I had wonderful parents. Maybe the first three or four times my mother took me down there. It changed after my father died when I was sixteen. After that I was shunted off to live with my grandparents in Arkansas and I was put into the care of three black men who worked for my grandfather. They looked after me for three years and were basically my friends, my companions, my teachers, my everything. So I wasn't alone much after my father died.

Bigsby: You left the South when you were eighteen. You spoke just now about the three black men who in effect helped to raise you. That was in Little Rock, Arkansas. In 1957, federal troops went into the South for the first time since the Civil War. Mississippi, where you spent your first sixteen years, was at the centre of Civil Rights activities in the late fifties and into the sixties. You left in sixty-two, but somehow I don't feel that that was what you were interested in at the time, or was it?

Ford: It was at the centre of everybody's life. I went to high school with no blacks at all. I never played sports against blacks. I never saw blacks as team-mates. I never had that kind of affiliation with black kids my age, so it was part of our life that we were separated from them. I was far from a rebel under those circumstances. My sympathies were not with segregationists, but the pressures of that life, in which everybody was clinging to a particular way of life, meant that I was buckling under right and left. In my heart of hearts, though, I was trying to find a way to resist. I had a kid stand up in class and call me a nigger lover, and I was shocked by that. I didn't quite know what I had done or what evidence there was that that was true, and I thought to myself, 'I got to get out of here' because I was on the wrong side of the race issues in the South and I just had to get out. Nobody was un-implicated. Nobody was un-involved. People made moral choices. I will say this, what I did by leaving Mississippi in 1962, and going off to Michigan to school, was not the brave thing to do. It was the self-surviving thing to do. People who were my age who stayed there and went to college in Mississippi, and live there to this day, are the real heroes.

Bigsby: When you went to Michigan initially you were doing a course on hotel management, which needs a bit of explaining.

Ford: After my father died I was shunted off to Little Rock to live with my grandfather because I was a kid in trouble with the police a lot. My mother knew when she was raising me by herself that she just didn't have whatever it took to raise me.

Bigsby: What did you do to get in trouble with the police?

Ford: I stole cars, broke into bowling alleys and stole the entire safe, got into lots of fist fights. I was just on the road to being a juvenile delinquent and in fact the guy I was running with at the time later went to prison. I was feckless. I don't excuse myself, although on the other hand it was rather fun to do that. But I was obviously heading for trouble and my mother had parents in Little Rock who ran a big hotel and could absorb me. They weren't very old. My mother was born to her mother when her mother was sixteen, and she married another man who was six years younger than she was. This is the South. They were all glutenated together in all kinds of ways. So the move to live with my grandparents in Little Rock was not a move to live with a couple of old people. I am sure they were younger than I am now when I moved up there with them. So I moved into the hotel.

Bigsby: Hence the hotel management course, but that only lasted a few weeks. Then you switched to English before briefly going to Washington University where you studied law. What were you thinking then?

Ford: I wanted to be a lawyer. It is as simple as that. I think I wanted to be a lawyer because I had seen, over the course of the early sixties, FBI agents who were I thought the forces of good going down into Mississippi and arresting segregationists and trying to arrest the people who had killed those three civil rights workers and buried them in a dam. I thought that to be an FBI agent was a good thing, but I was in love and after three months in law school in St. Louis, with my girlfriend, who is now my wife, in New York, as a model and IBM engineer having the time of her life, I just thought I am going to lose this if I sit down here in law school. I am not going to have somebody I am in love with any more, so I quit and moved to New York.

Bigsby: I seem to remember you saying that when your father died the impact was less directly on you than on your mother?

Ford: That's right. My father died in the morning about 7.30 by waking up and having a heart attack, as is often the case when people have heart attacks. They happen early in the morning. I woke up to hear him gasping for breath and went in and got into bed with him and tried to breathe air into his lungs. He died in my arms and my mother was standing at the door. She just went completely hysterical. Of course she would. It just wasn't possible at that point to be anything other, but I was not hysterical. I didn't cry. I just kind of bucked up in some instinctual way. It always made me wonder for years afterwards. I never cried very much and it wasn't until my mother died that I ever did. I was thirty-seven then.

Bigsby: She died shortly before you wrote *The Sports Writer*. Is there any connection between those two things?

Ford: I don't know whether this is just hindsight but there is definitely a connection. When I started to write *The Sports Writer* I was doing what people do when they write novels. They pull together things in advance of writing so that you don't hit a blank wall. I was looking for something for this character I was going to write, Frank Bascombe. What were the furnishings of his life, what were the impediments, what were the conflicts this book was going to contain? And I thought he would have been the father of a child who died. I had never had a child but what I had was grief and this is something that I thought I could write about, grief for my mother dead three months earlier. If you are the parent of a child who dies, and if you are the child of a parent who dies, those griefs would probably seem entirely distinct. For me, though, one stood for the other and was a way to write about it.

Bigsby: Frank Bascombe is somebody who loses people. He lost a child, as you say. He loses a son to a kind of derangement. He loses, in one way or another, two wives. Things slip through his fingers. How far is that an explanation of the man? Does he go on looking for something?

Ford: I don't know the answer to that. In a sense you write a book and give it to the reader and the reader makes what sense of it he can. That is the sense you made of it. I sort of fall into line with that by saying when I set about writing *The Sports Writer*, in 1982, I had just suffered my job as a sports writer to go away and came back down to Princeton where I was living with my wife. I didn't know what to do and I said, 'Maybe I will write a novel,' because I had quit writing novels a couple of years before. I thought I had had my shot and it hadn't worked out very well. And Christina said to me, 'I'll tell you what, why don't you write a novel about a person who is happy for a change?' because I had been unhappy. I thought serious novels were about people who were not happy. It is a young novelist's failure. At least it was mine. And so I thought, how can I write a novel that is about a man who is happy that is also interesting? And I thought, well, I can write a novel about a man who is trying to be happy when fate has dealt him bad cards.

Bigsby: What was the attraction of the present tense in *The Sportswriter*, which in many ways goes against the grain of the novel?

Ford: The obvious thing is you gain a sense of immediacy. To set something in the present tense does not restrict you as much as you might think because in the present tense you can always invoke the past. In the past tense, invoking the present is much harder, much trickier. But if you have present-tense verbs you can invoke the past if you need it. It not only makes for a sense of immediacy but it makes the present seem where life takes place, and if that happens to be one of the concerns of your book it is apt. It makes the present seem, in the way that novels and art can do, feasible and examinable in a way that life never permits us to do. It should be said there are wonderful novels which are set in the present tense, and I am far from the first to do it. Joe Heller's book *Something Happened*, a wonderful novel which has fallen off our life syllabus now, and Walker Percy's great novel, *The Movie Goer*, are written in the present tense.

Bigsby: I am struck by the fact that you rewrote your second novel, *The Ultimate Good Luck*. You changed it from first person to third person. I imagine people think, well that's easy, you just go through and cross out 'I' and you put 'He'.

Ford: I wrote *The Ultimate Good Luck*, which I thought was a just-can't-miss book, and I wrote it out to the best of my ability. It was ninety-eight pages long and I thought, 'Well, shit, this isn't a novel.' I felt very bad about it because it wasn't long enough and I realised it just didn't have enough stuff in it. So I showed it to my friend Geoffrey Wolff, who ran the creative writing programme at the University of California, Irvine, where I had studied (he is the brother of the writer Toby Wolff, who is my great pal) and Geoffrey said, 'I am really sorry to have to tell you this, but you are going to have to change the point of view of this novel from first to third.' I thought, 'Well, okay,' and I did.

We were living in Princeton then. I had a nice office in Princeton University as I was teaching there, and I just sat in my office for about nine months changing the point of view of this novel from first to third. I can't really make very intelligible what you have to do to change from first to third. A first person narrator is up against the action and the third person narrator is slightly apart. It is that aesthetic space that distinguishes one point of view from another. And in that aesthetic space I found there was an opportunity for more language because the language I had available to me in the first person was fairly sparse. So I rewrote it in the third, which does in fact require changing all the pronouns but once you change all the pronouns then that occasions an opportunity for you which you sense in an entirely instinctual way. It occasions an opportunity for you to say more, in other words to treat the reader to more language.

This is one of the lessons I learned about writing novels very early in my writing life, which was that when you write less or more, when you decide to make a sentence or paragraph longer or shorter, it largely has to do with the fact that you want to expose the reader to language. As Victor Hugo used to say, when language becomes a medium for communication it is dying. The reason you want to expose readers to language is not just to tell them something, which you do, but also to render to them all of language's multifarious possibilities, its sonorities, its poetical qualities, its rhythms, its chosen-ness. So that when writers write, and readers read, one of the things that is happening is that you are being given language to experience. What difference does it make if I have more words in this book than I had in its earlier incarnation? I had more opportunity to expose the reader to language which I could then choose and make as good as I could.

Bigsby: You are placing enormous emphasis on language but am I right in saying you have suffered from dyslexia?

Ford: Yes, and I do still. I am dyslexic.

Bigsby: So here you are talking about language and precision of language etc. yet language poses problems.

Ford: Language poses problems. I am not severely dyslexic, though. There are people who are and who have very profound problems. For me the classic dyslexic situation is that what you see on the written page doesn't register in your brain in the way it is written on the page. There is a disconnect there. Something registers but it is not always what you see and for me to be a good reader – and I was never told I was dyslexic until many years later – I would have to fix my eyes on the words and read them as carefully as I would were I reading aloud, but silently, because when I read a passage I couldn't remember anything I had read. One of the things that that exposed me to was the qualities of language which were non-cognitive, all of those rhythms and sonorities and all of those things which make language lush and agreeable to us. I don't think that was so bad. It would only be bad if my job was to read real fast, but that wasn't my job. I think one of the consequences of being dyslexic and of reading at the pace I do is that my sentences invite the reader to slow down.

Bigsby: Your father, like Frank Bascombe, was a salesman, an iconic figure in America.

Ford: The death of a travelling salesman is one of the great stories in American literature.

Bigsby: Were you drawn to putting him in that role partly because of the significance it plays in that culture?

Ford: In writing *Independence Day* I chose Frank to be a salesman because I wanted to give him a new vocation, because I was writing a new book. In American culture you can become a real estate salesman just by proclaiming yourself one. You don't have to train or anything. For me, it is always important for a character to have a vocation that the reader understands because when I grew up what a person did for a living was one of the ways that one became plausible. You knew who someone was by what that person did. I am just old fashioned enough to think that that still works. I don't know that I was very conscious of the salesman as a figure outside of my own divining in writing that. It just so happened, because I am American, we think a lot about real estate.

Bigsby: Also because you have lived in so many places?

Ford: That's right. I also remember that when I was a kid my father, on the weekends when he was home, would get my mother and me in the car with him and we would go out from the centre of Jackson, this little tiny burg in the middle of Mississippi that was beginning to have suburbs, and his idea of progress was to move out of the centre of town into the suburbs and buy a house. It is a typical part of the American dream and I always associated real estate with progress. Real estate was the consummation of people's hopes for themselves. So it seemed fundamentally to be an optimistic thing to do. We live, in America, in a totally mercantilised society in which sales, the making of money and the transference of goods and services one to another, is synonymous with progress.

Bigsby: There is something else about being a real estate agent which comes out of these books and that is that he meets people who are at key moments in their life. They are looking for a house because they have got married, because they have got divorced, because they have got old and decide they can't function any more, and that is what engages him. He is not just selling property.

Ford: No, he is selling life in a sense. He is selling access to a life and that I have to tell you was just fortuitous. I just wanted him to be a guy who sold real estate because I needed a profession for him to have. It was only after I started creating situations for him that I realised that being a real estate agent, something I hadn't really ever thought about, gave access to all of these people's lives and dreams. Moreover it afforded me an opportunity to have a say about the American spirit based on the American economy, things I just never plotted. I am not the kind of guy who can do that, so I have to depend on luck a lot of time. It should be said, I think, that anybody who writes novels has to fall heir to some modicum of luck because you know relatively little about what you are doing when you start as compared to what you come to know when you finish. So some providence has to assist you to make what starts off as just rudimentary stuff become whole and integrated and full.

Bigsby: Are you optimistic about this America?

Ford: I am quite optimistic about art. I am quite optimistic about the virtues of narrative and writing novels which is a way to renew our sensuous and emotional life and learn new awareness. But about my Republic, I am not optimistic at all. It is a dark time to be in America.

In Conversation With Jonathan Franzen

- 4th October 2006 -
- 6th October 2010 -

Jonathan Franzen was born in Illinois in 1959 and raised in suburban St. Louis. He graduated from Swarthmore College in 1981 with a degree in German and, indeed, spent time in Germany. His first novel, *The Twenty-Seventh City*, was published in 1988, followed four years later by *Strong Motion*, but it was his 2001 novel, *The Corrections* which won him a national and international reputation winning the National Book Award for Fiction in the United States and the James Tait Black Memorial Prize for fiction in the United Kingdom. In 2009 he published *Freedom*.

Part I – 4th October 2006

Bigsby: Your latest work is a memoir. What drew you back to writing about your mother at this moment in *The Discomfort Zone?*

Franzen: I had undertaken to write some kind of non-fiction about myself and to my surprise and horror it is really hard to write about my childhood without talking about the two giants who loomed over it. It would almost be okay to just leave myself out of the picture entirely and have the two giants. I feel I am mostly there as a foil for them. They terrify me, they protect me, so I think it is just implicit in the project. The question I really asked is why did I choose to write a memoir? My mum and I did not enjoy each other's company after we had been together about seventy-two hours. It was great for the first seventy-two hours and then it was time for me to go. She hated to admit that but I think she knew that, too, or so I tell myself now. But the instant she died, of course, I started missing her terribly and basically I miss her more and more.

She described herself in the last year of her life as her family's matriarch. She was the oldest person in her extended family. She was the oldest daughter of the oldest daughter. She was the one who sent the

Christmas cards to everybody up in Minnesota and Illinois and the cousins and former friends who are now retired in southern California and Florida. She held all that together. In her really beat up body her mind was just totally sharp and she held everything together. She was this link, not just for me but for everybody in my family, to the nineteenth century, to an old Protestant America. But how can a person be completely alive, somebody you can talk to on the phone, and eight hours later all of these connections are utterly extinguished. The book came not really through design but just through an investigation of what changed in the country and also maybe what changed in me between the late sixties and early seventies, when I was a kid, and this incredibly polarised and unequal brutish country that I live in now. I think there is an additional symbolic weight that she carries as the stern embodiment of all of those old-fashioned values, like thrift and egalitarianism and not judging others and so on.

Bigsby: It seems to me that what you are doing is giving the kind of attention to a person that you had accused yourself of not giving.

Franzen: Yes. Couldn't have said it better myself.

Bigsby: When you wrote the first novel you choose to set it in St. Louis but not quite a St. Louis that one might recognise.

Franzen: My first book was about the South Asians, some of them terrorists, planting a cell in the middle of the country and for reasons that are very hard for Americans to comprehend, waging a war on my parents' way of life. Needless to say I was not a terrorist in high school. I was a benign prankster. I was all over the clandestine part of terrorism but it was all completely innocent and playful, and that was an embarrassment. I learned two hours into my college experience that no one was interested in the interesting fun things I had done in high school. I learned to shut up about what an innocently western childhood I had had and had a lot to prove as a young novelist. I wanted to prove that I was a man and not a boy, wanted to prove that I was closer to sixty than to sixteen. This is the kind of chronicle of what I left out which is the somewhat embarrassing reality that I, with a certain amount of literary chest puffing, tried to turn my back on. In the same way that I have come around to missing my parents, in a sometimes almost hourly way, I am now in my mid forties and finally, having felt that some people read my books, feel brave enough to go back and look at what a goof I was.

Bigsby: You were taken back to your house once by a television crew for reasons which you may or may not want to get into, but what struck me was that you would not go into your house with the crew. I still don't quite know what it was that stopped you going into that house.

Franzen: I was taken back with a film crew of Oprah Winfrey's to emote over my parents' house and it is true that I had my back up because I didn't like the project. It was phoney to the bone, but even the night before, when I was there with another TV crew, I couldn't even bear to look at the house. One of my experiences, as I have got older, is that I keep thinking I am done with stuff I have not even started with. I did a lot of crying the week after my mum died and I thought the fact that I am crying less toward the end of the week, and am starting to interest myself in other things, means I am done, this terrible grief I have been worried about I am almost done with, and then of course that is revealed to be a sad joke. I behaved just insanely for the next year driven I think by a wish not to experience grief. That year of insanity passed and people could stand to be around me again and I thought, well, now I am done. There is such a wish to be done maybe because I am a guy, or we don't live in a terribly emotional time, we don't rend our garments the way many people used to. But I am just so afraid of feeling. I am just terrified of strong feeling. Even as I long to have strong feeling I am terrified by it. I particularly feel this as a writer because if there is not strong feeling there is no writing, no writing worth talking about. There is no writing really worth keeping and yet the last thing I want to do is experience it.

Bigsby: You have been talking about emotion and investing writing with emotion as well as life with emotion, but your first two novels were much more constructions.

Franzen: There was a lot of the emotion of rage in the second one. I don't know if lust is an emotion or if it is just a deadly sin, but there was plenty of that as well.

Bigsby: Your father didn't like it.

Franzen: My father admired the first one, which made my decade. I am very sorry to say it mattered a lot that he would be impressed and appreciate the first novel. I think in many ways it was a bizarre first novel, with its control and leather-arm-patch preoccupations with urban sociology rather than the kinds of things you normally think of a twenty-four-year-old being preoccupied with. I think a lot of that has to do with just a very straightforward wish to write a novel that would both satisfy some of my literary yearning and also seem serious and worthy to an extremely pragmatic person who never read books. And conspiracy was the flavour of the decade. Pynchon was still happening back in the late seventies when I first started thinking of being a writer, though I didn't know about him until a friend quickly pointed out that I was writing like him. I did read him but I had an acquaintance with clandestine activities from high school. Even though I was amazingly innocent I was also profoundly deceptive. I told my parents absolutely nothing. I completely sold them a different picture of me. I literally spent a lot of time climbing out of windows and sneaking out. It was only later, re-examining the evidence, that I realised they knew I was keeping everything from them and they were just kind enough not to call me. That is actually something I didn't figure out till twenty minutes ago. It is one of the reasons I miss them.

The funny thing is, and actually I am now completely at a tangent, but there is a chapter in this book about these rather ambitious pranks that I and some friends engineered in high school and when my mum was dying we talked about a lot of stuff. We spent a couple of weekends in my brother's house in Seattle and I tried to tell her about these ways in which I had deceived her and the kind of fun and interesting things we had done. In fact the President of the School Board had singled us out for being exceptionally responsible and good pranksters. She just cut me off right away. She didn't want to hear anything about it. She didn't even cut me off. She just picked up a magazine. She just truly did not even now want to know what I was doing in my secret life.

Anyway, conspiracy made perfect sense to me, the notion that everybody else is at work while I am breaking into the house rummaging through drawers, which was a staple pastime of my childhood, going through my parent's closet and drawers and finding things out about them. It was where I lived. The south Asia part was the weird part.

Bigsby: Most parents probably are not very keen if their son suddenly says I am going to be a writer.

Franzen: My mother was relentlessly discouraging, relentlessly critical, although to her credit, after the first book was published, she said you were right and I was wrong. She had one note and the note was that there are millions of aspiring writers, so what makes you think you can do it. It is wonderful as an avocation but you need a job. My dad was benignly sceptical. He actually trusted me, I think, in some fundamental way, probably inappropriately. Anyway he was disappointed with the second novel because it had tampons in it. Really that pretty much disqualified the entire enterprise.

Bigsby: After the first two novels, 1988 and 1992, there was going to be a nine-year gap before your next one. Can you explain something about what was going on?

Franzen: I was writing the book which came out after *The Corrections*, which was non-fiction, just to support myself. My dad was dying, my marriage was ending, I was running out of money and going into debt. I was trying to quit cigarettes. Then I listened to some new music and felt alive again and decided to try to write this three thousand page novel and tell everything I knew about the world and couldn't do it because there wasn't a bit of emotion in it. So I got a lot younger, I got much, much younger. I had been a functioning sixty-year-old throughout my twenties.

Bigsby: So you were reconstructing yourself in that period?

Franzen: It's complicated, and possibly more autobiographical than I care to be in a live format. I got married when I had just turned twenty-three. All I can say over and over again is I was this sixty-five-year-old and my mum was still alive. My dad had gone through this terrible illness and had died and I felt liberated by that. He had been sick for so long and had not wanted to be alive himself for much of the last several years. When I say to my surprise, here tonight, that it made my decade that my dad liked my first book, that is some indication of what the implications might be when that person finally goes. His approval is now mute, and he was a very controlled person and very terrified of emotion himself. Something so psychological I am just sinking into my seat.

Part II – 6th October 2010

Bigsby: Given the success of your new novel *Freedom* you must have come across the Atlantic on a high but England has done its best to bring you down, from the man who at your book launch snatched your spectacles and ran off, demanding a hundred thousand dollars ransom, to the rather more disturbing moment when you began reading for a television review programme only to discover that it was not actually the final version you were reading from. As a result your publishers have pulped eighty thousand copies.

Franzen: Yes, the first galleys which were made up from the manuscript.

Bigsby: Was it simply a matter of typos and spellings or was there something more fundamentally different between the two versions?

Franzen: Well, you know what its like. You get the galleys back and see all those things you haven't seen before so you change lots of sentences and take out the worst sentences. You fix the infelicities. I changed the shadings of a couple of characters, took a tone of stridency off one of them that I felt was too pronounced. You do those things for a reason.

Bigsby: Do you ever sense, when you are reading your work to an audience for the first time that, now you hear it aloud, there is a word, or phrase, that maybe shouldn't be there or should have been different?

Franzen: Yes, and I am having it with this book because this book was not read aloud from except for the first chapter while I was writing it and that was different from *The Corrections* which was dragged out over so many years that I ended up reading many different parts of it before it was published. As a result I cut a lot and changed a lot based on those out-loud readings.

Bigsby: When you were writing *The Corrections* there came a moment when you changed direction. Was that at all true of *Freedom*? What was its gestation?

Franzen: I knew enough with *Freedom* not to write hundreds of pages with something that wasn't working because those all got thrown away with *The Corrections* which was pretty much ninety per cent of the chunk I had written. So I was at pains not to repeat that. The false starts never went more than twenty pages at most before not getting pursued. You can't speak in terms of a change of direction because I just wouldn't have got far enough into it to have a direction.

Bigsby: Is it possible to say how long it took to write the book?

Franzen: I had about twenty pages on November 1st of 2008 and I finished it in December 2009, so thirteen months basically.

Bigsby: You have said that the book really began when you heard the voice of Patty?

Franzen: Yes and no. I had the voice of Patty seven years before I had anything else. It just languished in a drawer. I knew I had it there and I just didn't know what to do with it.

Bigsby: Is it right that it is female characters who have led you into your books?

Franzen: Often, yes, because they are easy.

Bigsby: Why?

Franzen: I perceive the world in somewhat gender terms. I walk around thinking about myself as male not female so to write about a female character is a quick way to be sure that I am not writing about myself. Writing about myself is what I cannot do directly. It will always shut me down.

Bigsby: Although you have said that this is the most autobiographical of your books. In what way?

Franzen: In the sense that the stuff that I have lost the most sleep over and that I am still tormented by, that I am most afraid of, most ashamed of, those are the stories I was determined to get into the book. It is not particular things that happened. It is the intense set of feelings I have, a suite of feelings I have in relation to certain large looming psychological objects in my head, like mom, my ex-wife.

Bigsby: There is a tension, in the book, between the figure of Joey and his mother, as there was an enormous tension between you and your mother. You said at one stage that you found it hard to be in the same room as her.

Franzen: Certainly three days was a lot of time during those years to spend with her though I was able to be in the same room as her once I got past say fifteen.

Bigsby: So are there aspects of you in Joey in terms of that relationship?

Franzen: Yes, but I couldn't get at any of that until it had all been translated into modern times and I had managed to establish a kid like Joey who is radically unlike me. He was unlike me politically, in his ease in the world and his good business sense. All these things are completely unlike me, right down to the intensity of his relationship with Connie in high school. It is all very unlike me, and it had to be unlike me. There was no hope of putting anything of myself in.

Bigsby: You referred to your wife. The relevance of that to the book seems to me to be that one of the things you are exploring under the name of *Freedom* is competition.

Franzen: Thank you for picking it out. I felt like I was flagging it with fluorescent markers but I don't think that in my entire tour and pre-publicity in the U.S. anyone came up with that once. No one ever asked me about it and I would think, 'Didn't you notice this?' People don't like talking about competition in the U.S. precisely because it is the elephant, or one of the elephants, in the room.

Bigsby: In terms of your own life you were married to a fellow writer and you became successful and she didn't. There was a kind of competition between you. You said something interesting in an interview which rang a bell with me. Arthur Miller's first marriage was breaking up and he went to an analyst, a therapist, and he explained to him that his marriage could be saved if he stopped writing.

Franzen: I didn't even go to a therapist but I came to the same conclusion, and I did substantially stop writing. I stopped trying to write fiction for a couple of years just to allow things to get back into some sort of balance.

Bigsby: But haven't you married another writer?

Franzen: Yes, I have.

Bigsby: This is a shrewd move?

Franzen: It is nice to enter into a relationship when you are forty rather than twenty-one. No formal pre-nuptial or pre-involvement document to sign, but there is a lot of vetting that occurs. You know the questions to ask when you are forty and you know the warning signs to look for. When you are twenty-one all the warning signs look incredibly attractive, wonderful. They are not warning signs. They are bait.

Bigsby: Can I come back for a second to Patty's voice because having said that it was important, and that you got it early on, there is an odd way in which the reader doesn't hear Patty's voice in *Freedom* because her therapist asks her to write an autobiographical account of herself which she does in the third person.

Franzen: So we are told, although the therapist is never really mentioned except in the title of the autobiography.

Bigsby: You mean I should distrust that?

Franzen: I am not sure distrust. That might be a strong word but I would just point out that we have really no objective verification except in the document. I should also just like to reassure anyone who hasn't read the book there is no therapist appearing in the book.

Bigsby: That section of the novel, despite being presented as an autobiographical account written by Patty, is not told in the first person. Later, there is another autobiographical section in which she says that she had tried the first and second person but that they didn't work. Did you try the first and second person when you started that autobiographical section?

Franzen: No, actually not. The phrase that was in my head often was the title of a Rosellen Brown novel called *The Autobiography of My Mother*, so for some reason the voice came to me in the third person, along with the notion of a jock writing about herself in the third person. I don't know about English jocks, but we have plenty of them in the U.S. and it is a great thing, one of the really beautiful things that has happened in our country in the last thirty years. There was federal legislation passed that required universities and educational institutions of all kinds to spend equal money on women's athletics. It was pretty radical stuff and came out of the second wave of feminism and it really has transformed the culture significantly because you suddenly had these really, really good female athletes with great facilities to train in. I wasn't thinking of any of that when the voice first came to me. The voice popped into my head along with the idea that she had been a jock.

It has been pointed out that Patty writes awfully well for somebody who is a B student jock, a basketball player, but even Humbert Humbert writes well in *Lolita*, in fact writes like Nabokov at his very best. He seems like such an unimpressive person in many ways so how did it happen that he has the best prose of the twentieth century? You can call it gimmickry, if you like. You can call it a conceit. I prefer the word conceit.

Bigsby: And she was very competitive as well.

Franzen: When I got around to writing the book it was very useful that she was a very, very competitive person because we live in a system founded on competition. It is built into our economic system and yet nobody likes to talk about it

Bigsby: Because she writes in the third person she herself becomes a kind of novelist, creating characters and creating her own story.

Franzen: Well she comes from an artistic family, or at least she comes from a family that encouraged her.

Bigsby: She says she doesn't like the artistic world.

Franzen: She hates it. At one point she says she feels that she was unlucky in many ways with her parents but she is very, very grateful that they didn't encourage her in any artistic way, the way her parents did encourage her sister. So, needless to say, she is also competing with her sisters. I don't think I am doing too much interpretation. She more or less says as much in the opening paragraph of one of her chapters.

Bigsby: The book begins in Minnesota, which is where your father was brought up.

Franzen: Where my whole family is from. I was the only one in my family not born in Minnesota. My brothers were both born in St. Paul like the two kids in this book and my father, like the father in this book, was from northern Minnesota.

Bigsby: They seem almost a perfect couple at first, very conscious of the environment, good neighbours with a sense of community. They remind me of something Chekhov once said. He wanted to write a play about people having dinner and talking inconsequentially while underneath their feet a gulf is slowly opening. Their perfect world begins to crumble beneath their feet and they go east, to Washington D.C.

Franzen: Right. Patty is from the East originally where she doesn't have the most successful relationship with her parents. Harm befalls her in the East and she imagines she can go to the Mid West which, in the Eastern imagination, is this innocent place, and attempts to restore her lost innocence, have a family and do things right. She goes to all the soccer games that her mother didn't go to for her. She is involved and listens and is available in all the ways that her parents weren't. So that is her enterprise, and for a long time it seems to work, until it doesn't.

Bigsby: Philip Roth has said that the older he gets the more, in his reading, he is drawn to non-fiction rather than fiction. Do you feel similarly?

Franzen: That is one of many differences between Roth and me. I actually spend more and more time reading fiction. I read plenty of non-fiction, because I need to know about the world, and I do a fair amount of non-fictional work because as a journalist I need to, but I am thirsty for fiction. I am hungry for fiction. A lot of new stuff comes in my door and I don't like most of it. I don't think it is good and a lot of things I used to like don't work so much any more, but I just started re-reading *The Sound and the Fury* this summer, which I have managed not to have read since I was a kid, and it is really remarkable. I feel bad because I don't read more history yet it is so rare that you find a good history book rather than a good novel. There are hundreds of really, really, wonderful novels. I feel sort of childish and regressive needing to have stories told to me but I am a dewy-eyed communitarian when it comes to the community of fiction readers and writers. These are my people and that is the way I want to connect with them. I need it and Philip Roth doesn't.

Bigsby: How far do you regard yourself as a satirist?

Franzen: I stopped being interested in satire because there is something beyond humour and irony. You need some anger and you need some self-righteousness to write good satire and I seem to have misplaced most of the anger I was in full communication with just ten years ago. I also increasingly consider it my job to resist self-righteousness. The project of the book is to morally complicate things and if you complicate things morally past a certain point satire becomes very difficult. The satirist has very little personally at stake. I increasingly think that, for me, good fiction, both as a reader and as a producer of it, is about personal risk.

Bigsby: Did *Freedom* grow organically or did you already know where you were going when you started writing?

Franzen: No, I figured out the ending of this book the day before I wrote it. A good inspiration is the shower and the broad outlines of it were figured out on the fly. If I had the whole thing planned out in my head before I start writing it, it would not be a book worth writing, which gets back to the personal risk thing. If there is not some serious unknown that has to be negotiated it would just be a boring project.

Bigsby: You have taught creative writing. To what extent can it be taught?

Franzen: I have taught a little bit and some things can absolutely be taught. There is no question that if you gave me twelve students in two years I could make them better prose writers and I think I could maybe spare them some circuitous routes to an understanding of some of the basic issues that a fiction writer confronts, both technical things, like point of view and first person versus third person, and also more vital stuff about how you use your own life, how to think about your loyalty to people you might be writing about. These are all things I had to figure out. I didn't have any teachers to speak of and I probably could have saved myself some very miserable seasons of struggle and failure. I think there are risks associated with programmes like this, too. Certainly in the U.S. there is a kind of cookie cutter workshop style and any given programme will have an idea of what is cool and what is not cool to be doing. I think if you are good that can be invigorating, unless you happen to be doing the thing that is cool. If you are doing the thing that is cool and everybody is thinking that is the cool thing to do that is potentially damaging, but fighting against the thing everybody else thinks is cool can be a rewarding experience.

Bigsby: You once said that you liked to translate bits of your work into German to see if the humour worked. If I were to pick a language to see if the humour worked it wouldn't be German.

Franzen: It is the ultimate test.

In Conversation With David Guterson

- 13ᵗʰ October 2008 -

David Guterson was born in 1956, in Seattle, Washington. He is a graduate of the University of Washington. He was a school teacher for twelve years during which time he wrote short stories, his first collection of which, *The Country Ahead of Us, the Country Behind* was published in 1989. In 1994, his first novel, *Snow Falling on Cedars,* won the PEN/Faulkner Award. His subsequent novels are *The Drowned Son* (1996), *East of the Mountains* (1999), *Our Lady of the Forest* (2003) and *The Other* (2008).

Bigsby: Your writing career began with short stories.

Guterson: My first book was a collection of stories, *The Country Ahead of Us, the Country Behind* (1989). Then I wrote a collection of essays on family and education about home schooling: *Family Matters: Why Home Schooling Makes Sense* (1992). I was a public school teacher, an English teacher, for ten years and during that time I was home schooling, or I should say my wife was home schooling, our children. I wrote the home schooling book while I was teaching and also while I was working on my first novel, *Snow Falling on Cedars*. I put it aside for about eighteen months in order to write the home schooling book. The novel really felt like a hobby for about ten years. I could handle short stories. I could write some essays. I could do some freelance journalism. If I could find a half hour here and there I could add a page or two to this novel that is sitting in my drawer. It always felt that way to me, something that was happening in the background of other things that seemed more important and more prominent, and it was very much a book based on the historical conditions of my own community. I really had no great expectations for it and was as surprised as anybody when *Snow Falling on Cedars* became as popular as it was, and that is an experience for which I am very, very grateful.

Bigsby: The success of that novel must have come as a real shock.

Guterson: It is not often that a writer with a first novel has an experience of that sort and I would never wish it otherwise. On the other hand the three subsequent novels have all been published in the shadow of *Snow Falling on Cedars*. There is a way in which each subsequent novel is compared to it and for some critics they somehow come up a bit short. The truth is that the subsequent three novels have been very different from *Snow Falling on Cedars* and that is just something I can't help.

I really don't feel entirely that it is an act of volition when I go to write a book and while I might in a practical sense want to write *Sleet Falling on Fir Trees*, that is not really possible. I have to write the book that wells up inside me. The four novels are similar to one another in the sense that they are all set in Washington State, although in very different parts of Washington State, which is a very diverse place. I think there are other ways in which a person might see that they are related and written by the same author. Ultimately they share a world view, or a sensibility that can be located in the text of each, but they are quite different from one another.

I think my new novel, *The Other*, is again a departure from the preceding three, and maybe dramatically so in a couple of important ways. One is that it is the first novel I have written in the first person, and because of that it lends itself to the suspicion, on the part of readers, that it is perhaps more autobiographical than the others. It is quite easy to go from the first person narrator to the authorial biography, to make the assumption that the narrator is in many ways the author. In the case of this book there is some legitimacy in doing that because this is far more autobiographical, in a strict sense, than my other three novels.

The narrator of this book was born in 1956 in Seattle, as I was, attended Roosevelt High School in Seattle, as I did, and then went on to the University of Washington in Seattle, as I did. He becomes a high school English teacher who has a languishing novel in his desk drawer. In the case of this narrator he has more than one languishing novel because his career goes on for many, many years. By the time he is in a position to write this story, at age fifty, he has got quite a bit of what he considers to be failed prose behind him and has accepted his mediocrity as a writer. He doesn't feel mediocre as a teacher, though, and has a lot of satisfaction in his profession. So this is a man living a very ordinary and conventional life who has settled down in essentially the same neighbourhood that he grew up in and who marries young and has children and lives a very modest, quiet, middle class existence because essentially this is my story up until *Snow Falling on Cedars* when things began to change.

This narrator, whose name is Neil Countryman, comes from very blue-collared, modest, Irish American stock. He is the first person in his family to attend college. His father and uncles work in the trades and, at a track meet in 1972, when he is a sophomore, he meets a boy from very, very different circumstances, a boy named John William Berry whose ancestors, both maternal and paternal, come from wealth and status and go back to the pioneering families that founded Seattle. Since he is an only child a considerable amount of wealth has been brought to bear on him. He is also, like Neil, a child of the late sixties and early seventies and his sensibility is formed by that era. He has a considerable and deep critique of the social, political, cultural and economic conditions in which he finds himself, as many young people did at the time. Because of this he feels the necessity to turn his back on the world, to renounce it and his wealth, to renounce all comfort. He gradually withdraws into the woods, the deep rain forest of my part of the world, and decides to dwell in a cave alone as a monk might, as a hermit. The only person who knows about this is his best friend, Neil Countryman, who, out of loyalty and concern, shows up on a regular basis with supplies, but also to engage his friend in an ongoing dialogue about the pros and cons of what he is doing and try to talk him out of it. So here are two boys who share a world view when they are sixteen, seventeen, eighteen, but who then go on very, very different paths. One chooses a conventional life and the other becomes very eccentric and withdraws from society.

The book covers two lives from childhood onward, in the case of the narrator into mid life. Both of these boys, at the age of about eighteen, meet young women and make the attempt to involve themselves in romantic relationships. Neil is successful in that regard, meets somebody he loves, marries and settles down. But for John William it is simply impossible. There is a chapter early in this book in which you see him make the attempt in the most awkward and uncomfortable way, and that chapter is told from the point of view of the young woman who is the victim of his narcissistic efforts, his absorption in his own ego. This makes it impossible for him to see her for who she is, as anything but a reflection of himself, and she was not prepared to enter into any kind of long-term relationship with a person like that. So when this fails, and when she pushes him away, he is devastated and never makes the effort again.

This is one of the elements that drives him towards hermitry. Neil, the narrator, his mother having passed away when he was thirteen, is left a very modest life insurance so that at age eighteen he can take the standard young American's trip to Europe for a summer with a backpack. He does that and it is on this lonely adventure in Europe that he meets another American who is travelling with her sister doing the same thing. They meet in the Dolomites in Italy and this is where he really begins to take a very significant turn away from John William. Rather than sharing John William's world view he begins to share Jamie's world view and to seek out another life much like the life that most of us live, a conventional life with its modest forms of happiness.

Bigsby: You said that the fact that it is in the first person shouldn't lead us to believe that this is autobiographical. You then went on to explain the ways in which it was autobiographical. I wonder if it is autobiographical in another sense. There is a reference to a Robert Frost poem in the book – *The Road Not Taken* – and it is tempting to think that you, the teacher, who went on to have a fairly normal life (if we forget the four million copies of *Snow Falling on Cedars*) might have taken a different path, the path identified in *The Other*. Is there any truth in that?

Guterson: I talked earlier about the autobiographical element in this book. I failed to bring in a whole other dimension to that which is that ultimately both these characters, Neil, who has this very conventional life, and John William, who is very eccentric, are ultimately parts of myself. I think all of us find ourselves engaged in an inner dialogue in which we recognise a sense of schism, a sense of carrying around a double, even more than one other, myriad contained personalities, a doppelganger, a shadow, a projection, an Other, as this book is called. And this other, this inner other, represents not only a path not taken, but a path that we carry without ever really actualising. So as much as the autobiographical facts in this book adhere to the narrator, the inner life of these two characters are part of my own inner life. In me is this other voice, always questioning the way I live and wondering if there isn't some other more appropriate path that is more in accord with who I am.

Bigsby: John Fowles used to talk about the writing process and said that for him it was like two gardens, the wild garden and the domestic garden. The wild garden was the garden of a free imagination that could take you anywhere, do anything, while the domestic garden was the control that you then had to impose on what could be the anarchy of the imagination. Do you think there is any sense in which that also applies to you?

Guterson: I think Fowles was articulating a principle about balance that is appropriate across the board in elements of fiction. You are always balancing. In the creation of character you are looking inward at those elements in yourself that are universal, and with the assurance that because love and death, family, friendship etc. are important to you they certainly are important to everybody else in the world, and you can count on that. But at the same time that you are working from a spirit of universalism about human beings you have to balance that with the opposite perspective which is that everybody is very, very different and ultimately you can't know somebody else, and you have to respect, honour and investigate that difference. So in the creation of character you are balancing the universal and the specific.

Fowles is bringing that same principle of balance to bear on something else and I believe he is right. There are two sides to the brain. The wild side, the imagination, must be given full force. It must not be tempered. It must not in any way be judged. It needs the opportunity to manifest itself when you are working. But the other side of the brain, the controlling force, organising force, rational force, also needs to be a player in balance with that other side. They are both necessary and, going back to Frost, he worked in rhyme most often and when asked about it he would say, 'I like the sensation of moving easy in harness,' so the rhyme was as if you were a horse pulling a wagon. You would move easy, but in harness. If you don't have the harness of rhyme, as far as Frost in concerned, you are floating freely. There are no borders. There are no boundaries. But if things are too rigid then there is no free rein. I find that balance operative in all aspects of fiction writing for me.

Bigsby: Before letting go of the autobiographical element, did you take any paces down that other road, the road that you did not take?

Guterson: John William is a hermit, who has renounced the world and completely turned his back on other human beings. In one way I feel that I take a step in that direction every day when I wake up at four thirty and am wide awake and energetic and have only one thing I want to do, which is to be by myself, living in my own head with the door to my study shut. There is something quite hermetic about that. There is a hermetic impulse in the writer. My brother often questions how I can spend so much time alone. He says he is not built for it, that he likes to go to work every day to be with other people. He enjoys the social life. I am not anti-social but I do very much enjoy the solitude that is inherent in the act of writing, so to some extent that kind of hermitry, that withdrawal, is inherent in what I do. On the other hand writing is the ultimate way to engage people. It is an act of communication. So, again, balance, polar opposites working hand in hand.

Bigsby: In reading *The Other* another literary figure came to mind, Herman Melville's Bartleby, a man who responds to everything by saying, 'I would prefer not to'. By the end of the story he negates himself out of life, that is to say he prefers not to go on living. On the one hand this can seem a celebration of that resistant self that is so strong that it can carry to an ultimate point. On the other hand, it is a denial of all sociality, a denial of what Melville used to call the joint stock company that is society. I felt that tension here, because John William Berry is not just a madman who withdraws and destroys himself. There is also something slightly magnificent about the act of turning your back not exactly on a mundane reality, but on daily life and progress as we define it in society.

Guterson: I also hear the voice of Bartleby but I think we all relate inwardly. There is some aspect of ourselves which feels that defiance of the world and there is a kind of heroism in it. In Bartleby there is something about the clerk who will not accept being a clerk, who nevertheless wants to embrace the fullness of his inner life and not be merely a clerk. There is also something existential about it, no matter what circumstances you find yourself in. You can be as absurd as you want to be, you can be as odd as you want to be, you can be yourself, no matter what is going on around you. The other element I see in Bartleby is that when we get to the end of the story we are a bit maddened by the fact that he remains just beyond our reach and forever a mystery. In other words we never quite understand why it is that he prefers not to. He just goes off, disappears out of the story, and the story comes to an end. I think that is accurate because another human being cannot be fully understood and in this story there is an ongoing motif that while the narrator is seeking to fully explain, in a sort of cause and effect way, what has made John William who he is, nevertheless the truth and clarity are always just slightly beyond reach and there is ultimately no way to know with complete certainty why somebody becomes what they become.

Bigsby: Your parents were Jewish. Is that simply an autobiographical fact of no particular significance or was it part of your life?

Guterson: My parents came from immigrant families who for the most part abandoned practice and theology and wanted themselves and their children to completely assimilate and participate in the life of Americans. My parents also grew up in the Jewish community, and with liberal Jewish reformed friends. Naturally the next generation, myself and my four siblings, were turned loose to participate in a much larger way in the society of public schools and friends who were not Jewish. The interesting thing for me was that my two older siblings grew up to be very, very orthodox Jews and myself and my two younger siblings not at all. Now why is that the case? Historically, I could say my older brother and sister were more influenced by counter-culturalism, that is because they were children in the sixties more profoundly than I was, or than my younger sister and younger brother were, they wanted to find a permanent counter-culture and lo and behold they found one in their own heritage. So they turned their backs on society by saying, 'No, I am not a modern person. I am this.' You see them, and you see Orthodox Jews dressed the way they are, outside the mainstream. It almost looks like an act of defiance of modernity, just in their appearance and what they choose to do, the rituals they choose to enact in their lives. They have chosen a form of renunciation of modernity. Why that stopped with me and my two younger siblings, why we didn't see it the same way, raised in the same house under the same circumstances, is because they were slightly older than us and their historical conditions were slightly different from us.

Bigsby: Nonetheless, at the age of twelve to thirteen you did what most children of that age don't do. You read religious books.

Guterson: I have been reading religious books my whole life, reading about a great variety of spiritual traditions. My previous novel, *Our Lady of the Forest*, is about apparitions of the Virgin Mary and delves deeply into Catholicism, though there are Catholics who will tell me that I got it all wrong, and I may have.

Bigsby: I wonder if in abandoning formal religion you weren't left with a space, and that that space is filled with a fascination for spiritual meaning and people who reach out for some sort of spiritual meaning. One of the things that John William is concerned with is Gnosticism, which is a kind of secret spiritual key to the universe.

Guterson: What I appreciate in that comment is that I see I have been read closely because this is really the centre of what drives me as a writer, and I would say it is going to be this way for the rest of my writing life. Ultimately, my concerns are spiritual and whatever spiritual life I have I think finds its way into my work. John William is consciously aware of Gnosticism as the driving force behind his choices in life. There may be psychological reasons, and familial reasons and childhood reasons, political reasons, all kinds of other reasons that are being brought to bear, but, as far as he is concerned, Gnosticism is at the heart of it and Gnostics are mostly considered heretics by the mainstream Christian church and the Catholic church. They were burned at the stake and all their gospels were destroyed, I think because what they say sounds very, very dangerous. If you embrace it you are taking a view of the world that is anathema to the mainstream western view.

In the cosmology of the Gnostics God is malicious and evil. He got bored and created the planet and then created us and spends all of his time entertaining himself by making us suffer, making us die, doing awful things to us, making us kill each other, inventing the atom bomb, causing the Holocaust, disease. Whatever he can think of to torment us, he torments us with it. The question of evil is at the heart of philosophy. Why is there evil in the world? People say, 'Well the ways of God are mysterious to men.' The Gnostics say, 'No, no, no. We know where evil comes from. It comes from God. God is evil. Turn your back on God completely. Do not embrace this God Jehovah. Have nothing to do with him. Renounce the world. Renounce him and you will see past him to the truth. Gnosticism is knowledge.' Gnostics are people who have a secret knowledge that the truth is beyond God and understand that when you denounce and renounce God you can penetrate the truth and escape from the prison of this world in which he has bound you. If you have that perspective life becomes anguish and this is what happens to John William. The deeper question is why do you embrace that world view?

Bigsby: Your siblings have something you haven't. They have an absolute confidence. You don't but you are aware of the fact that there is a space there that needs to be filled.

Guterson: The space that needs to be filled for John William, and for Neil, is the missing mother, in that Neil's mother died when he was thirteen and John William's mother was largely absent. In Gnosticism Sophia, the goddess of wisdom, the true goddess of the universe, is what you are reaching towards. That is why I wrote the book about the Virgin Mary. The Catholic church tried to suppress the so-called feminine divine but it kept rearing up and saying, 'No,' because human beings ultimately know that the divine has much to do with the feminine. You can't have a Trinity that doesn't include the feminine. It is absurd. Gradually over the years the will of the people wore down the church and the Virgin Mary was given larger status. So what is the empty space that needs to be filled? For me, as well as in this piece, the missing mother.

Bigsby: The other thing that strikes me is that powerful tradition in America, especially in the nineteenth century, of defining yourself against the natural world, looking for an identity. That notion, in Cooper, Melville, Twain, of pitting the self against the natural world as a way of finding who you are seems to me strong in your novel.

Guterson: It is the American story and it makes complete sense when you think about the geographic and pastoral conditions of the continent. You have these people coming over from Europe and landing on the seaboard. Why have they come? To redefine themselves, to reinvent themselves, and as they begin to settle the seaboard and look westward what did they see? They saw this dark and troubling forest at their back which is what I worked with, the haunted forest. What is out there, we don't know. There are dangers but there is also promise. There is also something to be discovered. And so the more restless among them began to penetrate and move westward, and this was ceaseless, ceaseless investigation and movement into the unknown until the people who settled the west were the most strongly committed to penetrating the unknown because, going back to the Greeks and Romans, the open unknown landscape is the landscape of the self. So you can feel as if what you are doing in moving westward into the mountains and forests is moving into the arena of life in which a deeper investigation of the self is being played out. The people who moved westward had this inner restlessness not simply to discover a new place. They were concerned with discovery itself. They may not have known it but they were inventing themselves and were restless in that way.

Bigsby: For Thoreau the natural world was not only a resource, it was a metaphor, and that is strong in American writing. You are an American, but you also seem to be very much from the northwest. You are Washington, Oregon, Northern California. Your attitude to the forests, to the woods, is reminiscent of Ursula Le Guin. There is a sense of there being something powerful, restorative, a context into which you want to insert yourself. And don't you do precisely that, going for walks and tramps through that wildness.

Guterson: I have, for most of my life, spent a considerable time in the mountains and out of doors. It is part of who I am. You use the word restorative. I see that that is how Thoreau might have viewed it. That is very Emersonian, that somehow there is redemption in nature. This is different in this book and it is different in *Our Lady in the Forest*. It goes back to Gnosticism. There is this American tradition of the romantic and the transcendental but there is another tradition of hermits, the desert fathers of Christian tradition, or the monks of Buddhist faith, who go to the woods for a different reason. They don't go in the romantic vein, in the transcendental vein. They go for a different reason and John William, I think, is more in that tradition.

In Conversation With Christopher Hampton

- 30th October 2005 -

Christopher Hampton was born in the Azores in 1946 but spent his early years in Egypt. His first play, *When Did You Last See My Mother?* was staged in 1966, making him the youngest playwright to debut in the West End. He followed this with *Total Eclipse* (1968), a work which featured the relationship between Rimbaud and Verlaine. *The Philanthropist* (1970), an ironic comedy, followed. Along with original plays – *Savages* (1974), *Treats* (1976), *Tales from Hollywood* (1989), *White Chameleon* (1991) and *The Talking Cure* (2002) – he has translated a number of works, most significantly *Les Liaisons Dangereuses* (1989), subsequently made into a successful film, and wrote the lyrics for *Sunset Boulevard*. He also wrote and directed *Carrington* (1995) and *Imagining Argentina* (2003) and is the author of the screenplay for Ian McEwan's *Atonement* (2007). Among his many awards are an Oscar, a BAFTA, a Laurence Olivier Award, a Tony, a Writers' Guild Award and a New York Drama Critics' Circle Award.

Bigsby: You were born in the Azores and then you were a number of years in Egypt. That was because your father had a job there?

Hampton: He worked for a company called Cable and Wireless. He was a radio engineer. It was a bit like being in the army because you got sent around the world for periods of time. But his favourite place was Egypt. Every two or three years he would come back to England and he would have to go up to head office to be told where he was going next, but he would always hope it would be Egypt and for a long period, in the first half of the fifties, it was. So, between the ages of five and ten I lived in Alexandria, which was then, and still is, a beautiful city but it was then very cosmopolitan and a nice place to be brought up, at least in retrospect. I think we all sentimentalise our childhood to a certain extent but it was a wonderful country to be brought up in.

I went to a school called The British Boys School. They were big classes. There were, I think, thirty in my class, none of whom were British except for me. One of the things we were taught was drama. We had two periods a week and were supposed to start writing plays when we were eight. A genial cove, an Englishman who was founder and chief director of Alexandria's Gilbert and Sullivan society, was very interested in the drama and so it was stimulating in all kinds of ways. It was also interesting to move around with a group of boys who could all speak five languages. Because it was such a cosmopolitan city every child could speak English, Arabic, Greek, Italian and French. The only problem for them was remembering which language they were talking in so people would slip from one language to another as they spoke, which was very interesting.

Bigsby: Was it then that you came across Ibsen?

Hampton: Yes. The first play I ever saw was a school play, Ibsen's *An Enemy of the People*. You wouldn't think it would be conspicuously enjoyable for an eight year old but I liked it very much indeed. I was particularly interested in a man wearing heavy makeup and a boiler suit sitting next to me, so I kept glancing at him and in Act 4 he suddenly sprang to his feet and shouted, because in Act 4 the audience joins in and criticises Dr. Stockmann as he stands there trying to defend his position. That was very, very exciting, people popping up all around the auditorium yelling at the stage. Anyway, the whole idea of theatre seemed interesting, even to a child who had never actually been to a proper theatre.

Bigsby: And decades later you adapted *An Enemy of the People*?

Hampton: Yes, I did for the National Theatre. It was Trevor Nunn's first production when he went to take over a few years ago. I decided to swear off Ibsen but when he asked me to do *An Enemy of the People* I found I wasn't able to resist.

Bigsby: Also many years later you wrote a play called *White Chameleon*, which is about your time in Egypt, in which you make a double appearance, as a young boy and then as an older person. Why at that moment did you decide to revisit your Egyptian experiences?

Hampton: All these things have slightly unexpected origins. In the case of *White Chameleon*, at the beginning of the nineties Richard Eyre, who had just taken over the National Theatre, decided that it would be very good, it being the thirty-fifth anniversary of the Suez invasion and the Hungarian uprising, to do two plays on these subjects. So he asked David Hare to do the Hungarian uprising and me to do the Suez crisis, because he knew about my background. David went to Hungary and did some research, thought about it a bit and then decided the subject was not for him. He couldn't work a way into it. I thought about it and went back to

Richard and said, 'I don't want to write about the Suez invasion. I want to write about me.'

I had never written an autobiographical piece before and as I was reflecting on being in Egypt at that time it suddenly seemed to me that a lot of my preoccupations, and a lot of my predilections as a writer, dated from that period. He very sportingly said, 'Okay, then we will do it in the Cottesloe and not in the Olivier,' and allowed me to revisit my past which was a very therapeutic thing at the time for me to do. The play, although it has not been done much and just ran for that period of time at the Cottesloe, was one of the most meaningful experiences that I had ever had in the theatre.

Bigsby: You were on the last boat out during the Suez invasion, just before the bombs started falling?

Hampton: We had been evacuated in 1952 when King Farouk was ejected from the country. It was thought that all hell would break loose. We had only just arrived but all the British were sent back to England and sat there for six months and then, rather sheepishly, came back again. Then we decided that this was just another storm in a teacup and kept ignoring the fact that they were telling us to leave until it became obvious that something dodgy was going to happen. Eventually, my mother and my older brother and I took a train to Suez, but the only ship we could get was an Australian liner which was passing by. They were somehow radioed and asked to stop and we got on a launch and went out and climbed up the gangplank.

My father remained in Alexandria all through the period of the invasion. His office, which was a communication centre for Cable and Wireless, was bombed by the RAF, or at least it was targeted by the RAF, but unfortunately they missed and demolished the Presbyterian church next door killing several, including the verger who was eighty. My father, who was not a man who reflected a great deal on politics and was a sort of natural unthinking Conservative, was very much transformed by the fact that the British government had launched this entirely unjustified attack. They had bombed his office and he was kept under house arrest with an armed guard at the front door, a very affable armed guard who at a certain point pointed out to my father that if he wanted to leave the back door was always available.

Bigsby: Then you arrived in England. Apart from that brief visit six months earlier, that must have been a bit of a shock after the idyllic life you had had in Egypt? You came back to a country that presumably you really didn't know too much about?

Hampton: No, I had hardly been here really, and it was very cold. I went to a prep school in Reigate, which had literally been picked out of some directory by my father with a pin, and I suppose the unwise thing I did was to repeat a number of things that my father had said about the British. Within seconds I was hauled up in front of the headmaster and told that this was very unpatriotic and that some of the boys had people whose fathers or cousins or uncles were serving in the forces and this was bad for morale and that I must keep my mouth shut. It was an interesting thing to happen to you when you were ten.

Bigsby: And then it was on to Lancing school, from which you got expelled?

Hampton: I think that is a little bit of an exaggeration. I took my exams for university and got into Oxford and I had been rather looking forward to the fact that there would then be a couple of terms when I wouldn't have to work so hard. I could put on plays and do all the things that I enjoyed doing. Then I was called up by my housemaster. I thought he was going to make me a prefect but in fact in the course of the conversation it became clear that he was asking me to leave the school, which I did. In fact I have seen him since and he maintains he could see that it would be much better for me to leave the school and go out into the world, but it was a little bit inconvenient because my father by that time was working in Zanzibar. He had a penchant for this. There had just been an enormous bloody revolution and the country was incommunicado so I somehow found myself, as it were, not quite knowing where to go.

Bigsby: You had some interesting contemporaries while you were still at Lancing, didn't you?

Hampton: David Hare was at Lancing as was Tim Rice. There were a lot of people who became musicians and artists of one kind or another, so I think it was fair to say that the school was very encouraging in that.

Bigsby: And somewhere in there you wrote a novel?

Hampton: Yes. That is what I did when I was expelled. I thought, I don't know what to do now so I will go to Paris and finish my novel. So I took a job in a factory. I was completely incompetent and they fired me in the end. It was lifting tubes and stacking them and it was very, very difficult, much too demanding for me. My coordination is not very good. Anyway, I earned the requisite thirty quid, or whatever it was, and went to Paris where I holed up for a month and finished this novel.

Bigsby: It was about someone who went to a public school?

Hampton: Yes, it was the usual first novel.

Bigsby: But you also wrote a play in a pub?

Hampton: After I had finished my novel I came back from Paris. There was a bit of a difficulty in Paris because I ran out of money and had to do menial jobs in order to be able to afford to come back to London. There was a marvellous placed called Les Halles where you could go and stand on the pavement and get hired to unload lorries all night. So, by that means I managed to come back to London where I got an incredibly boring job with City and Guilds of London wrapping up exam papers and sending them off to various schools, but in the evenings I started to write this play called *When Did You Last See My Mother?* I wrote it in the pub because it was quieter than the flat I was sharing with my brother and five Australians.

Bigsby: So when you got to Oxford you had already written a play?

Hampton: I had a play, but I had no idea what you did with it. The novel I understood. I had sent the novel to every publisher in London and they had all rejected it, so I understood that process, but I didn't know what you did with a play. It sat in a drawer for eighteen months until it was announced that the Oxford University Dramatic Society was going to do two plays by undergraduates. So I typed it out – I hadn't even typed it out – and handed it in and went away for the vacation. I came back the first week of the next vacation and there was a meeting which I went to and discovered, to my horror, that they hadn't chosen my play. They had chosen two other plays, but one of them proved to be too expensive for them to put on. My play had one set and five characters. About two or three weeks into the term this chap David Jessel, who works for the BBC now and who was secretary of OUDS, came and banged on my door and said, 'Can you get it on in three weeks?' So we did, and we got a very good review in *The Guardian*. I don't know if *The Guardian* is conscientious enough to cover plays by undergraduates these days, but it did then.

Bigsby: And that was followed by another play, *Total Eclipse*, about two writers, Rimbaud and Verlaine, two very different kinds of writers. Rimbaud believed he could change the world through writing and at the age of twenty-one decided he couldn't so stopped writing.

Hampton: I think he stopped at nineteen actually. It is hard to establish since the documentation is not very exact, but he stopped around that time. He just gave up. Sod this, he thought, and went off to make some money, which he also failed to do.

Bigsby: While Verlaine was a professional writer who soldiered on. I remember you once said that when you started writing that play you were drawn to Rimbaud but by the end you were drawn to Verlaine.

Hampton: Absolutely true. I think I wrote the play when I was twenty-one, so I was exactly half way between the ages of Rimbaud, who was sixteen, and Verlaine, who was twenty-six when they met. Initially I had been attracted by the uncompromising nature of Rimbaud's quest, his complete fierceness and his revolutionary desire to change everything, and of course less attracted by this weak snivelling boulevard poet he had shacked up with on his way. The more I worked on it, though, the more I felt drawn to Verlaine, who was a hopeless human being but as a writer decided he was in it for the long haul. And he did write a poem a day for the rest of his life, eventually by necessity because by the end of his life he was in abject poverty. He used to write a poem every morning and go to his publisher who would give him five francs for it. But at least he kept going whereas Rimbaud decided he wanted his writing to do something – i.e. to change the world – and realised quite quickly that it wouldn't and gave it up.

That is admirable in its own way, except what he didn't realise was that his writing did change the world, but not in quite the way he had anticipated. It changed the world because he was the first modern artist in the sense of all those artists who followed in the early part of the twentieth century and who derived something from him. So he had changed the artistic landscape by these few poems he wrote in a frenzy when he was sixteen or seventeen. It is a very interesting story. You can see why it attracted me and it is a play that I have kept going back to and have had various cracks at and done in various versions ever since.

Bigsby: Is there a sense in which there is a little of those two writers in you? I don't mean the snivelling bit, I mean the notion of art transforming things and the professional writer who is writing sometimes commissioned pieces. In *Savages*, you wrote a play in part about the plight of the Indian and the poor in Brazil. *Bright and Shining* is a film about Vietnam. *Imagining Argentina* is about the disappeared in Argentina. Is that still part of you, that feeling that art should go out there and do something in the world?

Hampton: I don't think that it can necessarily change specific situations. It is very rarely that something like the television play *Cathy Come Home* can actually bring about a change in the law of some kind. I just think there are these subjects that engage one politically, or make one feel strongly in one way or another, and you can prolong the debate or you can heighten awareness or you can do one of those minor but useful tasks. I think there has always been a strand of work that has not been as well known as other work that I have done, partly because it is very difficult to get people to fund these projects. I wrote a film for the BBC about the war in Sri Lanka in 1984, just as it was beginning. I went to Sri Lanka and spent some time there and visited both sides and got together a plot which turned out to be not unlike the plot of *The Constant Gardener*, I discovered, when I saw that the other day. I put together a film based on that and we could never get it funded or made and that was my main piece of work in 1984, i.e. that took the first nine months of 1984. The remainder of 1984 I adapted *Les Liaisons Dangereuses*, which did rather better in terms of reaching an audience. It is disproportionate, the attention that goes towards certain parts of one's output compared to other parts.

Bigsby: I am going to come on to film in a second but I have one more question about a play because the next one was *The Philanthropist*, currently playing again in London. It is called a bourgeois comedy, and it is a comedy, yet outside the window terrible things are happening, most of the cabinet are being wiped out. Some of the reviewers have gone back to that play and said they now see it as a different play, not quite the play they remember. The emphasis, they suggest, somehow has shifted. Do you find it any different?

Hampton: No, I don't. It is just that people have noticed different things this time. On the whole it was well received the first time, and it has been even better received now because I think it has settled. It is easy to understand now. I don't think any of the reviews mentioned those satirical/political references at the time of the first production. It is as if those bits of the play hadn't happened because they were focusing on something else, and that is quite interesting. It is very, very, interesting to have your plays revived, I must say, because you can see all sorts of things yourself in them that you didn't necessarily see at the time you wrote them, some things that you approve of and some things you disapprove of. It is a very interesting exercise to watch an old play. What you always hope is that the play will not be dated. *The Philanthropist* is very much of its time. You couldn't really update it, I don't think. It is very much late sixties. It is the kind of thing people were talking about in the late sixties. But it doesn't seem to have dated, which is very gratifying.

Bigsby: You were also writing for television at this time, and I'm thinking particularly of your adaptation of Malcolm Bradbury's *The History Man*, which, despite its success, didn't go down well with absolutely everybody.

Hampton: No, I think Mrs. Whitehouse [a campaigner dedicated to 'cleaning up' television] foamed at the mouth. At that time I had two small children and was living in a village in Oxfordshire and I went into the Post Office after the second episode and there was this big chill in the air. I spoke to some neighbours about it afterwards and they said, 'Oh, yes. They were discussing whether or not they would serve you.' So it certainly ruffled some feathers. I should say that it was much the most enjoyable piece of work that I ever did for television and worked out much the best. It was a wonderful piece of television, especially given the fact that we made it in I think twenty-one days of shooting and a couple of weeks in the studio. It was very quickly made but it just hit the target it was aiming at, I thought, rather accurately. I have very happy memories of it, although as far as I know it has never been repeated by the BBC or indeed put out on DVD or any of those nice things that they do. There was a huge sense of energy in Birmingham which is where we filmed it, at Pebble Mill. It was the very first production of a producer called Michael Wearing who went on to great things afterwards and it was at a time when the drama departments of both the BBC and Granada, for example, were absolutely fizzing with interesting stuff. The book is a masterpiece and the television wasn't half bad.

Bigsby: The principal actor in that was Antony Sher, who is one of those wonderfully edgy actors. You have come across a couple of others, Alan Rickman, for example, and John Malkovich.

Hampton: I like actors who are dangerous, who have an air of danger. Jonathan Price was another. In fact, the first actor I worked with, the actor who was in my first play *When Did You Last See My Mother*, and then played Rimbaud in *Total Eclipse*, was an actor called Victor Henry who was terrifying, terrifying. There was a scene where he was supposed to beat Verlaine up and if he didn't like the way the other actor was acting that evening he really would punch him. I once went into the pub next door to the Royal Court because they were worried about him. He would go on benders and he was sitting a hundred yards from the theatre on a bender, so I was despatched to see what I could do. I said to him, rather feebly, 'Victor, I don't believe you have eaten anything for a couple of days have you?' He said, 'You're quite right.' He picked up his glass and bit a piece out of it, crunch, blood running down his front. So he was quite dangerous. I am afraid, in a ghastly irony, he was killed before he was thirty by an alcoholic hit-and-run driver, but he certainly contributed a great deal to the success of my first couple of plays. I have always thought that danger is the rarest quality on stage and when you see it, it is like gold. It just energises the whole theatre or the whole room.

Bigsby: I remember we met in a bar in a theatre when *Les Liaison Dangereuses* was transferring to the West End and I asked how Alan Rickman was doing and you said, 'I don't know. I am waiting to find out.'

Hampton: Yes, he certainly liked to ring the changes, and he is a much calmer, milder man than Victor. He is more brooding than violent so you never quite know what he is going to do, but he is always interesting.

Bigsby: For a while you were making good money by writing films that weren't made.

Hampton: Yes, there are many, many writers in this country, and certainly more in America, who make extremely good livings by remaining invisible. Sometimes I think it is a way of keeping these people quiet by paying them enormous sums of money to write films that are then not made. The films are often not made because they are thought to be un-commercial or disturbing or difficult in one way or another. And so it is a very good way of keeping all that stuff away from the public.

Bigsby: What is the unmade film that you most regret?

Hampton: I think I most regret *A Bright Shining Lie*, because I spent about two years on it. It was a magnificent book about Vietnam, about a

265

man called John Paul Vann who went to do his tour of duty in Vietnam as an officer and got very interested in the Vietnamese, which was a rarity among Americans who, not uncharacteristically, and it is still going on, were quite happy to invade countries but were not so happy to work out what those countries might be thinking, what the people might be like or what the people might be interested in. Anyway, this man found that he loved the Vietnamese and when he finished his tour of duty and went back to America kept thinking about Vietnam. He went back as a member of the Peace Corps, staying in Vietnam for ten years. At the end of this his expertise was recognised by the American government and they started involving him in the war again. He was so pleased to be recognised that he colluded with them. They made him a General. He was the first civilian General ever to lead an army in battle in American history, and he went completely bonkers. In a way it is the American equivalent of Lawrence of Arabia, i.e. it is a story about a man who understands a people, falls in love with them in a sexual way, as Lawrence did, as well as in every other way, and then betrays them because he can't help being who he is and where he comes from.

In that sense it was a classic story and it was chosen by this man Neil Sheehan, who was the man responsible for the release of the Pentagon papers, as *the* representative story of the Vietnamese war, and he spent sixteen years writing the book. I spent a couple of years writing the screenplay with a young director who at the very last moment was replaced by Oliver Stone who became discouraged because his then current film, *Heaven and Earth*, which is about Vietnam, came out and did nothing at the box office. So he decided that Vietnam was over and decided not to make this film. So it wasn't made and it is a great source of regret to me, but several of them are.

Bigsby: What is the pleasure to you of writing for the cinema when sometimes they don't get made or you suddenly discover that you are not on the credits or have been replaced? In the theatre the writer is the central figure, in the film world not always so.

Hampton: My affliction is that I really love films. Logically, you would stay out of it altogether. A lot of people assume that you might write films because you earn more but by a strange chance, in my particular career, I have always earned more from the theatre than anything else, I suppose because the plays go into the repertoire and they keep being done. The only reason I spend so much time and energy writing films is that I like it and the satisfaction it gives. When a film emerges out of the other end as you wanted it – it doesn't happen very often, but it happened with *Dangerous Liaisons*, it happened with *Carrington* – then the satisfaction is absolutely enormous because you have had to fight all those battles to get there, whereas theatre is wonderfully civilised. You write a play, give it in, and if they like it they put it on. They consult you on casting and they are very deferential to you. They try and do the play pretty much as you wrote it. I find writing plays incredibly difficult and they take me a very long time and they are technically very difficult. I find writing movies comes rather more easily.

Bigsby: You say plays take you a long time but some of your films have taken decades.

Hampton: Well, that is a different thing. *Carrington* took seventeen years from the time it was first written to the time it reached the screen. *Imagining Argentina* took fourteen years but that is just because you are fighting all the time to try and find the money to make them. The actual process of writing a film comes more naturally to me than writing for the theatre. I certainly like working in the theatre much more than the process I have just described. The theatre is so much more pleasant than all the battles involved in getting films off the ground.

Bigsby: There was a curious aspect to *Les Liaison Dangereuses* in that you found yourself in a race to produce it?

Hampton: Yes. We signed a contract guaranteeing that our film would be out first. There was a very odd series of circumstances. I was invited to dinner with Milos Forman, who I knew had seen the play several times and was interested in making a film of it. I went to this restaurant in London and he wasn't there. I sat there all evening and he didn't turn up, so I thought, film directors, what can you do. I went home and two or three months later I read in the paper that he had announced that he was going to make a film based on *Les Liaison Dangereuses*, which was very galvanising.

I had been engaged in a dispute with the Royal Shakespeare Company, a rather arcane dispute, which, made simple, was that they wanted me to sell the film rights to the highest bidder, because they participated in the film right, and I wanted to sell the film rights to the people who would allow me to make the film that I wanted to make, which was obviously going to secure not such a handsome sum. So they had the right to impede me and they were exercising this right. The one thing that this announcement of Milos's meant was that I rang up the Royal Shakespeare Company and said, 'Okay, fine go, go, go.' So we sold the rights to a company called Lorimar and then, after that, this film should never, never have been made. It was a total miracle and aberration that it was made.

I had it in mind to make this film directed by Stephen Frears. Stephen Frears at that point had not made any large scale films. He had made *My Beautiful Launderette*. He had done a tremendous amount of wonderful work on television, but he was not the director that any American company wished to hire to direct *Les Liaison Dangereuses*. So my script went to every fancy director you could think of, and they all turned it down. They turned it down for a very simple reason, because they knew Milos Forman, this six hundred pound gorilla and a friend of theirs in many cases, was making a film. That meant that in the end the only thing they could do was to agree to have Stephen Frears because he was not concerned about Milos Forman.

The other amazing stroke of luck was that Lorimar was going bankrupt. I wish I had been there because there was a shareholders meeting at which the chairman said to the head of the film's division, 'You are out of your head. You have paid a lot of money to buy the rights of a play based on a book that is out of copyright and that is about to be made into a film by a man who has just won two Oscars on the trot. What are you thinking of?' Bernie Brillstein, who bought the rights, said, 'I know what I was doing.' And the chairman said, 'On top of it all the company is going bankrupt,' at which point Bernie said, 'Well, if the company is going bankrupt what the hell difference does it make whether we make this film or not?' Baffled by this logic, they went ahead and made it.

When I arrived in New York with Stephen Frears Bernie Brillstein took me aside and said, 'Is he going to ask for pay or play?' Now pay or play is the system whereby a director signs a contract and they have to pay him whether the film is made or not, and most American directors, when they sign up for a film, are pay or play. So, if Milos Forman signs a contract and the film doesn't get made he gets his five million dollars anyway. So the guy said to me, 'Does he know? Is he going to ask for pay or play?' I said, 'Not until he finds out what it is.' It was a very, very good meeting because he then said to Stephen, 'We are in a bit of a hurry with this movie. When can you start work?' And Stephen produced an incredibly battered little black book and consulted it and said, 'Tuesday.'

So we started work on January 1st and started shooting on May 30th and it was in the cinemas by November.

But the further miracle was that Lorimar went completely out of business. They went totally bankrupt, belly up, during the first week of shooting so we shot for three days, then they stopped us, and Warner Brothers, for some unknown reason, bought the film, sight unseen, I suppose because of John Malkovich and Glenn Close and Michelle Pfeiffer. They just bought it. It was shooting in France and it was a very small budget and they couldn't be bothered to send anyone to check. So we had the money and we made the film.

In America they screen the film in front of an audience that gives its opinions and the audience liked it, so there was absolutely nothing needed doing and it was a miracle all the way down the line. The other miraculous thing that occurred was that our publicity lady in Paris went to pick up some dry cleaning and in the dry cleaning store there was a script lying on the counter and she picked it up. It was the script of Milos's film which she brought back and we all had a quick read of it and decided we were all right. We didn't have to worry. Milos Forman's film came out six months or so after ours and it was called *Valmont,* with Colin Firth, I think in a wet shirt, and it looked exquisite because they had spent a colossal amount of money on it. It cost at least three times as much as *Dangerous Liaisons* but unfortunately nobody actually liked it or went to see it. Many years later I was invited to dinner by Milos Forman, again in London, and I thought, 'Oh, alright.' So I went along and I notice that we both arrived fifteen minutes early. At this dinner he told me, and I still don't know to this day whether to believe it or not, that he had gone to a restaurant that evening as well and that I hadn't turned up, so that may or may not be true. Anyway he was incredibly generous about *Dangerous Liaisons* and said a number of very kind things about it. Then there was a sort of terrible pause and I said, 'Your film looked absolutely exquisite.'

Bigsby: What were the problems of adapting *Les Liaisons Dangereuses* for the stage and the cinema?

Hampton: The real challenge was that the central characters in the novel never meet so I found myself doing a big map. I didn't actually have figures but I moved people about from one location to another so that they would be in the right place to talk to one another and motor the plot forward in the same way as it is motored forward in the book. That was a really complicated jigsaw puzzle of the kind that I really enjoy doing.

Then I had to do it again when I came to write the screenplay because Stephen Frears said, 'I don't want it to be like the play,' which by the way he hadn't seen. He said, 'I want it to be like a movie. I want it to be like a proper film.' So I started again and in fact the film is closer to the book than the play is. The film is more faithful. I have this theory, and I don't know how accurate it is but it is a pet theory of mine, which is that film and novel are much closer to one another than film and theatre.

Bigsby: There was a director of one of your films who knew less than Stephen Frears about directing, namely you. You directed *Carrington*, and you were going on to direct other films. Were you not petrified at the idea of running this big machine, which is what directing is?

Hampton: It was very, very frightening, but of course I discovered two things, one is that what everyone will say to you about a film set is that it is so boring, everyone is hanging about, there is nothing to do, it is dreadfully boring. Well of course there is one person on the set who isn't bored and that is the director, because everybody is waiting for him so it is not at all boring to direct a film. In fact it is incredibly absorbing and enjoyable. The second thing is that it doesn't matter how ignorant you are yourself if you are sly enough to hire a great cameraman, a great editor, and all the rest of it, people who have been doing it for years and years and years. It is their job to give you what you want and insofar as you can explain it to them they will do it for you.

One thing I didn't have to worry about was working with the actors because all those years in the theatre I have worked so much with actors that I am quite comfortable with them. I think for first-time directors it is often very scary, that aspect of things, working with the actors. I was old enough also not to be at all worried about saying, 'I don't know. What do you think?' I think if you start directing a film when you are young the tendency would be to need to know everything and control everything and want to. If a problem came up I would say, 'What do you think?' And usually there would be some very good answer at the end of that, or at least it would stimulate a discussion which would lead to a good answer.

So to my amazement, though I didn't really ever want to be a director I found it was really enjoyable and of course the propaganda is that it is much more difficult. It is not as difficult as writing, I can tell you that. I should add a cautionary note. Before I directed *Carrington* I was on a stage at the British Film Institute with Stephen Frears and Tom Stoppard, and Tom had just directed his film of *Rosencrantz and Guildenstern* and he was saying much the same as I was, i.e. it is not as difficult as writing. You have all these wonderful people to help you. And he said, 'In short, I found it immensely enjoyable,' at which point Stephen Frears leant forward and said, 'That is because you are not a director.'

Bigsby: You have written a musical, *Sunset Boulevard*, but now you are writing an opera.

Hampton: Yes, I have just written a libretto, well I wrote it last year for Philip Glass. Philip wrote the music for *The Secret Agent*, which was my second film, based on the Conrad novel. While we were doing it, eight or nine years ago, he said, 'Would you ever like to write an opera libretto?' and I said, 'Well, yes, sure.' A couple of years ago he phoned me and said, 'This is the time.' He sent me a novel, *Waiting for the Barbarians*, by J. M. Coetzee, which is a marvellous allegorical novel about the state confecting a war to paper over cracks at home. It seemed to me both a very good subject for an opera and very timely, so I did the libretto and it opened in Germany. Opera is quite strange. You do all this work and then they play for six performances. There was great excitement the other day. It has done very well and there are two extra performances announced, so they will be doing eight performances and half a dozen performances in Amsterdam and Austin, Texas, and Cincinnati, and so it goes.

It is very different from anything else, and most enjoyable. It is really a question of massive compression. I said to Philip, 'Look, what do you want from this libretto? What is your advice to me? I have never written a libretto before.' He said, 'Keep it very, very short because I have got to write all the music.' He said, 'I did an opera with Doris Lessing. She wrote the libretto, and it was sixty pages. I suppose the skill of it, if there is any, was to somehow capture the essence of this novel in forty pages.

Bigsby: Now you have been working on an adaptation of a work by one of today's leading novelists?

Hampton: I have just finished adapting Ian McEwan's, *Atonement*, which is going to be directed by a very lively young British director called Joe Wright who has just directed his first film, *Pride and Prejudice*. I hope they are going to do it next spring. This is a weird thing about writing films. I did three drafts and then Joe came on and, for perfectly good reasons of his own, wanted the whole thing rewritten, root and branch, from beginning to end. So I did. You don't mind if they know exactly what they want and it seems to make sense. But film is so much a question of rewriting and rewriting and rewriting, which is not my experience in the theatre where you give them the play and they do it.

Bigsby: Why have you done more adaptations than original plays?

Hampton: As you can imagine it is something I have thought about a lot myself. I do the work I feel inclined to do at the time, and it may be that the things that come easier to me are the things I gravitate towards, but I am trying to do more theatre work. The last thing I wrote, *The Talking Cure*, which is about the early years of psychoanalysis, about Freud, took me five years because of the quantity of research. I am not saying that it wasn't worth the five years but I needed to do other stuff during that five years in order not to go demented and end up in a psychiatric unit myself. It was a fascinating five years, but that is the length of time it took. Of the two plays that I have on the boards at the moment, one, on in London early next year, is an adaptation of a novel called *Embers*, by a Hungarian novelist called Sándor Márai. I read it and it moved me enormously. I felt it would work very well on the stage, so I adapted it. The big project I am working on at the moment, and probably will take another couple of years, is going to be taken from a book called *White Mughals*, by William Dalrymple, a book about the East India Company around the turn of the nineteenth century. I guess it won't be ready until the end of next year at the earliest. In the meantime I tend to take on other jobs while that is on the back boiler because, here's the thing, I actually find the preparation period is what takes the time, the notes, the structuring, the working out of what to leave out and what to put in. That takes an enormous amount of time. The actual writing will then be relatively quick.

Obviously the advantage of working on material that is already there is that you don't have to grapple with inventing a narrative. I think that is probably what I find very difficult, inventing a narrative, and what I have tended to avoid in one way or another. It is a question that has not exactly troubled me but it certainly goes through my mind from time to time. Certainly the quality of attention that you get from having a play on, and indeed the money you earn, is really second to no other medium and so it would be nice if I could write more plays but I guess I have written ten or eleven.

In Conversation With
David Hare

- 22nd October 2008 -

David Hare, writer and director, was born in St. Leonards-on-Sea in Sussex in 1947 and was educated at Lancing School and Jesus College, Cambridge. In 1968 he was a founder of the Portable Theatre Company, a radical group which performed around the country. It was for this company that he wrote *Slag* (1968). He subsequently worked at the Royal Court Theatre, the Nottingham Playhouse and the National Theatre. Among his many plays are *Plenty* (1978), *Racing Demon* (1990), *Murmuring Judges* (1991), *The Absence of War* (1993), *Via Dolorosa* (1998), *The Vertical Hour* (2006), *The Power of Yes* (2009) and *South Downs* (2011). He has also written for television while his films include *The Hours* (2002) and *The Reader* (2008). His awards include a BAFTA, a New York Drama Critics Circle Award and an Olivier.

Bigsby: For Arthur Miller, at the start of his career, theatre was a place where he could enter into a dialogue with his society, a place where people would naturally go to discover things about themselves and about their society. Is that how you see it?

Hare: Completely, yes. I started in the fringe theatre, which was a principled movement. It was essentially a political or revolutionary or an anarchic or a hedonistic theatre in the sixties. When the National Theatre was built it was seen as the enemy by most people on the fringe. It was going to be this great maw into which everything was going to vanish and in which talent would disappear but I felt, 'Oh, fantastic. They are building a national theatre. That is exactly what the country needs, and I want my plays to go on there because I would like to speak to the nation,' exactly that.

People were absolutely horrified when that was my reaction because they said, 'Why would you wish to join an establishment theatre?' to which the reply is, 'It is only going to be an establishment theatre if everybody who has something to say refuses to take part in it.' To this day people say to me, 'Do you see some contradiction between wanting to have a theatre that actually has something to say and working at the National Theatre?' to which I reply, 'No, of course not. Why on earth would you?' So it was always incredibly exciting to me, that big open Greek stage in the Olivier Theatre. It is brutally difficult to write for it, and very few living writers have been willing to do so, but it has always seemed to me exactly what a theatre should be.

Bigsby: When was that interest in theatre born? When you were growing up in Sussex did you have any interest in theatre at all?

Hare: My mother was Scottish and so she was roped in to teach Scottish accents at a local kiddies drama school. She was in a production of Molière's *The Imaginary Invalid*, and there was an incredibly attractive girl playing in this at the Bexhill amateur drama school. I was nine but the sight of Julie Christie at fourteen pretty much wed me to theatre for life.

Bigsby: You went to Lancing, which was then a boys school and where Christopher Hampton was also a pupil. Because it was a boys school he played women's parts in school plays. Were you ever in the embarrassing position of doing that?

Hare: No. But Christopher had a gift for it. We had this extraordinary situation where a lot of us were at the same school at the same time. Christopher Hampton was there and Tim Rice, who used to write with Andrew Lloyd Webber and now has written *The Lion King*. So the three of us were there at the same time. It is not that we particularly picked each other out, because, actually, it was just a school with very, very good liberal arts teachers. Although it was a school for children of the clergy, and was principally an Anglican foundation, it was at exactly the moment that public school ethics were falling apart and we had very fine first rate liberal arts teachers who introduced us to all sorts of things of which we would never otherwise have heard.

Bigsby: But what were you doing there in the first place because your background wouldn't have suggested that this would be a natural place for you to study?

Hare: I was a scholarship boy and essentially I got everywhere I did by winning scholarships.

Bigsby: Which includes Cambridge?

Hare: Yes. Everybody of a certain age knows the gradations of the British class system in the nineteen fifties and sixties, which were unbelievably rigid, so it did mean that I arrived at a private school with a sense of *outsiderishness*. An awful lot of playwrights come from places like Bexhill both because you feel outside but also because the metropolis and the culture seems incredibly glamorous in a way that it does not seem to those who are born into it as a matter of privilege. When I travelled up from Bexhill the sixty miles to the metropolis seemed absolutely like crossing a barrier. I got to see plays and famous actors. I loved it. To see John Gielgud on the stage, or to see Laurence Olivier, or Edith Evans or Peggy Ashcroft still seems incredible. The terrible thing, the pathetic thing, is that it hasn't worn off. I still feel the theatre is residually glamorous in some way though it is childish to believe this after you have spent forty years in it. But I still get terribly excited by going to it and when I go to a play I have a fantastic sense of expectation.

Bigsby: Did you still feel an outsider when you went to Cambridge?

Hare: Yes, very much so.

Bigsby: Wasn't there a story that you were going to be thrown out at some stage?

Hare: No, I had a problem with authority, it is true, but I think what happened was that I had been to California in what is now called a gap year, though the concept in those days didn't exist, and I had gone to work for a primal scream therapist in Los Angeles. It was just a wonderful time because I would be sitting with my ear to the keyhole listening to people saying completely extraordinary things and then I would get out their files and read these unbelievable things. British culture of the sixties and Californian culture of the sixties were much further apart than they are now. Things have got much closer. So I arrived in California at the age of seventeen and girls had their jeans cut off around their knees and the hippie revolution was in incipient flow. To be truthful it was more surfing than hippiedom. Hippiedom was just about to arrive. So I thought I had woken up in heaven and therefore to go back to Cambridge and study was not really what I most wanted to do, and actually the teaching wasn't as good as the teaching had been at my school. So I think I had a sense of wanting to get out and do things. University was rather a frustrating time for me.

Bigsby: Were you involved in theatre while you were at Cambridge?

Hare: Not much. I directed *Oh What a Lovely War* with Germaine Greer as the recruiting sergeant striding around in fishnet tights and singing "I'll make a man of everyone of you." You have never heard that song until you have heard Germaine singing it.

Bigsby: When you left Cambridge you were a co-founder of Portable Theatre. What were you setting out to do with that group?

Hare: We started with the assumption that all regular theatre was completely terrible. The theatre of the day was completely boring, corrupt, worthless. Harold Pinter was a joke. John Osborne was terrible, the usual young people's stuff. We wanted to go on a social mission to take theatre where it wasn't usually seen, so that might mean prisons or army camps or anywhere. The principle was to try and get a new audience for the theatre, not an audience which went all the time. Secondly, it was to deal with the problem of aesthetics. The glory of theatre is that it has a following who make judgements basically on aesthetic grounds, in other words how well the thing is done, rather than what it is that is being done. So the core theatre audience will go to *Hamlet* every two years and say, 'I saw so and so's Hamlet. He was good but he wasn't as good as the person who played in this earlier production. The lighting is better in this. I loved the set when it was done at Stratford. I like it less at the National Theatre.' That is all about aesthetics. Very few people go to *Hamlet* and decide whether to be or not to be.

How to get the audience to ask themselves the questions that Hamlet asks is the challenge of theatre, in other words, how not to reduce it to an art form in the sense of being about aesthetics. One way of doing that is just to say we are going to do the plays so crudely that there is no chance of you worrying about the lighting because it will be four lights stuck up on the floor. There is no point in worrying about the acting. It is going to be crude. There isn't going to be a set. We are just going to tell you things, or act things out for you which we think you ought to know. The thing we felt everybody ought to know was that we felt capitalism was on the imminent verge of collapse. We wanted to go around the country and dramatise the imminence of this collapse as violently and shockingly and unpleasantly as we could. So most of the plays were very short. They were very crude. They were apocalyptic and they were mostly very unpleasant and lurid, I suppose is the word.

Bigsby: On one occasion you played to an audience of one, but that person turned out to be significant?

Hare: There used to be an Equity rule which even though we were meant to be a revolutionary theatre group we observed, which is that you have no obligation to play if there are fewer people in the audience than there are in the play. If there are five people in the cast and five people turn up you have to play. If there are five people in the cast and four people turn up you don't have to play. So only one person turned up and it was Howard Brenton. So that is how I met him and I said, 'I don't think we are going to play because you are the only member of the audience.' So we went off to the pub and started talking. Then he became Portable Theatre's most distinguished and brilliant writer.

Bigsby: You were a director at first?

Hare: I was a director. I was not a writer.

Bigsby: But then you did start writing plays?

Hare: I started writing a play because a playwright who had promised us a play didn't write one. It was a one act play, *How Brophy Made Good*. On a Wednesday I was told that we needed a play for Monday because the person had lied. He said he had written a play but had not. This is a syndrome I was to encounter many times over the years and they always lie bare faced. They don't lie apologetically and they don't say sorry when they haven't got it, they just say, 'You know the play I am writing, I haven't written it.' There is no apology. So I had to write a play and I had never thought of myself as a writer. I wrote this one-act play. We started rehearsing it and put it on and I got the first review of my life, which was from *Plays and Players*. The reviewer said, 'It was the most pointless evening I have ever spent in a theatre.' But an agent came to see it and a producer from the West End came to see it and was convinced I was a playwright. So I then started leading a very split life. I was going around in vans doing dirty-minded theatre and at the same time a producer was trying to get me to write plays for the West End.

Bigsby: When did you realise that you were a playwright?

Hare: I think I discovered the minute I started writing dialogue that I had a facility for it. It was a dangerous facility because at first I thought that writing dialogue was writing plays. Then you slowly begin to understand that dialogue is only the means by which you will write the play. Noel Coward is plainly a genius at dialogue but he is less of a genius at playwriting. As the years went by it almost became too easy for him.

Anyone who can write a play in a weekend has a genius but it is unfortunately not necessarily a genius for playwriting.

Knuckle opened in the three-day week, which you have to be very old to remember, when Edward Heath shut down half the country for reasons too obscure to relate. It was a bad moment to open a play in the West End. Also the reviews were very, very bad and this is very difficult. We staggered on for four months with a loyal cast in the West End playing to empty, freezing, houses and to a panning in the press. It tempers you because you think, 'Oh, I see life is going to be fantastically unpleasant and uncomfortable but I have to believe that I have something that is so important to say and do that I really am prepared to put up with this.' That is what I mean about discovering I had a play. I thought, 'I don't know if this play is any good but I know that it is fantastically important to me that it is heard.' So that tempers you and accounts for my extreme hostility to critics.

I have never ever accepted their judgement at any level because they weren't right then and I don't believe they are right now. I don't believe they are right about anything and I have to believe that to keep going. It distresses me when I hear playwrights accepting the judgement of critics. There is a new thing now where playwrights have websites and they say, 'Go to my four star review from *The Guardian*,' and then there is a link. They say, 'Read what Michael Billington says about my play,' and you think, well, if you are going to put a link when Michael Billington says your play is good, what are you going to do when Michael Billington says your play is bad? Are you going to put a link then? Are you going to accept that Michael Billington knows more about it than you do? Once you go down that path you are really in trouble.

It shocks me in young writers that some of them seem willing to accept such judgements because in the theatre you are going to be fighting the judgement of the audience and of the critics all the time. I have always felt the audience was against me. I know they are and I have to swing them round. It is not true of some writers. There are writers they are disposed to like, but they are not disposed to like my plays before they see them. They are disposed to dislike them and I have to win them round. I have to fight them. Certainly for about twenty years it was arm to arm wrestling with them because I was telling them something they didn't want to hear.

Bigsby: About four years after *Knuckle* came two works, one was a television film, *Licking Hitler,* and the other was a stage play, *Plenty. Licking*

Hitler is set during the war and is about a black propaganda unit. The job of those who work for it is to lie, to deceive the Germans. It brings together people of different classes. The nature of the war time experience was that those class divisions you talked about earlier, which are so basic to British society, had to collapse and people were brought together in a most unlikely way. Later on, though, you suggest, these people survived the war to go on lying, to become part of a culture that lied to itself and to other people.

Plenty also begins in the war. Its central woman character, who had been an SOE agent, registers the subsequent betrayal of wartime values. Neither work, surely, is about nostalgia. They seem to be about the loss of values, about people who no longer know what it is they believe in. Is that the thrust of those two works?

Hare: Totally, completely. There was a famous sketch in *Beyond the Fringe*, a revue with Jonathan Miller, Alan Bennett, Dudley Moore and Peter Cooke, in which they satirised the way the British cinema had treated the war, a war in which seventy-eight million people died. You would certainly not know from the British cinema that seventy eight per cent of European Jews were exterminated. The British cinema had not begun to deal with the phenomenon of the Second World War except as a stiff upper lip personal psycho-drama, so there seemed this huge gap in the culture about the way people talked about the Second World War and what had actually happened. I was very affected by reading a book by Angus Calder called *The People's War* in which Calder argued that the defeat of Churchill in 1945 was not this anomaly that is completely inexplicable. It was not that people came back from the war and ungratefully threw out Winston Churchill. On the contrary, people came back from the war and had been radicalised by their experiences in the war. They had met the officer class. They had often found the officer class to be foolish or deficient, people who had to be covered for. They had seen the ruling class and the ruling class was no longer entitled automatically to pull privilege because in the battlefield an awful lot of ruling class, officer class lives had been saved by an awful lot of working class soldiers. So it is demonstrably true as a piece of social history that people came back having been in the army wanting to change the way the army was run, the way the country was run. And yet this was a piece of hidden history, just like feminist history is hidden. We have heard nothing of it.

I didn't know that we had black propaganda radio stations where we targeted individual Germans while they were at the battlefront and told them that their wives were being unfaithful to them back in Cologne. This came as news to me and was so not part of what you were generally told about the British war effort. I literally did not know that twenty million Russians had died and that the crucial engagement was in Stalingrad. This was never explained to me as a kid and so the whole way in which we saw the war in those days was totally false. So opening that subject out felt incredibly exciting. People are still doing it you know. The number of works of radical revision now about what the Second World War was actually like is a huge field now.

Bigsby: Yet wartime solidarity survived the war in terms of the Labour government which introduced so many key changes in British society. There was still a society that shared values. But that seems to have come to an end. If I were to say there is something that connects your plays it would be the loss of a sense of transcendence, a sense that people live for something other than money. People have lost sense of there being a purpose behind things.

Hare: They have to find a purpose in their own terms and in individual terms.

Bigsby: Well they were about to find it in a Conservative government at the end of the 1970s.

Hare: The political analysis of people like me was completely wrong. We basically thought that history was going to turn left and we were wrong. History turned right and when history turned right I personally couldn't write for a while. I couldn't write a play for some years because I had been so wrong about everything. I had never believed there was going to be a revolution in this country. I never thought there was going to be a left-wing utopia, but I did think violence was coming and social breakdown. Well, far from violence and social breakdown Thatcherism arrived and I don't know of anyone who prophesised Thatcherism. I literally don't know of anyone, be they journalists, social historians, playwrights, who saw Thatcherism coming. When it came we all had to do a double-declutch. You had to rethink what it was you were writing about and that, for me, was more or less a four or five year period when I wrote very little. I didn't know how to write about what had changed and then I slowly began to acquire an analysis about what was going on and was able to write again.

Bigsby: But you did write about the Right in *Paris by Night?*

Hare: By then I was getting going and by then I could see exactly what you are talking about. There were a whole lot of people who were still trying to find value in their work and in their lives, but obviously the victims of Thatcherism were those who were not doing it for the money. Throughout the nineteen eighties everybody who did things not for the money was told they were foolish. They were devalued and were told that money and efficiency were to be the criteria for everything and that therefore if you were in public service, in anything like teaching or the church, you must be an idiot and you must be an idiot because if you had any gifts at all you would be making money like anybody else.

The violence of the propaganda in the eighties is now almost impossible to recall, including attacks on theatre. Suddenly subsidy was being withdrawn from the theatre. Suddenly you could not open a newspaper in the nineteen eighties without somebody saying why I hate the theatre, why the theatre is terrible. We became the whipping boys because we were still interested in collaborative ventures and things which were against the mood of the time. But I began to become interested in people who were having to construct their own values without the approbation of the propaganda of the period. So I turned to the dear old Church of England because you can't work with much less approbation than a Church of England vicar. You have to do it because you want to do it. You can't do it because you believe anybody is going to thank you except God.

Bigsby: There is a sense, particularly in the first two of what would become a trilogy of plays (*Racing Demon, Murmuring Judges, The Absence of War*), that they are partly to do with the collateral damage of Thatcherism, that is to say the damage to those not in the magic circle. Someone had to deal with the fall-out from Thatcherism and priests turned into social workers not quite sure whether they should be concerned with God or with the people who they could see suffering in some way. The police likewise, were left with the fall-out from the Thatcher world.

Hare: When I went to police stations at that time, which was 1992 – and I spent a lot of time with the police whose company I really enjoyed – the surprising thing was I had expected them to be very right wing and of course they weren't. They were absolutely furious with Thatcher and they were furious with Thatcher for landing them with all the social problems. They would just say, 'Look, she has created splits in society and we are the people who patrol the splits. We patrol these people who have been left behind. It is our job to look after them and it is absolutely impossible because of the tensions that have been created by what she did.'

I am not saying they were a universally radicalised group of men and women, but there was much more political awareness about how they came to be doing the job they were doing than I was expecting. So they were in the front line in the way priests were in the front line. There was this wonderful phrase which the clergy would say to me: 'We don't push Christ down people's throats.' In fact, they didn't mention Christ at all. They were simply trying to fill in people's social security forms or explaining how they could get stoves. In other words they were doing the most menial low-level social work, citizens advice bureau stuff really, or counselling without a religious element in it at all, and all for the love of God, not in order to convert people to God. So I was used to the idea that there would be a Labour party that abandoned socialism but the fact that here was a Church that had abandoned religion was very, very striking. On the other hand, you could see the reasons why they were doing the things they were doing and in most of the parts of London that I was visiting you were extremely grateful the churches were there to do what they were doing.

Bigsby: The other thing that comes out of these plays is a strong sense of coteries, not necessarily class based, though sometimes they correspond with that, but within professional groups, who are much more interested in the rules of their own game than they are with the function they are supposed to be serving in society.

Hare: Well, what is the Bernard Shaw line about all professions. They are conspiracies against the laity, and that is exactly so, isn't it? Have you tried talking to a doctor? They are talking to themselves, aren't they. What is wrong with me? Why do you want to know? There are two major streams in modern theatre which you can say are represented by Beckett and Brecht. Beckett said that, to me, incredibly depressing thing: the sum of human tears is constant. He is basically saying there is nothing you can do. There will always be a certain number of people weeping in the world and if people aren't weeping over there they are weeping over here. It is a Manichean view. If one group goes up another group goes down. People are weeping and there is absolutely nothing you can do about that weeping. So he writes about what he would call the human condition, and it doesn't matter to him whether a play is set in Pakistan or the United States because there is something called the human condition and essentially humans deal with it in the same way. The contrary view is the

Shakespearian view which is that who you are has a great deal to do with what has just happened before you were born, the historical circumstances in which you find yourself and the turn that the times are taking.

That kind of theatre, the theatre where history is blowing across the stage, to me is much more exciting but also truer. In other words I don't think I suffer in the same way as a Chinese peasant. You might say that at the most basic level I suffer the same fate as the Chinese peasant, that I am going to be born and I am going to die without knowing why I was born, but saying that doesn't really get me very far. So what I am interested in with respect to the plight of the Chinese peasant is by what process did he or she come to be in this particular situation and what chances have he or she got of getting out of it. Is there any realistic chance of getting out of it? I don't think these are questions that much bothered Beckett.

Brecht is a very confusing subject. I have adapted two of his plays, *Galileo* and *Mother Courage*, but I find in Brecht, if I am honest, a complication that I can't quite reconcile myself to. *Galileo*, which is a play I absolutely love, I think is one of the greatest plays ever written. It is about one man's decision publicly to disown his own discovery, which set back civilisation for seventy-five years. Brecht says, look at this moment of moral failure. It is a moment of the failure of western civilisation. He says, one man fails and the results are catastrophic for everybody. In *Mother Courage*, a play I like much less, he is saying the exact opposite, and yet he said the two things within a year of each other.

In *Mother Courage* Brecht appears to be saying it doesn't matter how anybody behaves because the war will get you and you will be destroyed. It is a very depressing play to work on and if you work on it for a long time it is a hard play to work with because every single hope, or piece of positive thinking in the play, is extinguished by the war. The story of his compromise with the Soviet regime is so chilling, really, and what happened to him as a man is so chilling that it is hard to be at peace with the Brecht story.

Bigsby: Beckett exists in a paradox. Here is a man who talks about the impossibility of communicating in a play which is designed to communicate and which rests on the assumption of communication.

Hare: It is very hard for me to wrap my mind around that. I am not turning this into an anti-Beckett Festival, because I know that I will be alone in a telephone box, but basically why if it is an act of communication would you not be interested to see how the audience respond and much as I am disturbed by the way audiences respond to my plays, and the ghastly things I hear them saying, nevertheless to me the play only exists when the audience is there. That is what it is about. It is about the collision between what is going on on the stage and what the audience is thinking, and if you are not there to hear what the audience is thinking (and Beckett never attended performances of his plays) then you might as well hand it into an art gallery. That seems to me inert.

Bigsby: The Left, as you say, was in a difficult position, not alone you, but a lot of other writers. Trevor Griffiths insisted that if you want to reach an audience you don't do it through the theatre. So he turned to television because that is where the audience is. What is your attitude? You wrote for television. Were you drawn to it for the same reasons as Trevor Griffiths?

Hare: It was an opportunity to reach a huge audience and I think it made me write better. I think one of the problems of theatre is that you tend to adopt a rather smart arse tone, if you know what I mean, because it easily becomes cultish. It can attract a smart arse kind of writing. The classic example of this, to be fair is, David Mercer. If you see a David Mercer television play his heart is on his sleeve and it is incredibly emotional yet when he wrote for the theatre he thought he had to write 'clever, witty, dialogue.' I think for me it was emotionally very liberating to know that eight million people would be watching, and these were the days when eight million people watched a single play. So if you are going to talk to eight million people you have got to open yourself up. You can't do that kind of defensive writing that you sometimes find in the theatre, of which I think I was guilty when I was a younger playwright.

Of course we all wanted to write for television because everybody was writing for television and it was part of a tremendous tradition. If you have a weekly slot in which you know there is going to be a single play and you know there is going to be an audience of six or eight million people it is a wonderful incentive to write. Now that has been thrown away, by the BBC in particular, but also by Channel 4 and now that most plays on television are simply biopics of failing comedians or biographies of Mary Whitehouse then you are not exactly drawn to write for that genre any more because there isn't a feeling that the audience knows any more what that is that you are doing.

Bigsby: You have also written for the cinema. How far is that a form to which you are attracted?

Hare: A film is a huge commitment. I have written two films in the last five years, *The Hours*, which took me three years, and *The Reader*, which took two years so far. Only a tenth of that time do you spend writing. Nine tenths of the time you spend as an advocate defending both the script and the film. The input, so-called, is now so mammoth. There are endless meetings. Instead of being a script writer you become an advocate for your own script and it is so tedious that you realistically ask yourself, 'Do I want to spend two years of my life doing this? Do I want to spend all the time I have to do this?' Tomorrow I have to go back to New York to yet again defend the script that I wrote two years ago against all the people who want to change it into something that they will recognise more. If the book is good enough, which *The Hours* was and *The Reader* is, then you are willing to do that but film is not something anybody should take on light-heartedly, because it will break their heart. It is for very good reasons, of course. Films cost twenty-five million and thirty million dollars and people don't want to lose that.

Bigsby: In dramatising *The Hours*, by Michael Cunningham, you were dealing with a novel that works in an interior way. How much of a challenge was that?

Hare: *The Hours* is a novel about what is going on in the heads of three different women in three different periods of time that are not connected. One is Virginia Woolf, before she kills herself, and her decision that she must move back to London. Another is a contemporary woman's life in New York, and the third is a housewife in the nineteen fifties. It is all interior monologue and the moment I read it I wanted to make a film of it. I couldn't see what the problem was and it was very, very worrying. I was very disturbed because everybody else said, 'Oh, my God. You are taking on that impossible book,' but I couldn't see what the problem was because it seemed to me obvious that I had to invent events which would correspond to, and bring out in the characters and in some cases articulate in the characters, the dilemmas that Michael in his gorgeous prose had been able to express through the novel. So I just rubbed my hands and went, 'Oh great, there is room for me here. I can invent the events and the novelist is not going to complain because we are not going to have voice-over, which was the first rule.' I absolutely under no circumstances was going to have voice-over. I said, 'If you have voice-over why not just have a bloke reading out the novel. There is no point.'

So I began to invent the events. But obviously what excited me about it was the time scheme and the idea that you could throw three periods together, and also the idea that you could make a film that was like a code, so complicated as to be uncrackable. You could never know that film because it is so complicated. You can't know it. It was fun moving the pieces around and working out how it worked. I always claimed it ended up exactly as I had written it, but the director says it didn't.

Bigsby: Writing plays is high risk. A novelist writes the novel, it is published, it is well received, it is not. Between you and the audience are actors, all of whom are in a sense interpreting your work at every level. Is that what drew you to directing your own work because it is possible to have a bad production, a bad first production, which kills a play for years, sometimes for decades? Were you drawn to directing your own work as a way of protecting it or because you thought you could hear something that other directors might not be able to hear?

Hare: Exactly that. I did it for ten years, and I did it during that period when I felt that people didn't understand what it was I heard, what I sounded like, and what I looked like that other playwrights didn't sound and look like. It is not vanity. It is simply that if you are an artist at all you want it to be exactly the way you want it and you want to be able to control it. Now it has a downside which is that in a collaborative form you can't have the same engagement with a group of actors that you have with a group of actors and a director as well. Now that people know what my plays sound and look like I don't need to do them myself.

Bigsby: When you are directing your own work do you discover things that as a writer you did not?

Hare: Oh yes, completely. And actors do. Actors are the crucial people because the wonderful thing about them is that they will put everything under a degree of scrutiny. An actor will say, 'Why is my character called such and such?' All the questions that actors have to ask in order to do their work are richly creative questions which if you don't have answers to you had better shape up quick. I don't accept the answer which I believe David Storey once gave which is that we cannot know the author's intentions. I think it is a cop out.

Bigsby: You have directed your own work but you have also acted in your own work, in *Via Dolorosa*. Did you intend to do that when you started writing that play or was it the process of writing that led you to believe that you should act in it?

Hare: No, I was sent to Israel and Palestine, or the Palestinian territory as it was then called. This was the late nineties and I was meant to be writing a play about the Mandate but I was so startled by what I saw, and by the people I met, that I came back and said to Stephen Daldry, who was the director, 'If we put a play on which dramatises what is going on in the Middle East, we will be able to find five north London Jewish actors and we will call them Israelis and then we will find one Pakistani actor and we will find one Egyptian actor and we will find one Jordanian actor and we will find one Syrian actor and we will call them Palestinians. We will then give them plastic machine guns and we will stand them at check-points and then someone will design a set that looks like the Holy Land and it is going to be screaming falsity. Everything about it will be wrong because you can't make it authentic. It is just impossible in London to make it authentic.'

When I made *Licking Hitler* you could still physically reach the Second World War. England looked enough like the nineteen forties. Now if you go to films about the Second World War everything is wrong. The actors are too fat, for a start, and everything is wrong with the clothes. Everything is wrong in the set. We have lost it. It has gone, and authenticity is really important. So I felt the only way that I could do something authentic, and which also the audience would trust, was if they could see me. So I said to Stephen Daldry, 'There is very bad news. I'm afraid it has got to be a monologue.' And he said, 'That's fine, I'm not worried about that.' And I said, 'Yes, but the very bad news is I have to act it and I have never acted in my life.' And he said, 'I will teach you to act.' So he attempted it. It was very interesting and it was very good for me after I had been thirty years a playwright to actually see what it was like.

Bigsby: I have suggested that you write political plays but you surely don't just write about flawed societies, you write about flawed men and women. Your plays have a tragic dimension. But they can also be funny. You also have a concern with love, different varieties of love, different temperatures of love. Arthur Miller once said that the problem he had with American critics was that they thought he wrote plays while in fact he wrote metaphors. And that would be true of you?

Hare: The plays, although they are ostensibly about particular subjects, are not really about those subjects, they are about some great metaphor. I will give you a very, very quick example. In the case of *Stuff Happens*, which was about the diplomatic process leading up to the war in Iraq, it has a classic Shakespearian theme which was that the man who is clever, Tony Blair, ends up with nothing and the man who is stupid, George Bush, ends up with everything. George Bush got everything he wanted out of the Iraqi invasion while Tony Blair got absolutely nothing. Tony Blair spent his whole time saying, 'I can control George. I can stop him doing stupid things.' But actually it was a Shakespearian theme because power will always roll over people who believe that they control power.

We had a real problem playing Tony Blair, and it is an interesting problem because it is exactly the same in the films *The Queen* and *The Deal*. Whenever you dramatise Tony Blair he seems foolish but he is not foolish. Every actor who has ever tried to play him, however, always has this problem that he seems foolish. Stephen Frears famously said that whenever he puts on a Kevin Keegan shirt or picks up the guitar he looks stupid, but the reason he looks stupid is because he loses all the time, he loses to George Bush, and yet George Bush ostensibly is stupid. But of course power can't be ridden and that is a great Shakespearian theme. So once I knew it was Shakespeare, and the theme was that, then the writing was just filling in because you know what you are doing and what you are doing is creating this massive metaphor of life.

In Conversation With Michael Holroyd

- 5th December 2007 -

Michael Holroyd was born in 1935. His first biography, of Hugh Kingsmill, appeared in 1964. It was followed in 1967-8 by his two-volume study of Lytton Strachey. Subsequent biographies included *Augustus John* (1974-5) and his four-volume work on Bernard Shaw, which appeared between 1988 and 1992. Subsequent books included *Basil Street Blues* (1999), *Mosaic* (2004), *A Strange Eventful History* (2008), a study of Ellen Terry and Henry Irving, and *A Book of Secrets: Illegitimate Daughters, Absent Fathers* (2010). In 2007 he was knighted for services to literature.

Bigsby: Perhaps, since you are a biographer, I could begin by asking you to make the case against biography?

Holroyd: How long have we got? I think in a nutshell the case against literary biography is that it is completely reductive. It traces everything to an autobiographical impasse. It narrows it down. What did Byron have for breakfast? It produces a lot of inert scholarship. Then authors copy down what other people have written and give that as a source. Then there is a tendency for biographies to come in two or three volumes, I mean for goodness sake! Why should poets or novelists value literary biographies? It is completely irrelevant in so far as you are looking for ideas about literature. Biography gets in the way. It stops you thinking. As for other sorts of biography, for example historical biography, it places completely undue emphasis on an individual with whom we can identify rather than looking at history sociologically, economically. All that. How long was Cleopatra's nose?

Bigsby: I suppose it is not surprising that authors are hostile to the idea of biography. Don't I remember that you are supposedly Doris Lessing's biographer but that you had a private agreement with her that you would never write it. It was simply a device for keeping biographers at bay.

293

Holroyd: We made this agreement in Hong Kong many, many years ago. I was placed as a shield which Doris could use against some other people who wanted to write her life. She wanted an alibi, an excuse, and here is the alibi. Here is the excuse. But she did think that I might. She wasn't going to write an autobiography herself, no, no, but time passed and, insofar as this exists at all, it is a fantasy which will be published on both our behalves posthumously.

Bigsby: As you imply there, the other defence against the biographer is the autobiography, and indeed she has published two volumes of her own. Do I notice the same thing going on with you in that in *Mosaic* you turn to your own life. Are you trying to occupy the space that some wilful biographer might occupy later?

Holroyd: I think there is less chance of people being attracted to writing a biography of me. Also, apparently I don't appear, I have been told, in my autobiography. Hardly at all. An echo, a reflection, an indication, perhaps. So it was really like doing another biography of people I knew, parents I knew, and stepparents, and finding where I was in relation to them.

Bigsby: It strikes me that there was something strange about your parents. They got divorced. Nothing strange about that, of course, but they seem to have botched it.

Holroyd: So you think all the other marriages were sort of illegal probably?

Bigsby: Bigamy was the word that comes to mind.

Holroyd: It was a sort of divorce, nisi not absolute. They didn't even mention technicalities. There were lots of marriages afterwards so what was interesting to me, if interesting is the word, is that each holiday I would be presented with a new figure who was a stepfather or a stepmother, Hungarian or French, whatever it may be, even English. What was strange is that a few holidays later I would look around and there was no such person. It seemed like a very bad play with people who say a few words and then exit never to appear on stage again.

Bigsby: You also had to invent both sides of the correspondence between your mother and stepfather?

Holroyd: Yes. My mother never took any decision without first asking my advice and my advice would be very chairman like. I would say, 'Well, on the one hand, nevertheless upon the other, but we must not forget so and so however,' and I would go on until I saw which way she was going. Then I would come in and say what I deduced she wanted me to say and then she would go and do what she wanted to do anyway. This could take some time.

She had met a very nice Viennese gentleman who lived in South America. She asked me should she go and live in South America with him? This was a tricky one. She decided to catch a plane and asked if I would leave a note for my stepfather who would be returning in the evening to explain matters to him. So I did. My style actually had fewer "howevers". 'She has gone.' My stepfather drank a certain amount and so did everybody in his company. I remember towards the end of an ordinary evening he would get very aggressive and bang the table. She thought he was very rude and it made her drink rather more. So by the end of the meal she was nearly under the table. My stepfather would bang the table and I was sick. That was a normal sort of evening and for some reason my mother thought she had had enough of that, so I left this note for him. He rang me up, because I was living in a flat in London, and he said could I come over, and we spent some time together. He showed me my note and I read it and we drank, man to man. He did not get aggressive and I wasn't sick that evening. 'Now you are a writer, perhaps you could phrase it on your paper for me?' So I wrote a letter on his behalf which he then posted to South America. A month or two later, I got a letter from my mother saying, 'Look, I have received this very strange letter from your stepfather and I wonder how I should reply.' I won't go on. Eighteen months of international correspondence with myself ended disastrously, disastrously. She came back and had to go again.

Bigsby: Unsurprisingly, you were brought up by your grandparents who did not get divorced but probably should have done?

Holroyd: That is absolutely right, which told me that there is no rule about happiness and sticking together or happiness and parting. They should have parted because it was a very unhappy home and they would have been well rid of each other and starting again. My grandfather did try but he gave his mistress so much money, whatever he had left, that he came back bankrupt. He had no more to give and suddenly she didn't want to see so much of him. I couldn't quite work it out.

Bigsby: With all this going on around you as a child, was literature a refuge?

Holroyd: Yes, I think that tends to be so with single children anyway and so I certainly could travel on a magic carpet by reading books, by reading novels and stories. I could find friends among these characters. I could forget other things around me. Yes, it was, I suppose, a compensation and an addition, an enrichment of my imagination. Early on I loved Rider Haggard and Conan Doyle, who is much in vogue at the moment I see. I loved all that adventure when I was very young and later on I read French novels, realists, Balzac, Zola and then Russians. I loved Dostoevsky, and so I really educated myself although I didn't read any of that stuff at school.

Bigsby: And then it was off to Eton?

Holroyd: Ghastly Eton.

Bigsby: Didn't you become head of games?

Holroyd: Eton is divided into houses so there were about sixty in mine and I was captain of games.

Bigsby: And you were a champion at squash?

Holroyd: True. The great thing about squash is that it wasn't a team game, I noticed. So one didn't have to turn up along with ten other people to meet eleven on another side and try to find out what you were meant to do. You could play squash on your own. I might have played tennis if ever I could have found the courts, but I never did. They were somewhere near Slough, I think, but I played squash because it was a solitary game in a way.

Bigsby: Weren't you British under-sixteen champion?

Holroyd: At the age of seventeen I absolutely crashed and never won another game.

Bigsby: You didn't go to Oxbridge. Why not? Do you wish you had or did you benefit from not doing so?

Holroyd: All those things. I felt at one stage that I had missed out on going to a sort of Eden where the sun always shone, people were brilliantly clever and in love, and I had missed it all. Then I got more revolutionary and said, well I don't have to forget all that second-hand stuff I would have learned at university had I gone there. Aren't I lucky.

Now I have come to in-between, really. My reading has great gaps in it because of what I wasn't given to read between say eighteen and twenty-one. I have great gaps. But the other thing is that I found, at what was my university, the public library, books that I thought were important which weren't on the syllabus and that was a compensation for that. It is an odd education I have had in literature.

Bigsby: Then you hit that hiatus that young men did at that time, namely National Service, and at a rather inglorious moment in British history, Suez?

Holroyd: I managed to avoid Suez, not so much for ethical reasons, as for reasons of ignorance. I was on leave when Suez broke out and I didn't read a lot of newspapers then, but I saw it on Pathé news when I went to see a film. It said that the Royal Fusiliers were in Egypt and I thought, 'My God, I am a Royal Fusilier,' and I saw people going up onto a boat including a person I knew. And I thought, 'My God, what should I do about it?' So next day I rang up the Adjutant. I had been transferred from the Green Jackets to the Royal Fusiliers at the request of the Green Jackets and the only difference between them is that they had different buttons, so I thought I will ring up the Adjutant and see what he says. So I rang up and he said, 'Book yourself under arrest and march yourself to the Tower of London.' So I went to the Tower of London and there he was with two senior officers who said, 'Why didn't you answer the telegram summoning you to active service?' I looked completely blank. I hadn't received any telegram. You could see the looks of frank disbelief. But next day they found that in the heat of war the Adjutant had actually written out this telegram but sent it to himself, but I was had up for having the wrong buttons.

Bigsby: After National Service you had to have a career. Your father had various suggestions, none of which appealed.

Holroyd: This is why I didn't go to university because my father had a point of view, which I didn't agree with but it is very popular now, the received opinion now really, which is you go to university in order to equip yourself for a job for life or several jobs for life. He knew, he said, that 'science was rising but nobody was interested. The men and women of numbers are rising as the men and women of letters are declining. You must study physics, chemistry and mathematics, which will equip your for the modern world. Then you will not be like I am, out of a job.' The trouble is I didn't have mathematics within me. I couldn't detect the beauty of it. Physics is largely mathematics and chemistry I just couldn't do. I did have a place. In those days you could get places without really passing exams. You went up and you answered questions, not necessarily correctly, but with the right accent. But I didn't go.

What I didn't realise was you go up to read mathematics and then, after a few seconds, change it to something else. I didn't know anything about universities really. I thought they were just more school, so I took a job as an articled clerk. My father said that if I could argue against his common sense so vigorously then I might be able to get a job by arguing in court. I should become a lawyer because that is where people argue so I was an articled clerk in a firm of solicitors for about eighteen months. In fact I paid them rather than they paid me, which is a Dickensian thing. It didn't help the finances of the family at all. I learned nothing except how to make the tea. They had never had an articled clerk before, so I had to give it up because it was really no good.

Bigsby: The strangest thing about your relationship to your father is that you collaborated on writing a history of the world in verse. This doesn't seem entirely likely.

Holroyd: On foolscap paper. We decided to send it to a publishers we had heard of which seemed to specialise in that sort of stuff, Faber and Faber. We hedged our bets and so after some months of silence we did provoke them and say, 'When is publication? Should you not be letting us know?' They replied, 'The satire is not sufficiently satirical.' Satire, is that what we have been doing? We later thought of trying to get the serial rights in *Punch* as a more comic element, but it failed. In one way I wish I had kept it. He did most of it because my father thought if I am going to do writing and have a book published he should start writing now and *A History of the World in Verse* couldn't go wrong. You encapsulate everything. He did write five unpublished novels. One nearly got published.

Bigsby: And you wrote one that you wished you hadn't?

Holroyd: Indeed, I wrote a book called *A Dog's Life*. It was accepted but I showed it to my father and he wrote to Heinemann and said if it was published he would look forward to seeing them in court. So they said to me, 'We are backing you completely. As soon as you have settled this we will publish.' So eventually I published it in the States where my father would know nothing about it. He was in very bad financial trouble then but I managed to rescue him with the advance on royalties from the book in the States. He then found out years later and managed to give me some completely worthless chairs that the family had once had in India before it was invaded by the Chinese. So we were quits really.

Bigsby: You first biography was of Hugh Kingsmill. In some way that was surely an odd choice?

Holroyd: I came across his books in the library. I think the first one which I was really taken with was his life of Frank Harris, which is a wonderfully funny, ironic, lyrical short biography. I was much taken by that. His life of Johnson is very good. His other biographies tend to be cases for the crown as it were. They are tactical biographies – the Matthew Arnold and the Dickens and so on – but there are passages of sheer brilliance in them. They start terribly well but then money always got in the way and they end very hurriedly. He didn't divide people – men versus women, Tories versus Labour, black versus white, anything like that – he was interested in men and women of will versus men and women of imagination, and of course in all of us there are both will and imagination. I could see my daydreaming and laziness as part of imagination but there was little will in it and I rather liked the idea. I also liked the philosophy in a way. It wasn't fashionable. It wasn't a cliché. It divided people in a way that includes us all and the enemy is within.

Bigsby: This wasn't commissioned?

Holroyd: None of the first sixteen publishers commissioned it. It was like a tennis match. You sent it to them and back it came and you sent it over and back it came. I got terribly obstinate.

Bigsby: Then came Lytton Strachey and Lytton Strachey, among other things, was a biographer and indeed had written biographies which were in some way challenging the norm of biography?

Holroyd: Well, it is true, he had, not at the beginning though I have found out. Kingsmill was accused of being school of Strachey. In the Kingsmill book I tried to argue against that and in doing so I became interested in Strachey. It started a pattern whereby a minor character, sometimes a significant minor character, in one biography gets my attention and becomes a subject for the next. That has gone on really throughout all of them.

Bigsby: Not the least interesting aspect of Lytton Strachey is his correspondence

Holroyd: I became fascinated by the correspondence between Strachey and Dora Carrington, a girl who fell in love with him and stayed with him for fifteen or sixteen years. After he died she committed suicide. That story was a tremendous one and I got so involved in their letters that in a way I was more in their world than I was in my own. I think it is quite possible to do that and what I wanted to do, since these were unpublished, was to try and make them live again on the page and to affect readers to some extent as I had been affected by just reading and handling them. That was I think the centre of my book anyway.

Bigsby: It raises an ethical question in that people spend much of their lives protecting their privacies, aspects of their sensibility or experience that they want to hold close to their chest for what seem to them good reasons, yet your function is to prise their fingers off these privacies and put them out there into the public world.

Holroyd: When we are alive we have one set of values and what we want by way of priorities. Who is to say, though, what we feel when we are dead? It may be completely different, with people crying out voicelessly to have these things live again through these words, which are their words. It seems to me that I wouldn't write about a living person. I would find that extremely difficult, but I think that to make the dead live again is alright. I think there is nothing wrong in that. Indeed I find it rather a good thing to do. Now of course you can do it badly, make them wish they were dead again, and the tendency in biography is not to do what Strachey is meant to have done which is to attack, to debunk. The real danger, when you live with these characters so long, is to give a rosier picture, to make them centre stage, to make them more important. That is the real danger. So you must always give the minor characters, who disliked the main character, the best words they have in order to make a drama of it, in order to show both sides, the shadow and the sunlight.

Bigsby: You once said that you learn about yourself by writing about others, and you have written about a whole series of others. Are you able to step back and say what it is you have learned about yourself from writing about them?

Holroyd: Only that I can be interested in things that I never knew I would be interested in and therefore something comes alive which wasn't alive in me before. That is really what the process is I think. What I like is characters who are neither good nor bad. I liked mixed characters.

Bigsby: Obviously you write about people because of what seems to you their innate significance, but the process of writing also confers significance. It fixes someone, because there is a tide always taking people away from us. People who were once central to the culture, dominated it, a point of reference, can be forgotten so quickly. Whoever would have thought that Shaw, who bestrode the world in all areas, culture, politics, everything, would slip away? Do you ever feel that in some way the process of writing biography is resisting the loss of memory?

Holroyd: Yes, I think that is certainly true. It always strikes me when people fade in that way that there is a pathos to it. Alongside that is the fact that they are no longer communicating. Maybe they still have something to say. Maybe you can catch it, maybe you can find out what it was, maybe you are a messenger one way or another, and that strikes me as a worthwhile enterprise.

Bigsby: So that is the case for biography?

Holroyd: Maybe.

In Conversation With Christopher Hope

- 11th October 2006 -

Christopher Hope was born in Johannesburg in 1944 and was educated at the universities of Witwatersrand and Natal and worked as a journalist before moving to London in 1975. His first volume of poems, *Whitewashes*, appeared in 1971 and his first novel, *A Separate Development*, banned by the South African authorities, a decade later. Subsequent novels include *Kruger's Alp* (1984), *The Hottentot Room* (1986), *Darkest England* (1996), *Heaven Forbid* (2002), *My Mother's Lovers* (2006) and *The Garden of Bad Dreams* (2008). He has also written plays for radio and television. His awards include the Whitbread Award and the PEN Award

Bigsby: Your father was killed in the war but you have said that it took a long while for the impact to hit you. How long did it take and what was the nature of that impact when it finally did overwhelm you?

Hope: It took almost a lifetime. It is so strange. My mother, rather like Kathleen in *My Mother's Lovers,* was engaged three times and each time the man to whom she was engaged was shot down and killed although she had only been married once, to my father, and he was killed about three months after I was born. I had a photograph of him, which is all I had of him, and my mother remarried so in a sense I lost touch with him, but not knowing him and having lost touch with him I did, I suppose, what children sometimes do. I built him up into a personage, into someone, and he meant a very great deal to me, even though in a sense he was a complete and absolute stranger.

I know absolutely nothing whatever about my father, although I filled in the space in my own peculiar way. When you have created a ghost and given that ghost flesh and blood, that ghost is in a sense a kind of interloper in the life of your family since after all he doesn't exist, he shouldn't be there, he should best be forgotten but one is unable to forget him. I think a lot of what I have written has been a way of recreating somebody who has gone, but it was only after my mother died

305

that I could actually tell the story in my own way, to myself, of how I came to create a father I never had.

Bigsby: And his name was not Hope?

Hope: No. It is so peculiar. Apart from the usual clichés it is of course filled with the most extraordinary ironies. My father was an Irishman. He had no need to go to the war. He was part of an entire family of Irish who consistently went out and fought and died in either the First or the Second World War for a cause they didn't entirely believe in, or perhaps they did, I don't know, but it was so peculiar they were all volunteers. So I had this missing Irish father and my mother then went and married a Presbyterian, and that was somewhat difficult given the background. When I was about fifteen my parents came to me, my stepfather and my mother, and said, 'You know your name isn't actually Hope.' I said, 'Really?' They said, 'No, it's not. Your surname is Tully and we have never actually changed it.'

Well, I had been writing Christopher Hope on my school books for ever and I was known as this. It was very difficult, the thought that I had this hidden father in the cupboard whose picture I took out and consulted from time to time. So they said, 'Because you are not actually named after us the only way we can name you after us is if you agree for us to adopt you, and because you are of an age when this is a serious matter we can't decide that you should be adopted. You will have to go and see the judge or the magistrate who will ask you whether you agree to this.' I said, 'You mean I have a choice?' It was so peculiar. They said, 'He will ask you if it is your free and open decision to no longer be Tully but to become Hope,' which is an odd position to be in since you have always been Hope and always wished you had been Tully and never were.

So it was most peculiar not just to grow up with a fractured patrimony and personality but actually to have one offered to you at a late stage, along with this extraordinary freedom. And indeed I was taken aside by this solemn fellow who said to me, 'Now this absolutely has to be your decision.' And I thought that actually there is no decision. It is perfectly impossible. What would I like to be? I would like to be Tully, thank you very much, but that would be ridiculous. I would have to go round for the rest of my life explaining to those who had known me as Hope who I am and that would have been too difficult by far. But that oddity, those spaces, it seems to me, are sometimes extremely fruitful for a writer. You fill the gaps which can't otherwise be filled in any other way, and I think I have probably done a lot of that.

Bigsby: People have asked whether the mother in *My Mother's Lovers* was your own mother and you have said, 'Yes and no.' Your mother surely was not an aviatrix, she didn't do three rounds with Hemingway, didn't keep pygmies in the garden, or did she?

Hope: I have given the mother in the novel my mother's first name, and there are glancing resemblances is all I can say. But there is also this extraordinary feeling I have about Africa. I spend a lot of time north and south, east and west, on a continent that people use easy glib phrases about. They talk about mother Africa. If mother Africa is indeed maternal she has got a very odd way of showing it, I have to say. It is a most peculiar place and if she is a maternal creature her maternal feelings are to say the least lacking, or marked by most extraordinary indifference to many of her children. And that also fascinates me. So I wanted to extend the notion of motherhood somewhat beyond my own actual mother.

Bigsby: You were four years old when the National Party won the elections, and that was going to be the world that you then inhabited. Your conscious life, growing up, was a world defined by that party and its various policies. Was there ever a moment in which you imbibed that ethos and behaved in a way that you would subsequently be ashamed of?

Hope: I will try and answer the question in another way. There was such a moment for Athol Fugard. The other person who is exemplary in South African terms is somebody like Alan Paton. His great novel *Cry the Beloved Country* is one which I deeply admire but with which I have very little to do in the sense that tears were shed and there were feelings of guilt. In Paton's case it was Anglican guilt, in Fugard's case a kind of Dutch Reformed feeling of guilt and remorse. I don't think I have ever suffered from those things. What I think I have suffered from, to excess, is a form of anger. A most peculiar thing about totalitarian societies is that they are, of course, lethal. They are, of course, murderous, but they are also excruciatingly boring. If they can't lock you up and do away with you they will bore you to death. The price they pay for this untrammelled capacity to bore their people to death, if they are not slaughtering them or locking them up, is that they also appear completely preposterous, absolutely fatuous. What struck me from the start was the oddity of what we were, the strangeness, the dark comedy that we carried out so effortlessly. I am afraid anger got in the way of any more noble emotions, like remorse or guilt. My inclination was to attack and to celebrate the multiple idiocies, the rich lunacies of this extraordinary place. That is what I have always been fascinated by.

Bigsby: But there must have been a question, in some sense, of identity because at the age of eight you moved from Johannesburg to Pretoria, which is substantially Afrikaans, and you are not, and Protestant. Although you mentioned the Presbyterian stepfather you are from a Catholic background. So there you were living as a Catholic person in a Protestant city, a non-Afrikaans speaker person in an Afrikaans-speaking area. How did you adjust to this situation?

Hope: With considerable difficulty but I always thought of us as living in a kind of Irish stockade on a very tiny island surrounded by a very rough sea populated entirely by man-eating Calvinist sharks, and sooner or later they were going to get us. On the other hand, they had John Calvin but we had the Pope, who wasn't much help because he was a long way away. But when I was a teenager we then had Elvis Presley. We had rock and roll. It was a futile sense of rebellion but, as Gore Vidal has said, the first duty of a patriot is to be rude about his own country. Ours was such an extraordinary place that it wasn't a country. It was a geographical, political convenience. There was no such place as South Africa. Not only could you not define whether you were Jewish or Protestant or Catholic or black or white or Asian or mixed race or Chinese, the question always had a political vocabulary and colour that attached to it which had to be explained first before your identity, such as it was, came through.

So what it did do was to reinforce my feeling that the great glory of South Africa is not its endless obsession with black and white but the richness of its erogenous mix which is so interesting and so powerful. In the end if anything will help it is that. One drew a certain kind of cold comfort from the fact that not only were we different, everybody was different. There were no majorities worth attending to. They were just oddities and individuals.

Bigsby: You said you had the Pope. You also had the Christian Brothers. I have talked to men and women who have been educated by the Christian Brothers and there is one theme that emerges from this and it is a kind of withering violence. I don't know whether that is just because corporal punishment was around for that generation or whether the Catholic church specialised in this.

Hope: I think it came naturally. I think as colonial boys we were regarded as gongs to be beaten regularly. It just went with the territory. It was also, of course, a rough place. I have often said that when people reach out, what South Africans do, if they don't understand what you are saying, is raise their voice. If they still don't understand what you are saying, they raise one of their fists. If they still don't understand they threaten you with something or other. Reaching for violence is their way of keeping in touch. It is a habit I have deplored but there is a lot of it about and the Christian Brothers seasoned one for the fray ahead, it seemed to me.

Bigsby: What were your feelings when public acts of violence occurred, because you were in your teens when that was going on?

Hope: I remember individual instances and I remember major instances. For instance, it was an open secret that people in the hands of the security police would succumb to an accident of one sort or another. So much was this so that it quickly entered the mythology of the time. People slipped on a bar of soap in the shower, or happened to plunge from a tenth-storey window. In cases of mass murder, like Sharpeville, it turned out that most of those shot were shot in the back as they ran away from the police. I suppose what struck me about it was this mixture of great violence laced in with an open and honest awareness of what had been perpetrated, followed almost immediately by a kind of gallows humour as if this was no more than to be expected. I found that very peculiar and very characteristic, and it still is, it seems to me, even despite the changes. It is an attitude to violence which is why I am always amazed when I read tearful accounts by people who served on the Truth and Reconciliation Commission who say, 'We had no idea. This is absolutely awful.' One thinks, well, if you didn't know you sure as heck weren't paying attention. It wasn't that one didn't know, it was that one couldn't not know. It was all over the damn place. That was what was so extraordinary. It was so known that one preferred to understate because the reality was too painful and too in-your-face to deal with it in emotional terms. So one dealt with it in ironic or understated, darkish terms.

Bigsby: You have said that there is a real challenge in writing about South Africa because it could out-imagine the writer in many ways.

Hope: It still does. So much of Africa still does. People have remarked about *My Mother's Lovers* that there are bits where I can't possibly be serious. The fact of the matter is that nine-tenths of this novel I couldn't have made up because people would have said I was lying. Nine tenths of it is based, in very secure ways, on things that actually happened. It is the most extraordinary continent and place that it easily out-invents the best of its writers. The material comes flying into you from every direction. The question is what should your demeanour be when the news hits you? What do you do with boy soldiers?

I will give you an example of what it means. By great good luck I was in Liberia when Charles Taylor left office. Taylor has perhaps more blood on his hands than anybody I can think off in Africa. We were in the presidential palace. He was dressed from head to toe in white. There was a gospel choir, among other things, singing "Go Down Moses," and when the gospel choir stopped they played, over the tannoy, the theme from *An Officer and a Gentleman*. Charles Taylor was about to leave for the airport to be taken to comfortable exile in Nigeria. In a town in which nothing was working and boy soldiers were on the streets, he compared himself to the Saviour. He made a very moving speech. There was barely a dry eye in the presidential palace. He was then taken in convoy down the road to be put on a plane, beside which stood three presidents – from Mozambique, Ghana and South Africa – who were like sheriffs who had come into town, I suspect, to guarantee to Charles Taylor that he would have safe conduct out of the country with whatever he was taking with him, and there was a large entourage. How could you make up a scene of that sort? It was in a strange way terrifyingly moving. He felt badly done by. It was rather like McArthur saying 'I will be back.' That these things should happen in what was a war zone, a place of terrifying suffering, was bizarre, but at the same time something that only a great comic-tragic opera could do justice to.

Bigsby: Even in the new South Africa there are people, like Thabo Mbeki, who deny the reality of AIDS, who are constructing their own reality.

Hope: I think one of the definitions of a South African is somebody who is almost obliged to lead several parallel lives. Who they are at the time depends on which life you happen to interrogate them about. Jacob Zuma is a case in point because not only was the rape case [he was charged with rape] notable in its disturbing features, but he had been the minister in charge of moral regeneration before this happened. He was also the minister in charge of fighting the AIDS scourge which afflicts something like one in five of the population of South Africa. Each day, at the end of the hearing, he would appear in front of his supporters and they would break into what became a kind of theme song which, translated, runs 'Bring me my machine gun?' It is a great tune. It is just a pity about the lyrics. Meanwhile, across the road there were people holding up signs saying "Burn the bitch," meaning the woman who had brought the rape charge.

Bigsby: How do you see the political future of South Africa?

Hope: I am one of those in whom cheerfulness keeps breaking through despite evidence to the contrary – the triumph of hope over experience. The reason I say that is because what one went through before showed that there were individuals perfectly prepared to go to jail and perfectly prepared to speak out irrespective of what the sanctions might be. I think those individuals continue to exist. There is something wonderfully, marvellously, perversely brave about certain people in South Africa and I think that quality is there still. Having said that, I think it is in some ways almost as difficult now to speak out, though there is no censorship. Of course there is none of the usual paraphernalia which was employed by the old regime, where books and speech and people were sentenced and silenced and locked up or got rid of, but there is a conspiracy of politeness, correctness, and indeed embarrassment which makes it very difficult for people to speak out. The short answer is, I am not unoptimistic.

Bigsby: When apartheid was over the pressure had gone and that could be threatening to the writer whose stance was oppositional. There were writers in eastern Europe who felt the same thing. When the Wall fell their significance was diminished. Was there such a moment for you when the old South Africa had disappeared?

Hope: You see it in the old Soviet Union too. Once you had a subject and then suddenly they went and shot your fox basically. Everything was so coloured and compressed and focused by the issue of the times that it gave you a subject which was this great gift, even if the subject was not altogether prepossessing. Suddenly it was gone and I do think it not only cuts the ground from under your feet, it takes your breath away. When I lived in Moscow the Russians used to say that we were always told tomorrow will be paradise, only today is hell, and this guy said to me, 'Why can't we just be told, sometimes, tomorrow won't be too bad?' Just a little bit of ordinariness will go a long way but the trouble with ordinariness is that then, like most countries and like most writers in those countries, you will inevitably have to start writing about love and the drains, and this is a considerable challenge to say the least.

Bigsby: Doris Lessing was a very different generation to yours. In fact there is a twenty-five year difference. But she left Africa at the same age that you did. To this day she says that at some levels she still regards herself as an African writer. Do you?

Hope: Yes, I would agree about that. Yes, is the short answer.

In Conversation With
Clive James

- 2nd November 2005 -

Clive James was born in Kogarah, a suburb of Sydney, in 1939. A graduate of Sydney University, he worked briefly for the *Sydney Morning Herald* before moving to England in 1962 and graduating from Cambridge University where he was President of the Cambridge Footlights. For ten years, from 1972, he was television critic for *The Observer* and has worked extensively as a reviewer and critic. While establishing a successful career on television, he has published many books of criticism, poetry and fiction as well as five volumes of autobiography.

Bigsby: You have done a fair amount of television. Were you ever tempted to be an actor?

James: Acting was one of my aspirations. It never quite came true because I was mixed up in television, which is a different kind of acting. In order to stay sane in television I tried to pursue a literary career as well. I kept writing poetry, and I kept writing essays, which is a glorified name for book reviews in my case. The book review is a much despised form and we are often told not to collect them afterwards by the kind of book reviewer who doesn't collect his book reviews because nobody asks him to.

I go on writing poems. I have done all my life and now that I have retired I am writing lyrics again and essays. I am writing a cultural study of the twentieth century, writing more memoirs, writing this, that and the other, but I go on writing poems because poems are the basis of everything and they are a one-man band. If you can write poems you can't be put out of business. Nobody might read them, but nobody can stop you except perhaps the law and I recently wrote a poem designed to get me into trouble with the law. That was its specific aim. It was designed to offend religious groups. There is a law coming here making it illegal to offend religious groups. I think religious groups are there to be offended and if they can't take it they shouldn't be religious groups. My own religious group, the Presbyterian Church, has been offended by me since I was a tiny boy and I am going to go on offending it. I, for one, will be dammed if I will pull my punches about religious groups, especially religious leaders to the extent that they believe the stuff they preach. Most religions are just advertising campaigns for a product that doesn't exist. Have you ever noticed how the leaders of religious groups resemble each other physically? Have you noticed the extraordinary physical resemblance between Osama Bin Laden and the Archbishop of Canterbury? How do we know that these are two separate people? Has anyone checked up on the phone bills, on the credit cards?

I have written a poem, and you will know how offensive my poem is when I tell you the title. It is called *The Australian Suicide Bombers Heavenly Reward*. I like to think that when the Australian suicide bomber shows up, and he will, it is inevitable, he will have a different slant on the business than the other suicide bombers. I would like to think that the Australian suicide bomber might even have a different view of paradise, about those seventy-two virgins. Whose idea was it that seventy-two virgins were going to be more interesting than one woman who knows what she is doing. That is a religious leader's idea isn't it?

Bigsby: You have a website, but not one, presumably, that makes any money. That is not its point.

James: No. It is to spend my money, which it is doing with terrifying efficiency. But it is I think the future of broadcasting. The logical conclusion is that everyone will have their own TV station. The problem will be to get anybody else to watch it, but that is where ordinary fame comes in handy I guess. But how will I make money? Nobody knows yet. I have got a few theories but all I know so far is how it loses money. But what I do know that is wonderful about it is that I can invite other people onto it. I have got young painters and poets already appearing on it and, as I gradually fade away, my aim will be to be crowded out of my own website by all these visitors and finally no one will know I am gone. It is a bit like a pyramid really. You will see what I mean if you log on. If you log on you will practically double the viewing figures for today but the great thing is the statistics. It has already attracted visitors from fifty different countries.

Bigsby: You have Cate Blanchett on the site?

James: That's true. She is one of the people I interviewed. She was a mate and she came in and donated her presence for nothing just to help out but I can't expect that to go on happening forever. I will do TV shows in my living room and radio shows but the main thing at the moment, apart from all my guests, is to get some of my past writings on there because they probably won't come back in any other form. You can't keep all your books in print. I am told by Picador that the maximum number of titles the market can stand is about half a dozen, otherwise the bookshops don't know what to order. At one time or another I have had fourteen separate Picador titles. They have to go out of print but I can't stand the idea of the writing going out of print. Like everybody who writes anything I believe that every sentence is deathless and writers one day might even write about this thing. Writers will have to be stopped preserving their stuff. There will have to be court orders against them.

Bigsby: You have an interview on your site with Julian Barnes?

James: Julian won't give a television interview because he hates TV. Everything about TV makes him nervous. He takes beta blockers when he goes on it. But on the other hand he doesn't mind coming into my living room, having a drink and talking. You see the advantage. It is not like television for the people who do it.

Bigsby: There is a series on your site in which you talk to Peter Porter. Did you originate them on there?

James: No, they originated on Australian radio. Peter Porter and I went to the Melbourne Literary Festival years ago and just started talking about literature and quoting from memory. The audience liked that and Australian radio asked us to do a series and for once in my life I got canny and I said we will do this for a very low fee but I will keep the internet rights. So now we have loaded them all up onto the website and they will be running in perpetuity. People are listening to them all over the world. Anyone learning English anywhere is usually quite grateful to hear advanced conversational English and you can't really get more advanced than Peter Porter talking about literature or music.

Bigsby: In fact one of the fascinating things about those conversations is the territory that you cover.

James: The big emphasis is on memory from both of us and that was quite common in our generation.

Bigsby: Learning things in school.

James: We had to or we weren't allowed to go home. That is more or less going out of the world now and that is a pity because it trains the memory and the memory is a treasure house.

Bigsby: People tend to be amazed if you can remember literature.

James: Yes, they tend to drop to their knees and worship you if you can remember anything.

Bigsby: I was really struck by the fact that you got interested in Latin poetry and so taught yourself Latin.

James: Most languages are best learned when you are a kid, especially hard languages like Japanese. Japanese is designed to be learned by children and used by adults. It is very hard to learn to read when you are older. I did manage it but I knew how to learn and gave it a lot of attention. Most languages you should learn as a kid if you can. If you can't, you should just go at them as an adult but you have got to be ready to make a fool of yourself and that is why the English on the whole are bad language learners because they don't like to be at a loss. You mustn't be afraid of making mistakes. So I got in there and learned Latin that way and a lot of people who knew Latin, who studied Latin at school under the classical system, saw me using a parallel text and got quite annoyed, and said, 'We weren't allowed to use those. You shouldn't use them. You will never master Latin until you can do without the parallel text. You should just have a dictionary.' And I pointed out the obvious. The parallel text is a dictionary, a convenient dictionary.

Use any method, cheat, borrow, beg or steal but just get some of the language into you and when you get a few lines of the poetry into you, you are off to the races. You have only got to get a few lines of Virgil into your memory and you are beginning to read Latin. It is the same with Italian – a few lines of Dante and you begin Italian, a few lines of Goethe and you begin German. A couple of memorable lines of poetry is the place to start. In Japanese it is the place to start. The first week I was learning Russian I read *The Three Bears* because *The Three Bears* in Russian is written by Tolstoy. So you get in there and you read something, get something to remember. That is the way memory comes in handy. Once it is in your memory it is yours. Nobody can take it away from you.

Bigsby: And learning the structure of languages, including English …

James: ... is very, very handy. If you get nowhere with other languages, and I am not a linguist at all, but if you get nowhere with other languages it is very handy to remind you that English too was an arbitrary system of sounds attached to things and you learn how the structure works. I have been learning about English all my life and reading other languages has helped, no question. English is a marvellous mechanism. It is the supreme language, but you will never know why unless you have a look at some other languages as well.

Bigsby: How important is it for you to be an Australian?

James: It is increasingly important. When I was young and stupid I didn't quite realise what a privilege it was and I had to be away the first few years and then for decades to realise that the country I had left was in a unique historical position as the exemplar country, the country of the future, the country that every other country wants to be. I have become prouder and prouder of my role as an expatriate because I think the expatriates have contributed something at least. But, as for Australia itself, I have learned more and more about it while I have been away and it is so important I still have an Australian passport and believe me that is a real sign of loyalty because that passport is practically useless. Australia has managed to achieve bad diplomatic relations with so many countries that you can't go ashore in Spain or France but I have still got my Australian passport, and that is the worst of both worlds because in Britain it puts you in the other passports queue. You land early in the morning and two jumbos have come in from Africa and India. There are a thousand people waiting in the other passports queue and there is you on the end of it, while through the EU queue ex SS tank commanders are being waved through, with palm fronds as they go through the fast track. That is the price, but I don't complain.

Of course I am very proud of being an Australian but I believe in the old empire. I was born under the old empire, raised up in the Commonwealth. I believe in what Robert Conquest calls the Anglosphere. I am very, very keen on the idea. At first blush it sounds like supremacism. It is not really. It is just the privilege of having grown up in a democratic tradition. There is nothing more precious than democracy and the English language exemplifies it. Australians speak a pretty good version of the English language. It is in some ways more vivid than the British. Shane Warne actually swears better than your guys.

Bigsby: Michael Blakemore, the theatre director, still has an Australian passport but he is thinking of ditching it for the very reason you are saying, just to get into the country.

James: He is only saying that. I know Michael well and he won't. He is blagging.

Bigsby: Have you got a view on republicanism in Australia?

James: I have. I am not for it and neither is the Australian public. It voted against the referendum when it had the chance and I am in favour of maintaining the connection. In other words I am in favour of keeping things complicated. I don't believe in the inevitable march of history. Suddenly you hear from people for whom the word history has never passed their lips in Australia. Suddenly you hear from people, who have never mentioned this word, insisting that history dictates that Australia become a republic. I don't believe any of that and I don't believe that the immigrants who came to Australia from all the countries in the world that suffered during World War II, and not just the European countries, do either. They were all refugees from political instability and the last thing they want is any more political instability in the country they came to. That is what they taught their children and that is the real reason why the referendum was defeated and will probably go on being defeated.

The Prime Minister, John Howard, who is a very canny individual, as many bald men are, got to his feet the night before the referendum and pointed out to the television audience that he was not in favour of a Presidential system because the framework that had been mooted would give too much power to the Prime Minister of the day. Now for a Prime Minister to stand up and say this system would give me too much power was a political masterstroke, and of course he was right. Suddenly there will be no limit to ambition. The great advantage of the monarchic connection is that it places a limit to ambition and Australia has some of the most ambitious men in the world. I have spent my life fleeing from some of the newspaper magnets, just to start with, and these men must not be let loose to contest against each other for the right, privilege, and opportunity of ruling Australia. It must not happen. We must keep things roughly as they are because everything is going to change anyway. We are now entering a phase of history where everything that continues will be precious. That is a very long answer to your question. But I am against it, though I will understand when it comes in, as it probably will if the Royal

320

family give up, for example, and if I was Charles I probably would give up on Australia. I mean, who needs all that crap?

Bigsby: Is it hard to be taken seriously as a humorous writer?

James: Yes, it is hard to be taken seriously as a humorous writer. I don't think I am a humorous writer, in the sense that I am a humorist. I can't imagine anything more deadly than to earn a living as a humorist. I have known many humorists and they are bleak people. Their fate is cruel. There are penalties you pay for being entertaining, or trying to be, especially as a poet. I am still not taken seriously as a poet and in my book, *The Book of My Enemy*, most of the poems were published either in *The London Review of Books* or *The Times Literary Supplement*, both very prestigious outlets in this country. I probably had more poetry published in *The London Review of Books* than any other poet they have ever printed. Did they review my collected poems? They did not. *The London Review of Books* didn't review that book, nor did *The Times Literary Supplement*. Why not? Because they think I don't need it, because I am really an entertainer. I am not really a poet at all, and that is the way it is going to be until I croak. Then, the day after I croak, I will get discovered. That will be too bloody late. My hand will be sticking up through the ground saying, 'Over here!' You have got to take the rough with the smooth, and that is the rough.

In Conversation With
Hanif Kureishi

- 20th October 1998 -

Hanif Kureishi, playwright, screenwriter, novelist, was born in London in 1954 and is a graduate of Lancaster University. His 1985 film, *My Beautiful Laundrette*, won the New York Critics Best Screenplay Award while his first novel, *The Buddha of Suburbia* (1990), won the Whitbread first novel award. Subsequent novels include *The Black Album* (1995), adapted for the theatre and performed at the National Theatre, *Intimacy* (1998), the film version winning a Golden Bear for Best Film, *The Body* (2003) and *Something to Tell You* (2008).

Bigsby: You were born of a Pakistani father and an English mother. Did you have a sense growing up that there were two conflicting traditions or did you simply choose your own?

Kureishi: I didn't think they were conflicting until later, until people said to me that they were. To me, it was just my life as we all have lives. We all have relatives who seem quite different from one another. It was only when people said to me, 'You don't know where you are, you aren't one of us and you aren't one of them,' that I began to feel rather disturbed. I was alright until then. Then I began to think about who I was and was rather worried about the whole thing. Then I came apart in those places and now I can see that having a Muslim Pakistani family and an English suburban family is unique and interesting. At the time, though, it scared the life out of me because I thought you weren't supposed to be like that. It was terrifying for me because it bothered other people so much and I could never understand what it was about me that made other people so violent, why they would chase you down the street shouting out 'Paki' and all the stuff that went on. I found all that very disturbing. I suddenly saw that I was a victim of people who were very angry with me for reasons that were not to do with me personally. I can see that that was a very interesting experience but at the time it was terrifying, awful.

Bigsby: When did that first impact on you? Was that at school or later?

Kureishi: I think when I went to school because in those days the teachers were quite racist as well. They all used to call me Pakistani Pete. I got into a lot of trouble because then I started to call the teachers by their nicknames. They were all called Bollocks, or whatever. They would say, 'Morning, Pakistani Pete' and I would say, 'Hello, Bollocks.' It got very traumatic and rather frightening and I got into a lot of trouble. I became alienated from the whole thing. I felt a sense of powerlessness. I suppose I thought it was something about me. Then I realised it was about race and I began to think about race and the way race works in a society.

The worst thing about race is that you internalise it. You think it is you, and the conflicts explode within you rather than in a sociological way, and it really disturbed and upset me for a long time because I felt that I didn't belong, that I couldn't fit in. I thought everybody else did belong and fit in. Then the sixties happened, which was a celebration of not fitting in, and that made it easier for me. Then I started to write about it, because I wanted to tell other people about what it was like from down there, how it felt, because people didn't know how vicious people could be about something like the colour of your skin, or your name, or whatever.

Bigsby: You were growing up when the rhetoric of Enoch Powell was the public language?

Kureishi: Yes, Enoch had a terrible effect on my life. I would go to people's houses and they would say, 'We're with Enoch,' and look at you as if they were about to smack you with a hammer. I was amazed that Tony Blair went to Enoch Powell's funeral because he was a deeply racist and unpleasant man and I am glad he is dead. It was terrifying, all of that. I suppose in the seventies, particularly, you felt that there were very powerful fascist groups which don't seem to me to be around in England now but there certainly are in France and when I speak to French Algerian writers you are aware of the terror they feel and the sense of exclusion and how awful that is.

Bigsby: You said the sixties made a difference but you were quite young in the sixties. You entered them at the age of six and thus were only sixteen when they finished. So where did you get your sixties from? Was it television, movies? Did you feel part of what was going on?

Kureishi: I watched it on television and also I had a very long adolescence. People do now, actually. My adolescence probably started when I was thirteen and ended just now when I got off the train. I finally matured. The sixties was such a pleasure to me because if you grew up in the suburbs you were expected to work in a bank, be commuters, but realised that the Beatles and the Rolling Stones were not working in banks. They were leading creative lives, and it helped me to believe that I too could lead a creative life, I suppose. After all, the British writers who were around in those days always seemed to me to be very posh, people like Graham Greene, whom I admired. He went to public school. I didn't. I went to a state school. I wasn't educated, really, so the sixties gave me a sense of possibility, that you could be creative and you could be young and you didn't have to work in a bank.

Bigsby: Did your father try and introduce you to the traditions that he knew, or was he resolutely British himself?

Kureishi: He didn't like India very much [the family had moved from India to Pakistan on partition] because he didn't like religion. He had been to Muslim schools and been beaten by the mullahs so he hated religion and he hated the mullahs. He liked books and he got me to read. He wanted to be a writer and lived his whole life as a failed writer. He would write every day, every morning, on these massive typewriters they had in those days. The whole house would shake, and I would get up and write. I had to live the life, as I do now, that he would have wanted for himself. He thought that being a writer was a grand job, and he was a commuter. So he opened the door and said, 'If you do that you will have a better time than I am having myself.' He made me fall in, love with books. He made me see that they were a pleasure. He gave me an appetite for literature. And he gave me loads of good advice which, really, I suppose, was about discipline.

I ran into a friend of mine the other day who is a writer and he was just getting out of bed at three o'clock in the afternoon and he hadn't written anything for three weeks. He was staggering around. He is rather a good writer and I thought I would never do that. I am so conscientious. I get up and start writing every morning at seven o'clock and I always have done and I always will. I get up and rush to my desk and this is ingrained in my head. That is what I do. Writing is something you do every day, whether you feel like it or not, and the idea that you develop your talent, whether you feel like it or not, and that you have to protect your talent and use it and develop it, that has stayed with me.

People sometimes have a romantic idea about writing. But I think most writers do get up and get on with it, apart from the bloke I met on the street the other day. My father wrote with relish. He wrote with love. He wrote because he liked to do it. It wasn't torture or punishment. He wrote because he loved to do it and I love what I do. In fact, you feel at your best when you are doing things that you like to do, that you love to do, and the love in a sense never runs out. I never run out of things to write about. I never think, God, I have finished something, now I don't have to do anything for five years. I always think I want to do more. This is fascinating, this is interesting to me, this is challenging, this is alive, this is full of juice and good things for me.

Bigsby: Could you have done what your father did which is to go on writing but not being published?

Kureishi: It was amazing. He wrote tons of novels. I have got some of them piled up in my house. He just carried on doing it, but it would be heartbreaking to do that because I don't think you develop as a writer if you do that. In a sense it would be like having conversations by yourself and after a time you would just say the same thing over and over again and you would become mad. You wouldn't develop. There wouldn't be anybody else there. There wouldn't be a challenge. There wouldn't be any conversation. You write books, you send them out, and someone responds. You have a chat about it. Writing is living and means something to somebody and that is interesting and that is why I do it. It would be very hard to carry on doing it on your own.

Bigsby: Were those books any good, his books?

Kureishi: Not really, no. They were goodish but they were not really good. It is rather tragic and heartbreaking to have to say that, and that makes it worse in a way for me. My father was always rather surprised that my books got published and his weren't because he thought his books were philosophical and mine were about people taking drugs and having sex. He couldn't understand that the public were so gullible.

Bigsby: You did eventually go to Pakistan. What did you learn from that experience about yourself or, indeed, the place?

Kureishi: I went to Pakistan for the first time in the early eighties and I was hoping for a spiritual experience. In fact, I got robbed as I left the airport, funnily enough. I got in a taxi and I was taken to a forest. I was terrified and I thought, 'I have come to my homeland and these guys are taking everything.' Then I realised that I was an English boy and that was rather terrifying because I thought that I would feel more at home there in some silly way and I didn't. I saw that all the things that I like – books, music, argument, intellectual discussion, alcohol, drugs, adultery – and that you could enjoy in London, you couldn't get in Karachi, which was run at that time by fundamentalists. It was during the period of Islamisation. One of my uncles said to me, 'The thing is we are Pakistanis and you will always be a Paki,' and that really disillusioned me. I realised that I couldn't live there. I couldn't belong there, in the same way that obviously my family did, so I had to go back to London and be a Paki in London as well.

Then I began to see that in a sense all of this was my material, my work, my writing, that this could be converted into words, into stories. In a sense these stories hadn't been told before, the stories of the immigrants coming to Britain in the fifties and sixties and their lives, and the shocks, and all that we were trying to do. All of that was quite new and I wrote plays and then I wrote *My Beautiful Launderette*.

I wrote plays because in London the theatre at that time was very exciting. Property was cheap and there were lots of lunchtime theatres in basements and a lot of theatre was using pop music and was about class and race and sexuality and I was very excited by that. The theatre wasn't really my thing though, and when I came to write a film, which Channel 4 commissioned, *My Beautiful Launderette*, I felt very released by the form of the cinema, by the fact that you can just cut and you are somewhere else. You don't have these people on the stage who have got to talk for a long time and can't go off and come on all the time. They have got to be there, whereas with a film the fluidity of the form really attracted me.

Bigsby: Then what has brought you back to theatre?

Kureishi: Well, the opposite, I suppose. Film and television are very quick. I wanted to write a piece in which people would talk to one another for a long time, as people often do in life. So I have written a play.

Bigsby: Obviously there is a sense in which your own life feeds into your work. What is the relationship between a fictive piece of writing and the life of the person who writes it?

Kureishi: When you are writing, when you are doing anything creative, when you are doing anything interesting, you have to go to where the action is. You have to go where the erotic is, where the life is, where the conflict and the difficult and interesting inner-life things are, and those things are usually in your unconscious, in your life. And usually, unfortunately, for writers, for all of us who want to write, in your family too. In a sense you need to go there in order to make your writing alive. I have always taken from life but I have only used it as an excuse. I don't think you can just take a bit of life and stick it in a book. I had an uncle who had launderettes and he used to take me round his launderettes and tell me I should run them. This writing stuff, he said, wasn't going to get me anywhere, so I wrote a film about a bloke running a launderette. I never ran a launderette. I just knew a bloke who did and it became that film. But that was just the starting point, where I began.

In a sense you look around all the time for things in life which are starting points, which are excuses, which are beginnings for what you are then going to do. You have to do that. I don't think you can just take people and stick them in a book. I have never done that, and you couldn't do it. You can only take a bit of them, like a nose or an ear or an eye. Then it becomes something else.

When I wrote *Intimacy* I set it over one night and when I realised it was to be set over one night then I could write the book because that was the form, that was the structure. This guy was going to go mad and in the morning he was going to leave. Setting it over one night was the excuse to write a book. Then I took bits and pieces of my own life and my friend's lives and stuff I made up, all kinds of other stuff, and mixed it up and imagined things. But it was the form of being one night that really interested me and that determined what went in it.

Bigsby: Did you have discussions with your family when you wrote *The Buddha of Suburbia*? Was there any tension that emerged from that book?

Kureishi: My father was rather annoyed because, in *The Buddha of Suburbia*, the father has sex with a woman down the road and then runs off with her. In fact my father wasn't doing any of that kind of thing at all. He was sitting at home watching *Panorama* on television and I think he was rather annoyed that I had given him this interesting, extravagant and highly sexualised life when in fact he wasn't doing any of these things at all. So in a sense it wasn't autobiographical. I hadn't taken him and put him in a book. I had taken a bit of him and then done other things with it, so it was very complicated. But I think he was rather annoyed that people would think he had been doing these things. It was difficult for him because he was a writer himself so he couldn't say much since he was always putting me in his books. I used to read his books and there would be some sullen teenager lying on the floor with a joss stick burning in the background which my father thought were drugs. You just have to do it, but you have to be aware of what the consequences are.

Bigsby: In your case is writing close to the erotic self?

Kureishi: I do write about sexuality, and I write about all that goes on around that, because clearly when men and women and other people want one another there is a lot of action, there is a lot of desire, there is a lot of intensity, there is a lot of love and betrayal and hatred. In a sense when one person wants another person that is when the action starts and I suppose most of our culture, most of western literature, is entirely about one person wanting another person and what happens when you do that. So yes, I would say that I write about the erotic, which is desire, the deepest and most fundamental human desire and need and how could you not write about that if you wanted to write about what people were really like and what they really wanted and out of that how the world works. Yes, there is romance, there are weddings, there are children, and everything else, but for me that would have to be the beginning.

Bigsby: Now that you have become successful and well known does the racial situation still stir anger in you?

Kureishi: I will be angry on behalf of other people. I don't get it myself because I don't have a job and I don't go to school and I think people mostly get it in environments like that. One of the reasons I didn't want to have a job was that I didn't want to be in a place where people would have authority over me and could abuse me but all of my life I have been very angry about injustice and inequality. I am also very puzzled by the idea of the strange. Here is somebody else and they are a different colour, or they are taller, or they are shorter, or they are this religion or that religion, or they are a different sex – how frightened we are by other people and how then we have to contain or control them by racially or sexually stereotyping them. How frightening other people are to us and how aggressive we are to other people. That seems to me to be a more general question about fear and aggression, which fascinates me, but a lot of people aren't racist as well.

On the other hand, I just want to be a story teller. I want to tell the stories that interest me and have meaning for me. I don't want to do propaganda because I think that is dull and patronising. It is uninteresting. When I first started to write, people would say to me, 'The Asians in your pieces are always buggering one another and taking drugs. You know that Asian people don't do that.' I would say that it is not my job to do propaganda. I can't do that. I wouldn't want to do that. Writers have to betray people on behalf of everybody else.

Bigsby: Are you annoyed that you are asked questions about racism rather than about your writing?

Kureishi: I think questions about race are very interesting. I think they are right at the centre, particularly of Europe. It isn't only black or Asian people who have to face this stuff. It is about all of us, about how we want to live, what kind of Europe we want, how we deal with something like Islam, which always seems to me to be a neo-fascist religion. But we want to be nice liberal people so how do we fit neo-fascist religions into a liberal society? These are all questions that will have to exercise all of us. I think race, colonialism, is right at the centre, not only in Britain but particularly in Germany, which is heavily racist, along with France and Scandinavian countries. These questions are right at the centre of what kind of society you want, what kind of people you want to be. What is a liberal society? What is a democracy? How are we going to live together? How do people live together without killing one another, which is the history of Europe in the twentieth century? I think these questions are very interesting. I don't think they are tiresome, but I don't think they are only questions for me. I think they are questions for everybody who has to try and live with other people.

Bigsby: Were you surprised by the attacks on *Intimacy*?

Kureishi: It got very hot around that time. The newspapers just devour you. They just go bonkers and ring you up every five seconds. The story is not about you any more, it has its own impetus. I was rather pleased because I thought there would be a fuss and I hoped that more people would read the book. I had no idea that my sister would get involved. The papers would ring me up and say, 'Your sister has given a press conference,' and I would be rather surprised that my sister, sitting in her front room, was entertaining journalists, my sister who had always wanted to be a writer and was furious. The envy is just unbearable. It did get hot and a lot of people didn't like the book and a lot of people didn't like me and a lot of people thought that it was all autobiographical and a lot of people thought I hated women and other people thought that men should never leave women and women should never leave men and everybody should always be happy and that people shouldn't write books that are about families breaking up because that is the one thing that none of us can bear, the idea of our parents not being together with us forever. I can see that it is an unbearable idea, but people do leave one another and you have to write books about it.

I felt somehow that people were very angry that I had written a book about smashing something that is sacred, which is the family, which is the couple, and that you can't smash that and you can't leave, and what about the children? It is always about the children. It is never about the parents. It is always about the children and they are brought in as the thing you can't damage. If you leave the wife you always damage the children. It seemed to me to be a very interesting debate about families and about how families survive and what we do in this day and age with each other and with our families and about what kind of families you want to have in the future and how we are going to reconstitute the family once it is broken up. It applies to all of us and we all have to discuss it. I haven't met anybody who hasn't thought about leaving their wife or their husband. I was rather annoyed that I was somehow scape-goated for bringing up something that seemed to me would be interesting to everybody.

Lightning Source UK Ltd.
Milton Keynes UK
UKOW050021100912

198683UK00001B/13/P